THE INSISTENCE OF THE INDIAN

THE INSISTENCE OF THE INDIAN

*RACE AND
NATIONALISM
IN NINETEENTH-
CENTURY
AMERICAN
CULTURE*

*Susan
Scheckel*

PRINCETON UNIVERSITY PRESS

PRINCETON, NEW JERSEY

COPYRIGHT © 1998 BY PRINCETON UNIVERSITY PRESS

PUBLISHED BY PRINCETON UNIVERSITY PRESS, 41 WILLIAM STREET,

PRINCETON, NEW JERSEY 08540

IN THE UNITED KINGDOM: PRINCETON UNIVERSITY PRESS,

CHICHESTER, WEST SUSSEX

ALL RIGHTS RESERVED

LIBRARY OF CONGRESS CATALOGING-IN-PUBLICATION DATA

SCHECKEL, SUSAN, 1958–

THE INSISTENCE OF THE INDIAN : RACE AND NATIONALISM IN

NINETEENTH-CENTURY AMERICAN CULTURE / SUSAN SCHECKEL.

P. CM.

INCLUDES BIBLIOGRAPHICAL REFERENCES AND INDEX.

ISBN 0-691-05963-2 (ALK. PAPER). — ISBN 0-691-05964-0 (PBK. : ALK. PAPER)

1. INDIANS OF NORTH AMERICA—PUBLIC OPINION.   2. INDIANS IN POPULAR

CULTURE—NORTH AMERICA.   3. INDIANS IN LITERATURE.   4. AMERICAN

LITERATURE—19TH CENTURY—HISTORY AND CRITICISM.   5. NATIONALISM—

UNITED STATES. 6. PUBLIC OPINION—UNITED STATES.   7. UNITED STATES—

POLITICS AND GOVERNMENT—19TH CENTURY.   8. UNITED STATES—RACE

RELATIONS.   I. TITLE.

E98.P99S34   1998   305.897—DC21   98-6185   CIP

THE BOOK HAS BEEN COMPOSED IN GALLIARD

PRINCETON UNIVERSITY PRESS BOOKS ARE PRINTED ON ACID-FREE PAPER

AND MEET THE GUIDELINES FOR PERMANENCE AND DURABILITY OF THE

COMMITTEE ON PRODUCTION GUIDELINES FOR BOOK LONGEVITY OF THE

COUNCIL ON LIBRARY RESOURCES

HTTP://PUP.PRINCETON.EDU

PRINTED IN THE UNITED STATES OF AMERICA

1   3   5   7   9   10   8   6   4   2

1   3   5   7   9   10   8   6   4   2

(PBK.)

To Peter

AND TO THE MEMORY OF

Adelaide Scheckel

1910–1996

CONTENTS

ACKNOWLEDGMENTS

THE LIST of those who have helped to strengthen and sustain this project is long. It must begin with Eric Sundquist, who as a teacher, first awakened my interest in questions of race and nationalism. His thoughtful criticism and encouragement throughout the (long) course of the book's development have been invaluable. I also wish to thank Richard Hutson and Michael Rogin for the care with which they read and responded to my work in its early stages. To Leith Davis, Catherine Judd, Ellen Lane, Kristen Mahlis, and Alix Schwartz I am indebted for many hours of exhilarating intellectual exchange and essential emotional support. Friends, colleagues, and students at The University of Memphis provided the intellectual community in which the book took final shape. To those who read and commented on portions of the manuscript, special thanks are due: Theron Britt, Barbara Ching, Leslie Ferris, Allison Graham, Kevin Hagopian, Paul Naylor, and Jennifer Wagner-Lawlor. The book has benefited from the incisive comments of Anne Norton and Cheryl Walker during the final stages of revision. My editors at Princeton University Press have been a model of professionalism and competence. I especially want to thank A. Deborah Malmud for her unfailing faith in this project.

A semester as a visiting professor at the University of Southern California gave me a chance to test in the classroom ideas that became part of this book. I thank my students, both graduate and undergraduate, for their contributions and my colleagues for making my time in Los Angeles so rich and enjoyable.

Several grants made it possible for me to devote time to research and writing: summer research grants from the Huntington Library and the South Central Modern Language Association; two faculty research grants from The University of Memphis; and a fellowship from the Marcus W. Orr Center for the Humanities.

Portions of this book have previously been published. An earlier version of chapter 2 appeared in *James Fenimore Cooper: New Historical and Literary Contexts*, edited by Wil Verhoeven (Amsterdam: Rodopi Press, 1992). Part of chapter 3 was originally published in *American Transcendental Quarterly* 10, no. 3 (September 1996) and is reprinted by permission of The University of Rhode Island. A version of chapter 4 was published in *Desert, Garden, Margin, Range: Literature on the American Frontier*, edited by Eric Heyne (New York: Twayne, 1992). I am grateful to Alan M. Hantman, Architect of the Capitol, for permission to reproduce photographs of the Capitol artwork.

My final and deepest expressions of gratitude are reserved for Lewis Jacobson, Kristen Mahlis, Deborah Scheckel Cobb, Stephen Scheckel, and Mary Langlois, who once again have seen me through; my mother, Elizabeth Scheckel, for her continuing encouragement; and Peter, whose sustaining presence—even when absent—makes it all possible.

THE INSISTENCE OF THE INDIAN

ONE

THE "INDIAN PROBLEM" AND THE
QUESTION OF NATIONAL IDENTITY

> Therefore, the essence of a nation is that all individuals have
> many things in common and also that all have forgotten
> many things. . . . Every French citizen is obliged to have for-
> gotten the Saint Bartholomew's Day massacre and the massa-
> cres that took place in the Midi in the thirteenth century.
> *(Ernest Renan, "What Is a Nation?")*

IN ONE OF THE earliest and most influential reflections on the
meaning of nationhood, Ernest Renan suggested that the nation depends on willed acts of remembering *and* forgetting.[1] The violence
by means of which the nation was forged and defined must be forgotten
so that it can be reimagined as "family" history—the history of the nation. Recent theorists of nationalism, such as Benedict Anderson and
Homi Bhabha, have taken Renan's moment of willed forgetting as the
starting point for the nation. Whether it unfolds like a realist novel in
"homogeneous, empty time" (Anderson, 22–36, 194) or emerges, as it
does for Bhabha, in a liminal space that reveals "the ambivalence of the
'nation' as a narrative strategy" (1994, 140), the idea of the nation begins in a moment of forgetting and is driven forward by an impulse to remember: to negotiate the gap between individual and collectivity; to fill
the space between "immemorial past" and "limitless future" (Anderson,
11–12); to narrate in "that strange time—forgetting to remember"—the
"liminality of cultural modernity" itself (Bhabha 1994, 161, 140).

The dispossession of the American Indians has been one of the most
troubling episodes in U.S. history. From the beginning, settlement and
expansion depended on it, and up to the present it is an act of violence that
Americans seem unable to forget. Despite innumerable attempts to re-
write the Indian as the subject of "family" history, the ghost of the Indian
as the object of genocidal violence has returned inevitably to haunt the
nation and its narratives.[2] This haunting marks the limits of that forget-
fulness out of which the nation arises. As such, it forms the focus of this
study, which concentrates on the first half of the nineteenth century. I
chose this period because it encompasses a moment in American history
when attempts to articulate a coherent narrative of national identity and

to define the status and rights of Indians within the United States intersected to create a pattern that reveals much about the forces driving both projects.[3]

On a conceptual level, these two concerns were linked because debates over Indian policy called into question the very principles on which the idea of "America" was founded, threatening to make explicit the contradictions implicit in American national ideology and social experience and to reveal deep and widespread tensions in the discourses of American nationalism: between republican and liberal values; natural rights and positivist theories of the law; federal and state power; and among differing visions of how race, gender, and property qualified "We the People." Attempts to articulate American Indian policy necessarily also involved attempts to absorb such tensions and incorporate them into coherent and compelling narratives of the nation as a stable, consensual union of virtuous citizens.

Rise and Fall: American Nationalism and Indian Decline

The War of 1812 marked a turning point in U.S. attitudes toward American Indians. With boundary disputes between the United States and Britain settled, and American claims to virtually all lands east of the Mississippi secure, it became difficult for Americans to imagine Indians uniting (as they had when they formed an alliance with the British) to pose a serious military or political threat to the United States.[4] The 1819 comments of Henry Clay, Speaker of the House, reflect this shift in attitude. When the colonies were established, Clay noted, "we were weak . . . and [the Indians] were comparatively strong; . . . they were the lords of the soil, and we were seeking . . . asylum among them." Now, however, things had changed:

> We are powerful and they are weak. . . . [T]o use a figure drawn from their own sublime eloquence, the poor children of the forest have been driven by the great wave which has flowed in from the Atlantic ocean to almost the base of the Rocky Mountains, and, overwhelming them in its terrible progress, has left no other remains of hundreds of tribes, now extinct, than those which indicate the remote existence of their former companion, the mammoth of the New World.[5]

Clay's tone suggests a combination of regret and resignation typical of nineteenth-century political rhetoric on the Indian question.[6] The following chapters will explore the basis and implications of this national nostalgia. Sad as the Indians' fate might be, Clay's language reinforces its inevitability. As Indians were transformed from "lords of the soil" to "poor children of the forest," so the nature of the threat they posed to the United States changed from a military to a moral one. Much as Americans might couch their accounts of Indian extinction in reassuring metaphors of natural processes, there was no denying that the "wave" that drove Indians from their lands was one of Euro-American westward expansion. Nineteenth-century Americans had to account, in moral terms, for the fact that the nation was built on the graves of Indians.

Postwar expansion focused new attention on Indians occupying lands U.S. citizens wished to claim as their own. In response, for the first time the U.S. government attempted to articulate a unified, clearly defined, legally justified Indian policy. The latter became the focus of particularly intense public interest during the 1820s and 1830s. The 1828 election of Andrew Jackson did more than any other event to bring the Indian problem into the spotlight. In his "First Annual Message to Congress" (December 1829), Jackson stated succinctly, "Our conduct toward these people is deeply interesting to our national character" (Richardson, 2: 456–59).[7]

Jackson's choice of language reveals much about what was at stake in defining American Indian policy. For an early-nineteenth-century audience the word "interest" was a potent term. Eighteenth-century political philosophy defined it as the basis of all moral calculation and action. According to Rousseau, for example, enlightened self-interest, which urges men to enter into the social contract, is the very basis and guarantee of civilization. Liberal theories of political and economic development envisioned self-interest as the engine of progress that could, in theory, benefit society as a whole. With the rise of capitalism and competitive individualism during the nineteenth century, however, by the 1820s Americans had begun to question the capacity of self-interest to sustain moral principles and communal values. American Indian policy brought into focus the tensions implicit in these various interpretations of the term.

But Jackson's formulation permits yet another interpretation that evades the very complexities the statement invokes. "Interest" is also an aesthetic term suggesting a somewhat distant if nonetheless intriguing engagement. To declare the Indian problem "interesting" in this sense would be to evade troubling questions of morality and rational responsibility. The number of novels, poems, dramas, captivity narratives, and visual artworks focusing on Indians that appeared between 1820 and 1860 suggests just how "interesting" Indians remained to the American public as a subject of popular representation during the first half of the nineteenth century. Thus, Jackson's simple yet enigmatic comment also suggests the trajectory of the chapters that follow, each of which considers the nature of the "interesting" connection between the Indian problem and the question of national identity by tracing how American attempts to define the meaning of the nation during the first half of the nineteenth century became intertwined with efforts to define the status and rights of Indians, and how these interconnected projects of self-definition became aestheticized in popular representations of Indians.

For Jackson himself the "interesting" problem posed by American Indians was clear; he had risen to national prominence fighting and negotiating treaties with Indians, and his views on American Indian policy were well known. As early as 1817, while serving as military commander in the South, he had repeatedly voiced his opinion that Indians were subject peoples without rights of negotiation. According to Jackson, "Congress ha[d] full power, by law, to regulate all the concerns of the Indians," including the right to occupy and possess their lands whenever national interest, broadly defined, made it necessary.[8] When President Jackson proposed the Removal Act of 1830, "friends of the Indians" familiar with Jackson's ideas on Indian rights knew that force would be inevitable and did their best to stir public opposition to the passage of the bill.

At the same time, events in Georgia were building toward another widely publicized debate over Indian policy. Even before Jackson had taken office, awareness of the new president's views had given Georgians the confidence to take the Indian problem into their own hands. Between 1828 and 1829 Georgia enacted a series of repressive laws that effectively stripped the Cherokees of their political and property rights. These actions set off a flurry of protests and led to the famous Supreme Court cases *Cherokee Nation v. Georgia* (1831) and *Worcester v. Georgia* (1832). These cases were followed closely by the public. Excerpts from and commentary on the legal arguments were reprinted in periodicals and pamphlets; the Cherokees published several appeals to the American people, which were printed in prominent newspapers, and went on speaking tours in the East to stir up support for their cause. Jackson's political opponents did all in their power to keep the issue before the public, hoping that it would damage Jackson's chances for reelection in 1832.[9] In spite of the Court's ruling on the Cherokees' behalf in 1832, the tribe was eventually forced to remove in 1838 along the infamous Trail of Tears to Oklahoma. The drama and pathos of this event once again focused public attention on American Indian policy and the moral questions it raised—especially among those living in the East, where the majority of books, debates, court decisions, and speeches on the subject were both produced and received.[10] As Michael Rogin has written of the Jacksonian period, "Indians had not mattered so much since the colonial settlements. They would never matter so much again" (1975, 4). Indians mattered during this period not primarily as a physical or political threat to the American nation but as a threat to Americans' sense of themselves as a moral nation—a threat, in short, to American national character and legitimacy.

Lucy Maddox concurs with Rogin's assessment: "Whether the American writer in this period wanted to address the question of the place of the Indians in national culture or to avoid it, there were few subjects that he or she could write about without in some way engaging it" (10–11). She focuses on (mainly canonical) works that do not necessarily appear to be about Indians and shows how the politics of Indian policy, however masked or "removed," remain central. Although this approach leads to illuminating new readings of familiar works, it does not attempt a fresh understanding of the Indian problem itself or nineteenth-century conceptualizations of it. Whereas Maddox focuses on one formulation of the problem—"civilization or extinction"—and examines literary texts that articulate or interrogate this logic, the scope of my project is different. Examining cultural productions that focus explicitly on Indians and American Indian policy, I explore how and why nineteenth-century representations mark a cultural problem that no single text or logic seems capable of containing, and how this insistence of "the Indian" in American popular culture and consciousness inflected national identity formation during the first half of the nineteenth century.

The Insistence of the Indian in American National Consciousness

During the 1820s, as Americans struggled to define the status and rights of Indians in the United States, the question of American national identity also provoked considerable attention. Having tested its strength against other world powers in the War of 1812, the new nation became self-consciously concerned with constructing an idea of "America" that could reach beyond the founding act of revolution to offer post-Revolutionary generations a source of national identity and legitimacy. This concern was heightened by a growing awareness that the founding fathers were dying. By the end of 1826 only one signer of the Declaration of Independence remained alive. As historian George Forgie has argued (52), as long as the founding fathers lived on, American national identity, born of the founders' military and political actions, and American national character, guaranteed by their morality and integrity, could be embodied in the founders themselves. But as the events and individuals actually responsible for creating the nation faded into the past, Americans of the post-Revolutionary generation attempted to find new means of affirming a sense of national identity.

One response was to turn from the historically defined realm of political action to the imaginative realm of language and symbol. From the 1820s through the 1850s, cultural critics repeatedly called on Americans to produce a literature, a drama, an art that would express and affirm the nation's distinctive identity. The Revolutionary War and the Declaration of Independence notwithstanding, the argument went, Americans would not achieve true independence from Britain until they had produced a national literature and art that dealt with American materials, celebrated American history, illustrated and simultaneously shaped American character, thereby binding individual citizens together as a people through a shared vision of the nation and a national culture.

Indians were often proposed as the perfect subject matter for a national literature. On a purely aesthetic level, the association of Indians with the distant past, together with popular conceptions of their status as a dying race, made them an appealingly romantic subject. More important, Indians were a uniquely American subject. According to William Gilmore Simms, one of the most vocal proponents of a national literature based on Indian themes, Indians could be claimed as America's Gauls and Goths; they represented the prehistory of the nation, offering the means to locate the origins of the nation in a distant, almost mythic past. Such sentiments resonate with Benedict Anderson's argument about the importance of historically distant origins (whether actual or invented) to imaginative constructions of the nation: "If nation-states are widely conceded to be 'new' and 'historical,' the nations to which they give political expression always loom out of the immemorial past and, still more important, glide into the limitless future" (11). For a nation originating in a recent act of revolutionary rupture, imagining such a vision of continuity with a distant past was not easy. But by claiming Indians, with their long history and mysterious origins, as part of their own national story, nineteenth-century Americans found a way to ground national identity in the distant, inaccessible, "immemorial past."

In his 1833 address entitled "The Importance of Illustrating New England History by a Series of Romances Like the Waverley Novels," Rufus Choate proposed just such an act of literary appropriation. Rewriting the history of Indians as the history of (Euro-) America, Choate suggested that King Philip would provide an excellent subject for literature illustrating the "heroic age" of the nation; Philip would become a "tragic hero" in the American national drama (Choate, 1:319, 336). Washington Irving's *Sketch Book* (1818) includes an essay on Philip cast in just such terms. The tragedy both Choate and Irving associate with American Indians points toward a serious moral paradox. While Indians might provide Americans with the materials out of which to create a sense of mythic origins, the actual history of Indian relations in America called into question the legitimacy and morality of that national identity. Nevertheless, the popularity of representations of Indians in literature, drama, and art during the first half of the nineteenth century provides evidence that many Americans found the subject quite compelling.

In her *Reflections on Political Identity*, Anne Norton suggests that moral paradox of the sort that surrounded nineteenth-century representations of Indians plays a crucial role in a nation's definition and legitimation. She describes the process as follows:

> The recognition of qualities that distinguish the polity from all others entails the propagation of abstract principles against which the conduct of the regime and constitution of the nation may be measured. The qualities definitive of the nation are abstracted from it and made objective. The citizens, having before them an objective principle of nationality, may thereafter determine whether the regime, or the regime's actions, are appropriate to the nation. This is the beginning of legitimacy. (53)

By testing the principles that governed the conduct of the United States, the Indian problem helped to define the nation. The debates over property, which were at the heart of the problem, were simultaneously debates over what is proper to, and thus constitutive of, the nation. But while Indians provided an occasion for the examination of national morality or "propriety," clear and definitive solutions seldom emerged. Thus, the ambivalences that characterized the Indian problem ultimately became part of the "principle of nationality" defined in relation to it.

As debates over the status and rights of Indians in the United States unfolded, Indians emerged as nationally liminal figures. Neither citizens nor aliens, at once symbolically central and politically excluded, Indians constituted the boundaries at which the meaning of the nation is defined.[11] Norton has explored the function of liminal figures in the process of national formation: "Liminars serve as mirrors for nations. At once other and like, they provide the occasion for the nation to constitute itself through reflection upon its identity. Their likeness permits contemplation and recognition, their difference the abstraction of those ideal traits that will henceforth define the nation" (1988, 54). In literature, drama, and art focusing on Indian subjects, nineteenth-century Americans reified "the Indian" into an object of contemplation that both reflected and provided imaginative space for reflection on the meaning of national identity.

In her recent study of narrative form and identity formation, Priscilla Wald examines the role of Indians. Her analysis in many ways parallels Norton's, but the quality that Norton identifies as liminal Wald characterizes as uncanny. Analyzing nineteenth-century debates over the status and rights of Indians and blacks, Wald locates the anxieties of white citizens in the recognition that these excluded groups were both similar to and different from themselves. Underlying debates over Indian rights, Wald claims, is the awareness that all rights are conventional, bestowed by a government that can just as easily revoke those same rights. For example, the Court's examination of slavery in the 1857 *Dred Scott* case led Justice John McLean to wonder what "stops a government from making 'white men slaves?'" (Wald, 45).

While Wald's formulation of the Indian (and slavery) problem provides insights into the cultural anxieties produced by these debates, I would argue that it misses the fundamental manner in which the Indian problem provided the occasion for, and space to reflect on, national identity formation. Although opponents of the *Dred Scott* decision might, for rhetorical purposes, have posed the question "What is to keep the government from making white men slaves?," few white Americans steeped in nineteenth-century ideologies of race would have been in danger of actually confusing their own status with that of blacks or Indians. Debates over the status of excluded groups created anxiety not because they stirred confusion between "us" and "them" but because they produced alternative, troubling, visions of "us" by calling into question the very principles by which white Americans defined their collective moral ascendancy and national legitimacy. In other words, the Indian problem (and the slavery question) disrupted not individuals' constitution as Americans but the symbolic systems according to which the meaning of the nation itself was constituted. While collective and individual identity formation cannot actually be separated—participation in a collectivity is part of the individual's identity—the shift in emphasis that I wish to suggest is significant. Whereas Wald employs a psychoanalytic model of individual development as a metaphor for national development, I focus instead on identity as it is articulated through symbolic systems that shape meaning by virtue of their capacity for communal recognition. I find such a model more useful than the metaphor of individual psychology in understanding the popular representations, and the communally defined idea of the nation, that are the subject of this study.

During the first half of the nineteenth century, Americans' unavoidable confrontation with the Indian problem frustrated attempts to create a unified, consistent idea of the nation. Efforts to define the nation in terms that could accommodate the complex disruptions produced by the Indian problem were much closer to the process that Bhabha describes than to the smoothly unfolding narrative structure governing Anderson's idea of the nation. According to Bhabha, the narrative of the nation is inherently unstable. In opposition to

THE "INDIAN PROBLEM" 11

the linear equivalence of event and idea that historicism proposes, [which] most commonly signifies a people, a nation, or a national culture as an empirical sociological category or a holistic cultural entity, the narrative and psychological force that nationness brings to bear on cultural production and political projection is the effect of the ambivalence of the "nation" as a narrative strategy. (1994, 140)

Bhabha alternates between locating this instability at the margins of the nation—the minority, the exile, the colonial hybrid, whose very presence disrupts the nation's claims to homogeneity, coherence, and unity—and defining it as a condition of language itself. Like Bhabha, I see the ambivalence of nationhood both deriving from and manifesting itself in problems of representation. I also agree with Bhabha that this ambivalence is best understood in terms of language—although not as conceived in Bhabha's poststructuralist understanding of the instability of all language and meaning but closer to the way in which Lacan describes the role of language in "The Insistence of the Letter in the Unconscious."

In this seminal essay Lacan explores how language structures both the individual unconscious and culture itself:

> The speaking subject, if he seems to be thus a slave of language, is all the more so of a discourse in the universal moment of which he finds himself at birth, even if only by dint of his proper name.
> Reference to the "experience of the community" as the substance of this discourse settles nothing. For this experience has as its essential dimension the tradition which the discourse itself founds. This tradition, long before the drama of history gets written into it, creates the elementary structures of culture. And these structures reveal an ordering of possible exchanges which, even unconscious, is inconceivable outside the permutations authorized by language. (104)[12]

Lacan's emphasis on the historical, communal meaning of language—as discourse—differs somewhat from classic (Freudian) approaches. For Lacan, language is not simply a symptom to be analyzed in order to illuminate the individual's psychology; rather, language itself constructs meaning—for individuals and communities—through the structures and relations it makes possible. This understanding of language informs my analysis of nineteenth-century American popular culture. I intend not only to decode particular uses of language for the meanings they reveal but to consider how Indians functioned as part of a larger discourse of nationalism and to explore the historical meanings and social relations this discourse made possible.

With this in mind, I return to Anne Norton's suggestion that liminal figures—those who, like Indians, belong neither within nor outside of the nation—serve as mirrors that permit the nation to be defined through reflection on its identity. Just as the construction of self-image during the mirror stage as something unified and controllable to some extent depends on a denial of reality, so the construction of the nation as a homogeneous union of citizens also depends on an essential denial of reality. If Indians provided a crucial site of reflection on national identity during the first half of the nineteenth century, they also represented that which had to be denied for a coherent image of the nation to be recognized. Thus, the insistence of the Indian in the American national consciousness can be understood as the driving force behind the repeated return to Indians as the subject of popular representation and the occasion for national imaginings.

The chapters that follow focus on representative works from several popular genres juxtaposed with contemporary political and legal rhetoric on the Indian problem and U.S. national identity. Chapter 2 considers James Fenimore Cooper's popular frontier romance *The Pioneers; or, The Sources of the Susquehanna* (1823) together with the Supreme Court's decision in *Johnson and Graham's Lessee v. McIntosh* (1823) as a means of exploring how nineteenth-century legal discourse and the discourse of popular fiction engaged and "managed" the morally troubling and politically charged question of Indian land rights. In their respective narratives, Cooper and Chief Justice Marshall attempt to legitimate American claims to land once owned by Indians and "inherited" from England by virtue of the Revolution. Both construct a story of the national past and a version of the American political "family" intended to assuage the guilt associated with the violence (of conquest and revolution) that characterized relations with both Indian and English forebears, projecting a stable, peaceful future for the nation despite its violent origins.

Chapter 3 explores an alternative myth of national origins as it was enacted on the popular stage. During the first half of the nineteenth century Indians were the most common subject of plays that presented themselves as "National Dramas," and Pocahontas was the single most popular figure featured in these plays. Focusing on James Nelson Barker's play *The Indian Princess or La Belle Sauvage* (1808), the first written about Pocahontas, and George Washington Parke Custis's *Pocahontas, or The Settlers of Virginia, A National Drama* (1830), the most successful of the Pocahontas plays, this chapter considers how these popular performances of the Pocahontas-Smith legend served to define and legitimize national identity. These plays illustrate the peculiar national and narrative problems posed by Indians during this period of intense nationalism. While the exclusion and removal of Indians was necessary to the founding and expansion of the nation, Indians, as the original inhabitants of the American land, also served to represent the potential of the continent itself and all that distinguished Americans from their European antecedents. Indians thus became the repository of an idealized and nostalgically distanced American identity that achieved its power in the national narrative by virtue of the impossibility of its ever being fully realized.

In chapter 4, I examine a best-seller of 1824, Mary Jemison's captivity narrative, in the context of early legal and political rhetoric that defined the policy of Indian removal. Known locally as "The White Woman of the Genessee," Jemison lived most of her life with her Seneca husband and children in a home she built herself, liminally located between a Seneca village and a white town. As her epithet indicates, the fact that she was a woman—emphatically identified as "White" although living with Indians—was central to her significance for white neighbors (and readers). I explore how the values and powers popularly associated with womanhood and whiteness during the nineteenth century were simultaneously contested by Jemison and enlisted by early editors of the narrative to make of her a figure representing Euro-American ascendancy over Indians. Jemison emerges in the narrative as a heroic mother embodying the principles upon which early justifications of removal were based. Examining both the captivity narrative itself and the extensive commentary provided by the book's editors, I center my analysis on points of disjuncture between the story Jemison seems to be telling and the story the editors prefer to hear. Such moments of narrative dissonance reveal how editors construed Jemison's story as a more palatable (yet, to Indians, no less destructive) maternalistic alternative to the government's paternalistic model of Indian-white relations.

Black Hawk's *Life* (1833), the focus of chapter 5, textually represents the loss of power that Indians actually experienced as a result of the (forced) removal policy implemented by Andrew Jackson during the 1830s. It is significant that this representation of an Indian as autobiographical subject occurred at the same moment that the nation debated policies defining the status of Indians within the United States as subject peoples without sovereignty or citizenship. Reading Black Hawk's *Life* and news accounts of his celebrated "tour" in juxtaposition with the Cherokee Supreme Court cases of the early 1830s, I explore how textual, legal, and political constructions of the Indians' subject status relate to and reinforce one another. In addition, I consider how this project of defining "the Indian" depends on and reinforces nationalistic constructions of the meaning of "America" and American citizenry.

In chapter 6 I examine guidebooks to the U.S. Capitol produced in the 1830s and 1860s. In particular, I explore the vision of national history these guidebooks presented and how they defined the American citizen-tourist in relation to it. The guidebooks' representation of history is revealed most clearly in accounts of artworks commemorating the contacts between Euro-Americans and Indians. Individual works of art were described in dramatic terms as part of a larger chain of events; guidebooks provided the prompter's cue, turning the Capitol into a theatrical space where symbolically charged moments from the national past were to be staged repeatedly within the minds of the "imagined community" of citizens who had come to tour the Capitol. Making these works of commemorative public art the occasion for national imaginings, guidebooks to the Capitol nostalgically constructed a past that never was and a citizenry that emerged through the very act of (guided) interpretation, in which "the citizen" was cast as audience and actor in an ongoing national drama.

The continuing popularity of Indians as the subject of representation during the first half of the nineteenth century indicates that none of the stories Americans told about "the Indian"—or about the nation as defined in relation to Indians—was the final word.[13] What this study ultimately explores, then, is the insistence of the Indian in American popular culture as marking a problem that the symbolic cannot solve, the threshold of resistance at which meaning emerges, the very gap that the nation is imagined to fill. The Indian question revealed to nineteenth-century Americans the deep ambivalence of a nation founded on the conceptual assertion of natural right and the actual denial of Indians' natural rights. This gap between nation as sign of Enlightenment principles and nation as "performed" in American Indian policy remained unclosed.[14] The gap itself became the imaginative space in which the nation emerged, not as a coherent idea or a realist narrative but as an ongoing performance that repeatedly played out, without resolution, the fundamental ambivalences of American national identity.

TWO

COOPER AND THE SOURCES OF AMERICAN

NATIONAL IDENTITY

AS SUGGESTED BY its subtitle, "The Sources of the Susquehanna," *The Pioneers* is a book about origins. For James Fenimore Cooper it represented an account of personal origins based
upon the story of his father's founding of Cooperstown, where he spent
much of his childhood. It is also a story about national origins, about the
desire of nineteenth-century Americans for an originary myth upon which
to found a sense of national identity. In *The Pioneers* Cooper attempted
to incorporate into a legitimating national narrative both the Revolution
that marked the beginnings of a new political identity and the process of
settlement by which the new nation took possession from the Indians of
the vast territory it now claimed as its own.[1]

In its examination of American origins, *The Pioneers* looks both forward and backward. One strand of the plot centers on new beginnings—the building of a new settlement, the progress of a new nation,
and the founding of a new line of legitimate heirs to America's future—
while another examines the nation's relationship to its past. The book's
final scene illustrates the crux of Cooper's struggle. Elizabeth Temple
and Oliver Effingham, now married and firmly established as the chosen
progenitors of the American future, discover the old woodsman Natty
Bumppo lying upon the ground above the graves of Chingachgook and
Major Effingham, representatives of America's prenational past. Inter-
rupted in this graphic display of mourning, Natty rises. Oliver and Elizabeth invite him to join them in the new world they are busily building
on the frontier, but he refuses. Instead he drifts away toward the setting
sun, running from but never escaping history. This final scene illustrates
a central problem: the new order is built upon the graves of the old,
and the ghosts of those supplanted do not rest easily. This chapter
explores how nineteenth-century Americans attempted—in popular
fiction, legal argument, and official Indian policy—to come to terms
with the restless ghosts of the national past, the legacy of a history of
conquest and revolution that threatened the moral foundations of
nationhood.

American Origins and the Problem of History

In *Imagined Communities: Reflections on the Origin and Spread of Nationalism* Benedict Anderson argues that nationalist imagining, like religious imagining (and, I would add, like mourning), is concerned with death and immortality. It entails the attempt to establish a sense of continuity and meaning in the face of historical change: "If nation-states are widely conceded to be new and historical, the nations to which they give political expression always loom out of the immemorial past and, still more important, glide into a limitless future" (11–12). By encompassing a past that is lost to memory and connecting it to a future that is yet to be, the nation makes eternal the space of the continual present which it occupies. Whereas religion promises transcendence in the face of loss, nationalism, like mourning, offers history—imagining a future that descends from the past.

While Americans of the early nineteenth century, with their optimistic faith in progress, would have had little trouble imagining a "limitless future" for the nation, where were they to ground a sense of continuity with the "immemorial past"? Envisioning the English as historical forebears would lead to a sense of patricidal guilt, for a patrimony (of nationhood) gained through violence against the fathers could not be considered legitimate. While nineteenth-century Americans could locate a historical beginning in the American Revolution and define themselves as the heirs of the founding fathers, the Revolution itself, representing a quintessential act of discontinuity with the past, provided not a sense of historical continuity but what many Americans feared would be a legacy of instability and discontinuity: the threat of repeated revolution. Locating the beginnings of nationhood in the recent Revolutionary War still left Americans without that sense of connection to the "immemorial past" which Anderson identifies as so crucial to the idea of the nation.

Many literary nationalists of the early nineteenth century suggested that the history and myths of American Indians could provide the new nation with a sense of "primitive" origins. Efforts by nineteenth-century ethnohistorians such as Heckewelder and Schoolcraft also illustrate the urge to preserve a record of the American Indians as a national legacy. Reviewing Schoolcraft's work in 1845, William Gilmore Simms drew parallels between the American Indians and the ancient Gauls and Goths of European history (136).[2] He urged Americans to incorporate the Indians and their legends in a national literature. Rufus Choate, speaking in 1833, likewise insisted upon "The Importance of Illustrating New-England History by a Series of Romances Like the Waverley Novels." He suggested that King Philip's war would be an especially appropriate topic. As Choate's suggestion reveals, grounding national history in an Indian heritage focused attention on the violence and coercion that characterized the history of Indian-white relations. It would be difficult, without experiencing a deep sense of patricidal guilt, to claim as forebears those whom Americans were in the process of destroying.

In *The Pioneers* Cooper grappled with the difficulties of establishing a sense of national identity in the face of the nation's complex and conflicted relationship to its past. This struggle is most clearly articulated in the central question that runs throughout the book: Who has the right to own and govern the land originally possessed by Indians and inherited through the Revolution? Cooper was not the only American of his day to grapple with this problem. In 1823, the year that *The Pioneers* was published, the Supreme Court examined the basis of American rights in the case of *Johnson and Graham's Lessee v. McIntosh*. In his attempt to define the principles underlying American claims to the land, Chief Justice Marshall confronted many of the same problems that Cooper dealt with in *The Pioneers*. In both narratives legitimacy depended upon the kind of story one told about the past.[3]

The case of *Johnson v. McIntosh* arose out of two competing claims to the same land: the plaintiffs received their grant directly from the Illinois and Piankeshaw Indians before the American Revolution, while the defendant's grant came directly from the U.S. government. Before it could decide the merits of each claim, the Court needed to determine "the power of Indians to give, and of private individuals to receive, a title which can be sustained in the Courts of this country" (Washburn, 4: 2537).[4] In his landmark opinion Chief Justice Marshall reviewed the history of Indian-white relations in America and undertook a broad examination of the status and rights of Indians in the United States. To determine the nature and extent of Indians' rights, the Court found it necessary to inquire into the basis of Euro-American claims to the land. This inquiry reached far beyond the narrow limits of Indian-white relations, ultimately raising questions regarding the United States' relationship to England and the extent to which nineteenth-century Americans were upholding the ideals that had justified the revolutionary break from England. Thus, the case of *Johnson v. McIntosh* implicitly helped to define the character of the new nation itself.

As the Court interpreted the history of Indian-white relations in America, it determined that Indian title could be extinguished only by the government of the nation claiming sovereignty over Indian lands. European claims to sovereignty rested upon the rights of conquest and the "Doctrine of Discovery."[5] By asserting direct ties of political kinship and inheritance between the United States and England, Marshall could claim that, as a result of the Revolutionary War, the rights of Great Britain devolved upon the new nation: "The British government, which was then our government, and whose rights have passed to the United States, asserted a title to all the lands occupied by Indians, within the chartered limits of the British colonies" (Washburn, 4:2544). In this account of history, the new nation's right to the American land derived from European principles transmitted intact from the Old World to the New, inherited from England by virtue of the Revolution.

It is not difficult to see how such a history might complicate Americans' sense of national identity. Claiming that the United States inherited its rights from England (Washburn, 4:2543, 2545) placed a nation defined politically by its separation from England in an awkward position. For example, the Court found itself upholding as precedent British colonial policies, such as the Proclamation of 1763 (2548), which the Revolutionary generation had denounced—and which had, in fact, been cited as a just cause for rebellion. In addition, many elements of British Indian policy, which the United States now claimed as its own, seemed to contradict the basic principle of "natural right" at the heart of American Revolutionary and democratic ideology. Such contradictions frequently were brought to public attention by speculators who wished to acquire Indian lands unhindered by government regulation. Speculators argued for their right to purchase lands directly from Indians by drawing specific parallels between Indians' natural rights and the principle of natural right that informed Revolutionary rhetoric and documents such as the Declaration of Independence.[6]

Marshall's language in the *Johnson v. McIntosh* opinion betrays his difficulty in reconciling the moral and ideological implications of the case, on the one hand, with the political and economic conditions of national existence, on the other.

> However extravagant the pretension of converting the discovery of an inhabited country into conquest may appear; if the principle has been asserted in the first instance, and afterward sustained; if a country has been acquired and held under it; if the property of the great mass of the community originates in it, it becomes the law of the land, and cannot be questioned. So, too, with respect to the concomitant principle, that the Indian inhabitants are to be considered merely as occupants, to be protected, indeed, while in peace, in the possession of their lands, but to be deemed incapable of transferring the absolute title to others. However this restriction may be opposed to natural right, and to the usages of civilized nations, yet, if it be indispensable to that system under which the country has been settled, and be adapted to the

actual condition of the two peoples, it may, perhaps, be supported by reason, and certainly cannot be rejected by Courts of justice. (2547)

Marshall seems to admit that the denial of Indians' full rights to the lands they possessed is a convenient fiction, but one that cannot be rejected by the courts of a nation whose very existence and future expansion depend on it. While he suggests that "it may, perhaps, be supported by reason," Marshall does not entirely succeed in justifying it. This "perhaps" locates the boundary of Marshall's legal narrative in the imaginative terrain of surmise, fiction, (historical) romance, somewhere between "the actual state of things" (2547) and the stories that make sense of things as they are.

In *The Pioneers* James Fenimore Cooper also addressed the question of who has a right to the American land. Like Marshall, Cooper attempted to construct a narrative that would legitimate American claims in the face of the nation's Revolutionary origins and the Indians' prior claims. For Cooper, as for Marshall, the rights of the new nation did not originate with the Revolution but were transmitted from the past according to principles of inheritance. The problem faced by Cooper, like that faced by Marshall, was thus twofold: to establish the basis of Euro-American rights to lands possessed by Indians and to solidify the lines of inheritance by which these rights devolved upon the present citizens of the United States. By manipulating the category of race, Cooper found a way to bring the prior "owners" of the American land—both the Indians and the English—into a narrative of kinship and inheritance as ancestors willingly bestowing their authority and property on their rightful American heirs. By invoking an attitude of mourning in relation to these historical forebears, Cooper enacted a symbolic affirmation of Americans' claim to the land and to the legacy of nationhood. While it achieved a stronger sense of moral resolution, Cooper's fiction was no less convenient nor contradictory than Marshall's. The balance of this chapter explores how Marshall's legal discourse and Cooper's fictional narrative encompassed and incorporated in the project of national identity formation the unavoidable contradictions that emerged from an American history characterized by revolution and conquest.

Revolutionary Revisions

The first scene of conflict in *The Pioneers*, an argument over who may claim ownership of a recently killed buck, introduces the key issues that will structure Cooper's narrative. Judge Temple, the great landowner and developer of the frontier settlement of Templeton, believes that his shot has killed the deer. He good-naturedly argues his case in mock-legal terms: "I would fain establish a right, Natty, to the honor of this death; and surely if the hit in the neck be mine, it is enough; for the shot in the heart was unnecessary—what we call an act of supererogation, Leather-Stocking" (Cooper [1823] 1980, 23). Natty, the old woodsman who lives on Temple's land, insists that the buck was actually killed by the shot of his young companion Oliver Edwards (later identified as Oliver Edward Effingham, son of Temple's boyhood friend and business partner). When the judge offers to purchase the buck, Edwards refuses to sell his property. In a later discussion of the incident, the judge's cousin, Richard, links ownership of the buck to ownership of the land: "Well, Duke, you are your own master, but I would have tried law for the saddle [of the deer], before I would have given it to the fellow. Do you not own the mountains as well as the valleys? are not the woods your own? what right has this chap, or the Leather-Stocking, to shoot in your woods, without your permission?" Richard, continuing the debate with himself, expands the issue of ownership rights even further when he raises the question of Indian rights to the land: "There is Mohegan [Chingachgook], to be sure, he may have some right, being a native; but it's little the poor fellow can do now with his rifle" (93). This brief, fairly lighthearted controversy prefigures the competing claims to the land that drive the plot of *The Pioneers*.

Natty's framing of the question during the argument over the buck firmly links justice to national identity: "[M]ight often makes right here as well as in the old country, for what I can see" (22). To prove that the new country has a distinct identity, Natty implies, one must prove that it is governed by principles of justice morally superior to Old World rule by force. The book's opening paragraph makes a similar point: "[T]he whole district is hourly exhibiting how much can be done, in even a rugged country, under the dominion of mild laws, and where every man feels a direct interest in the prosperity of a commonwealth, of which he knows himself to form a part" (16).

Natty challenges the authority of the judge, and the law he stands for, on the basis of his own understanding of "natural law." The opposition between natural and civil law has been identified by many critics as the central theme of *The Pioneers*, and Natty, the main spokesperson for natural law, had already been recognized by early reviewers as its real hero.[7] But Natty remains outside the lines of inheritance by which the conflicts that drive the plot are resolved and legitimacy is ultimately established. I will return to Natty's role later in this chapter to explore how his marginal position in the plot structure actually adds to his power. For now I wish to underscore his structural marginality as one of the strategies by which Cooper attempts to contain the troubling moral questions Natty raises.

As representative inheritor of the American land, Oliver Edwards/Effingham is the official hero of Cooper's story of national origins; it is Oliver's challenge, based upon the rights of inheritance, rather than Natty's, based upon natural law, to which Judge Temple finally responds and succumbs. The plot of *The Pioneers*, in fact, is centered upon Oliver's efforts to regain his lost inheritance—the land now claimed by Judge Temple. Justice—and resolution—are finally achieved in the novel not by the power of civil law nor by the moral authority of Natty's natural law but by virtue of Judge Temple's personal loyalty to Oliver's father and his respect for the principles of inheritance.[8] Cooper's focus on inheritance as the determinant of who may own and govern the American land radically simplifies the question of legitimacy: if rights to the American land were established in the past by others, then the only issue becomes the smooth transmission of past rights to the present.

Oliver's unusual ties to the past serve to reinforce structurally his inherited right to the land. The reader fully understands the basis of Oliver's claim only toward the end of the novel, when it is revealed that Oliver is the grandson of Major Effingham, a retired British officer, who is himself the adopted son of the Mohican Chingachgook. The land upon which Templeton now stands was first given to Major Effingham by Chingachgook's tribe as a sign of gratitude after Major Effingham saved the chief's life.[9] With the outbreak of the Revolutionary War, Oliver's father, a loyalist, left the family's property in the hands of his friend Marmaduke Temple. When the Loyalists' property was confiscated and sold after the war, Temple purchased the Effingham lands—an action that Oliver sees as a breach of loyalty and a violation of his hereditary claim to the land.

By playing upon Oliver's relationship to Chingachgook, Cooper conflates the question of Indian rights with questions of inheritance, thus simplifying the path toward structural and narrative resolution. But the racial masquerade simultaneously complicates the moral ground the novel must traverse to achieve resolution. Throughout the novel Oliver speaks proudly of his Indian lineage; Natty and Chingachgook both call him Young Eagle, son of an Indian chief, and the townspeople believe that his bitterness toward Judge Temple is based upon his sense of the Indians' violated rights. The statements by Oliver and those who speak for his rights call into question Americans' treatment of the Indians and the moral legitimacy of American claims to the land once owned by them. At one point Mr. Grant, the minister, openly expresses his doubts: "I know not that he who claims affinity to the proper owners of this soil [the Indians] has not the best right to tread these hills with the lightest conscience." Chingachgook responds by suggesting a solution that most readers would be reluctant to apply to the problem of Indian rights in the United States: "[Judge Temple] will cut the country in two parts, as the

river cuts the lowlands, and will say to the Young Eagle, Child of the
Delawares! take it—keep it—and be a chief in the land of your fathers"
(142).[10]

Through Natty Cooper proposes another equally disturbing solution.
On Christmas Eve, as Chingachgook is drinking and singing of his past,
Natty suggests that the violation of Indians' rights will lead to violence:

> Why do you sing of your battles, Chingachgook, and of the warriors you
> have slain, when the worst enemy of all [Judge Temple] is near you, and
> keeps the Young Eagle from his rights? . . .
>
> And why have you slain the Mingo warriors? Was it not to keep these
> hunting grounds and lakes to your father's children? and were they not given
> in solemn council to the Fire-eater? [Major Effingham's Indian name] and
> does not the blood of a warrior run in the veins of a young chief, who should
> speak aloud where his voice is now too low to be heard? (165)

Chingachgook responds to this reminder of his injuries by reaching for
his tomahawk, which, fortunately for the judge, he is too inebriated to
use.

But even as Cooper flirts with the threat of violence, he is simultaneously framing the conflict in terms that contain that violence. Natty's
account of the series of crimes committed by the Indians' "worst enemy
of all" actually shifts attention away from Indian rights per se. First Natty
notes Judge Temple's violation of the Delawares' ability to preserve the
land for future generations—of Indians, the reader naturally assumes.
Next he suggests that Temple has compromised the tribe's act of giving
the land to Major Effingham. By the end of the passage, Oliver has replaced Chingachgook as the wronged party, the one whom Natty chas-
tises for his complacency; he is the "young chief" whose voice should be
raised against the injustices he has suffered at the hands of Judge Temple.
Thus, through displacement Cooper defuses the more radical implications of the questions he raises regarding the justice of American Indian
policy.

Later in the novel Cooper expands this logic of displacement from a
personal to a broader, historical dimension. Just before he dies, Chingachgook explains to Elizabeth Temple the nature of the injury he feels
he has received at the hands of the whites—an injury he associates with
the general decline of his people:

> John [Chingachgook] was young when his tribe gave away the country, in
> council, from where the blue mountain stands above the water, to where the
> Susquehanna is hid by the trees. All this and all that grew in it, and all that
> walked over it, and all that fed there, they gave to the Fire-eater—for they
> loved him. He was strong and they were women, and he helped them. No

Delaware would kill a deer that ran in his woods, nor stop a bird that flew over his land: for it was his. Has John lived in peace? Daughter, since John was young, he has seen the white man from Frontenac come down on his white brothers at Albany and fight. Did they fear God? He has seen his English and his American fathers burying their tomahawks in each other's brains, for this very land. Did they fear God and live in peace? He has seen the land pass away from the Fire-eater, and his children, and the child of his child, and a new chief set over the country. Did they live in peace who did this? did they fear God? (401)

Once again the crime against the Indians is defined as a violation of the rights of inheritance: the transmission of the land from the Fire-eater (Major Effingham) to his children and from them to his children's children. Once again this right is premised upon the Indians' right "to g[i]ve away the country, in council." This is one Indian "right" that most Americans were quite willing to acknowledge.[11] Chingachgook imagines the transfer of property in terms that Americans would find quite reassuring: the granting of Indian land to Major Effingham is presented as a voluntary act of love and appreciation; once they have given the land to the white man, the Indians respect his absolute ownership of the land.[12] Thus, in Cooper's account of dispossession the only violence associated with the loss of the Indians' land and the violation of their rights is not that between Indians and whites but among whites themselves—the conflict between Oliver and Judge Temple and, in Chingachgook's broad historical vision, fighting between the Indians' "English and . . . American fathers."

Near the end of the novel Cooper finally makes explicit that the true object of criticism (voiced by Oliver, Natty, and Chingachgook throughout the novel) is Judge Temple's purchase of the Effingham lands after the Revolutionary War under conditions Oliver interprets as a breach of loyalty and honor between two white men. Thus, the judge's right of ownership is challenged not by Indian but by English prior rights to the soil. The crucial event underlying the conflict has nothing at all to do with Indians but is strictly a matter among whites: as Cooper ingeniously constructs the plot, the American Revolution (fighting between the Indians' "English and . . . American fathers") becomes the ultimate source of the conflict over who has the right to own and inherit American land. While these narrative strategies structurally displace the moral threat posed by Indians to American national legitimacy, the radical implications of the questions the novel raises regarding the justice of American Indian policy continue to reverberate in the background even as Cooper attempts to shift the focus to American Revolutionary origins.

While this strategy allows Cooper to evade one set of complications, it calls attention to another. As an act of patricidal violence, the Revolution tainted the legitimacy of the nationhood thus acquired. Even for those who accepted the moral validity of the founding act of revolution, the question of national legitimacy was far from settled. As George B. Forgie has pointed out, many Americans of the post-Revolutionary generation experienced anxiety regarding their worthiness to assume the authority of the fathers and their ability to preserve the nation they inherited. According to Forgie, they attempted to ease this anxiety through repetition: by repeating the actions, and thus revealing the same character, upon which the father's authority is based, the son proves his right to that same authority. But, as Forgie goes on to argue, America's Revolutionary origins complicated the task of imitation: repeating the violent action by which the fathers gained their authority would endanger the very inheritance the sons hoped to preserve; even imitating the virtue of the fathers was difficult since virtue may be proven only through action, and the task of preservation in prosperous times did not provide many opportunities to display the kind of heroism upon which the founding fathers' authority rested. In the absence of an appropriate field of action, Forgie concludes, those with ambition to imitate the fathers were drawn toward a patricidal course. Forgie sees the American Civil War as a manifestation of such tendencies (63–71).

Cooper offers a different answer: revision. Throughout his writings Cooper attempts to redefine the meaning of America's Revolutionary origins.[13] In *Notions of the Americans Picked Up by a Travelling Bachelor* he describes a visit to George Washington's home with the reverence of a pilgrim at a holy shrine (Cooper [1828] 1991, 409–420). When he writes about the Revolution itself, however, Cooper betrays a deep ambivalence toward the nation's Revolutionary origins. At one point he goes so far as to deny that a revolution ever took place. According to Cadwallader, Cooper's representative American spokesman in the book, "We [Americans] have ever been reformers rather than Revolutionists. Our own struggle for Independence was not in its aspect, a Revolution. . . . We have never been in a hurry to make unnecessary innovations. Reform marches with a dignified pace; it is revolution that is violent. The States continued the practice of the Colonies" (228 and 287, resp.).

By distinguishing between reform and revolution, Cooper is able to accept the radical changes occasioned by the Revolution while still stressing the value of political and social stability. In Cooper's reformulation, the Revolution wass neither violent nor disruptive of an essential continuity between (English) colonial and (American) national "practices." Like inheritance, reform is a process of gradual change based upon unchanging principles, a process that is ultimately conservative rather than revolutionary.

In *The Pioneers* Cooper also redefines the meaning of the Revolution in American history. In place of models that imagine the new nation emerging as a consequence of a violent rupture with the past, Cooper offers a model in which continuity with a more distant, pre-Revolutionary past becomes the fundamental principle underlying U.S. national identity. Cooper's rewriting of the Revolution edits out the violence of conflict: none of the major characters in *The Pioneers* actually fought in the Revolutionary War. Judge Temple, the founder of Templeton, is the closest thing to a "founding" father in the book. Although his Quaker beliefs prevent him from actually fighting, he does gain possession of his lands through the purchase of property confiscated from Loyalists after the Revolutionary War. Like other American founding fathers, he presides over his newly acquired lands, occupying a position of moral and political leadership. By the end of the novel, Judge Temple's authority and property have been transferred to Oliver, a representative of the post-Revolutionary generation, whose claim to authority is untainted by violence, having originated in the pre-Revolutionary past, and founded upon principles of inheritance that encompass both Indian and English prior rights. In Cooper's version of history, American claims to the land—and to the legacy of nationhood—are not legitimated through imitation of the founding fathers, who violently wrested from England both nationhood and the land which the English, in turn, had seized from the Indians. Nor, as in Marshall's narrative, are they simply "inherited" intact from England. Rather, Cooper attempts to purify the national inheritance of violence and guilt that undermine legitimacy in Marshall's narrative through a series of displacements that set the stage for a ritual mourning of the ancestors, both English and Indian, who willingly bequeathed their authority and property to the new nation.

Indian Problems

By eliding the question of Indian rights with the problem of American Revolutionary origins, Cooper simultaneously attempts to address and dispel the Indian problem. The book's final resolution of the various complications—of loyalty, land ownership, inheritance—caused by the American Revolution is meant to resolve both problems. Neat as this strategy appears, it doesn't quite work. The voices of protest that echo throughout the novel, and the figure of the wronged Indian that hovers just beyond the surface meanings, are too distinct to be ignored or forgotten yet too marginalized narratively to be fully encompassed by the resolution of the plot's central concerns. A gap remains between the historical questions Cooper raises in *The Pioneers* and the narrative strategies by means of which he attempts to resolve them.

When removed from the narrative world he created and viewed in relation to the social and historical realities of his day, Cooper's solutions to the problem of national legitimacy appear even more limited. For example, the resolution presented in *The Pioneers* depends upon the bringing together in one family lineage America's Indian and English forebears.[14] But this directly contradicts contemporary justifications of American Indian policy. In *Johnson v. McIntosh*, for example, Chief Justice Marshall attempts to explain the European (and American) denial of Indian property rights on the basis of the absolute impossibility of uniting Indians and whites as "one people":

> Although we do not mean to engage in a defense of those principles which Europeans have applied to Indian title, they may, we think, find some excuse, if not justification, in the character and habits of the people whose rights have been wrested from them.
>
> The title by conquest is acquired and maintained by force. The conqueror prescribes its limits. Humanity, however, acting on public opinion, has established, as a general rule, that the conquered shall not be wantonly oppressed, and that their condition shall remain as eligible as is compatible with the objects of the conquest. Most usually, they are incorporated with the victorious nation, and become subjects or citizens of the government with which they are connected. The new and old members of the society mingle with each other; the distinction between them is gradually lost, and they make one people. Where this incorporation is practicable, humanity demands, and a wise policy requires, that the right of the conquered to property should remain unimpaired. . . .
>
> When the conquest is complete, and the conquered inhabitants can be blended with the conquerors, or safely governed as a distinct people, public opinion, which not even the conqueror can disregard, imposes these restraints upon him; and he cannot neglect them without injury to his fame, and hazard to his power.
>
> But the tribes of Indians inhabiting this country were fierce savages, whose occupation was war, and whose subsistence was drawn chiefly from the forest. . . . What was the inevitable consequence of this state of things? The Europeans were under the necessity either of abandoning the country, and relinquishing their pompous claims to it, or of enforcing those claims by the sword, and by the adoption of principles adapted to the condition of a people with whom it was impossible to mix. . . . (Washburn, 4:2546)

Unwilling to include Indians in the American "family" and unable to justify Euro-American policies toward them on the basis of natural right

(2547), Marshall is left with "conquest" and "force" as the principles upon which American claims to the land ultimately rest.

Marshall's references to public opinion and the demands of humanity reflect his anxiety over the moral grounds of this position. The relationship he posits between fame and power reveals the political significance he attaches to public sentiment. Questions of morality are clearly at the center of Marshall's opinion in *Johnson v. McIntosh*. Although he repeatedly acknowledges that American Indian policy, specifically the American claim to Indian lands, seems illegitimate—"opposed to natural right, and to the usages of civilized nations" (2547)—he refuses "to engage in a defense of those principles" directly or rationally, his strategy remaining purely rhetorical. In the longer passage, Marshall's struggle to affirm the legitimacy of Euro-American claims to the land emerges as a struggle to encompass American Indian policy within a consistent legal narrative. He turns first to the conventional narrative of conquest that "humanity . . . has established." Marshall recounts that "[a]s a general rule . . . the conquered shall not be wantonly oppressed. . . . Most usually, they are incorporated with the victorious nation." But the history of American-Indian relations does not fit this established narrative. Rather than simply tell another story peculiar to the American experience, Marshall attempts to retain the authority of the familiar narrative by making the American exception a part of—and proof of—the "general rule." Americans, Marshall suggests, accept the principles established by humanity, but the fierce and warlike Indian character places them outside both the principles and the humanity that informs them. This is, of course, the Indian character as characterized by Marshall. By the 1820s, however, Indians were no longer considered a serious military threat. Tribes such as the Cherokees were, in fact, living proof of the Indians' ability and willingness to adopt the ways of nineteenth-century Euro-Americans. Marshall's convenient fiction of the Indian character illustrates the gaps between the legitimizing narratives of conquest available to him and the American experience for which he must account. By locating the narrative perspective at a moment, early in American history, when conquest and the subjugation of Indians were necessary to national survival, Marshall makes "inevitable" a policy that by the 1820s was not only avoidable but unjustifiable.[15]

Marshall's written opinion in the *Johnson v. McIntosh* decision reveals another problem which undermined efforts to establish national legitimacy: the gap between natural and civil law. In his introductory comments Marshall writes

> It will be necessary, in pursuing this inquiry, to examine, not singly those principles of abstract justice, which the Creator of all things has impressed on

the mind of his creature man, and which are admitted to regulate, in a great degree, the rights of civilized nations, whose perfect independence is acknowledged; but those principles also which our own government has adopted in the particular case, and given us as the rule for our decision. (2538).

Marshall articulates a clear distinction between natural law, which is universal and unchanging, bestowed by God upon all men, and civil law, which is historically determined, devised by particular governments for "particular case[s]." Ideally, he suggests, these two laws should coincide: the laws of God should "regulate, in a great degree, the rights of civilized nations." But Marshall's later comments reveal his difficulty, in this particular case, in reconciling the universal principles of natural law with the historically determined forces shaping civil law. While he must admit that the denial of the Indians' full rights to the land "may be opposed to natural right, and to the usages of civilized nations," from a practical, historical viewpoint he finds it "indispensable to that system under which the country has been settled" (2547). Once again Marshall's solution highlights rather than resolves the moral problems he grapples with.

The authority of natural law in American jurisprudence was a topic of intense debate during the first half of the nineteenth century. Surveying legal commentary written between 1816 and 1836, historian G. Edward White concluded that during the years of the Marshall Court natural law was an important source of law in the United States: "A recurrent theme of the treatise literature was the idea of natural law as the foundation of all other laws" (677). Nathan Dane, in his *General Abridgment and Digest of American Law* (1823–29), went so far as to declare that all laws contrary to natural law were invalid (6:429; quoted in White, 677). Still, there was considerable debate regarding the relationship between and relative authority of natural law and written laws and documents—including the Constitution—as the basis for American jurisprudence. Whereas the common law, which was based upon universal principles consistent with natural and divine law and recognizable by reason, had dominated the law of England and the early United States, the nineteenth century saw the growing ascendancy of what historian Morton J. Horwitz has called instrumentalism, a pragmatic rather than idealistic jurisprudence more concerned with immediate policy than timeless principles (1–30). White has described the transformation in American law during this same period as a move away from the authority of natural law (which, in America, embraced natural rights principles) and toward positivism, or a reliance upon written laws. What both historians have described is a shift from the timeless, universal principles of morality to contingent, local, practical policies as the basis of American law. The significance of this change in terms of national identity formation becomes clear in light of the American Revolution. According to White, "The idea that human beings, by virtue of their humanity, had been tacitly granted certain freedoms . . . was given a dramatic reformulation in the eighteenth century, when it was associated with republican forms of government, the sovereignty of the people, and the proposition that 'all men are created equal' " (676). Thus, to question the authority of natural law and its role in American law was to shake the very foundation of national ideology.

White has noted that the relationship between natural and constitutional rights was tested most severely and redefined most radically in cases, such as *Johnson v. McIntosh*, that examined the status and rights of racial minorities. The rights of black slaves and Indians had not been specifically defined in the Constitution or written laws, but since unwritten natural law was generally considered an authoritative basis for judgment in the early years of American jurisprudence, this omission was not viewed as critical (681). The meaning of race and natural rights in American law remained to be determined through specific cases. Given the significance of natural law arguments to Revolutionary ideology, the written opinions explaining and justifying the Court's decisions were important not only because they helped to define the principles of American law but also as part of an ongoing project of national identity formation.

Law and Legitimacy

Marshall never fully reconciled the Indian policy upon which national existence depends with the natural law principles central to national ideology. In fact, his opinion in *Johnson v. McIntosh* participated in the process of evolution by which natural law gradually lost authority as a principle of American law (White, 681–82). Cooper, however, was not willing simply to allow the conflict to stand. In Cooper's view, national character and prosperity depended upon the moral authority and power of the law, and in *The Pioneers* he was determined to reconcile justice and the law upon which American claims to the land and nationhood rested.

In the figure of Natty Bumppo questions of natural law, morality, and justice come together. Throughout the novel Natty repeatedly challenges the moral authority of Judge Temple. He questions the judge's claim to the buck that Oliver has killed and expresses opposition to the Judge's game laws. Perhaps most dramatically, in the famous pigeon hunt Natty's restraint is contrasted with the weakness of Judge Temple's claims to moral and social authority.[16] Despite repeated assertions that he will use the law to protect and preserve the resources of nature from the wastefulness of the settlers, here Judge Temple joins the other settlers in what Cooper describes as the "wasteful and unsportsmanlike execution" of pigeons (Cooper [1823] 1980, 244). When Natty reminds him of the immorality of such waste, the judge is unable to control himself: "Even Marmaduke forgot the morality of Leatherstocking as it [the flock] approached, and, in common with the rest, brought his musket to a poise" (249).

Notwithstanding his supposed commitment to the rational, morally responsible use of nature's resources, the judge is overwhelmed by the sheer excitement of such a dramatic enactment of mastery over nature, which is, as Natty repeatedly suggests, the final goal to which he, being a settler, is committed. Judge Temple's authority, based upon his association with the law and social order, is seriously called into question: he is unable to control even his own passions, much less bring order and moderation to others; nor is he able, despite his protestations, to rise above the destructive excesses of the process of settlement in which he participates. In contrast, by shooting only the single pigeon he needs for food, Natty reasserts his commitment to the "natural laws" he believes should govern the use of nature and becomes the sole voice of morality and restraint in this scene. Thus, Cooper seems to affirm the authority of natural law above that of civil law.

But while Cooper embraces Natty's morality unreservedly, he does not fully accept the actions that follow from it. In practical terms, Cooper presents Natty's opposition to the laws of Templeton as a threat to social order. When Natty ultimately violates the game laws by killing a deer out of season and then rejects the warrant to search his hut, the sheriff proclaims, "He has set an example of rebellion to the laws, and has become a kind of outlaw" (355). Although these words are spoken by a representative of the law who has little personal integrity, Cooper supports the general principles expressed. Natty is finally brought to justice in a trial scene that emphasizes Judge Temple's struggle to rise above personal feelings and administer justice impartially.[17] Here Cooper seems to be upholding the authority of civil law and its abstract forms. Though many critics have examined the conflicted relationship between the rule of civil law (Judge Temple) and the natural rights of the individual (Natty), I wish to emphasize the ways in which this conflict brings into focus the interrelated problems of law, dispossession, and national legitimacy.[18]

These problems lie at the center of *The Pioneers*, and they come together most clearly in the figure of Natty. As the conflict between Natty and the law reaches a climax, so does Natty's heroism. This is not because Cooper rejects the authority of the law or romanticizes Natty as the rebellious individual but rather because Natty fulfills a strategic function in Cooper's management of the conflict between natural and civil law as it intersects with the problem of race—a conflict that was becoming ever more apparent and troubling to nineteenth-century Americans (including Cooper). Natty, the white man who lives as an Indian and urges Chingachgook to seek revenge for the injuries to his race, is set in clear opposition to Temple, the Indians' "worst enemy of all," the champion of settlement and the representative of civil law. As the conflict reaches its climax, Cooper redefines the opposition in terms that contain its dangerous implications. By the time a posse arrives to take Natty to jail, he has already ceased to be a threat. As he stands amid the dying embers of his hut, which he has torched in order to protect it from intrusion, he tells the posse, "I have come to mourn, not to fight" (357). At this moment Natty assumes his full stature and meaning as hero. With this pronouncement Natty himself contains the threat he had represented more completely than the law possibly could (this is emphasized by the fact that Natty breaks out of jail after only a few hours). When he adopts an attitude of mourning, Natty's challenge to the principles Judge Temple upholds becomes an expression of allegiance to the past. His resistance does not disappear but rather is transferred from the realm of action to that of sentiment. Once defined in terms of mourning, Natty's resistance no longer threatens but actually serves the cause it would seem to resist; the mourner's expression of resistance is simultaneously an assertion that all resistance is futile, since we mourn that which we admit to be beyond our power to regain. By association with Natty, natural law and the Indians' rights are included in this vision of mourning. In his role as representative mourner, Natty opens a safe channel through which opposition to or anxiety over change can be vented under conditions that obviate the need to translate opposition into action.

According to Thomas, at the end of the novel, "when Natty removes himself from society, he exists as a continual reminder of the inability of man's written laws to coincide with the higher laws of nature" (41). It is true that Cooper never fully resolves the conflict between natural and civil law, but he no longer really needs to once he has removed Natty from the realm of historical and social reality, represented by Templeton, and situated him in the realm of sentiment and deferral, represented by the state of mourning. This, I would argue, is the crucial moment of Natty's "removal" from the world of Templeton and all that it represents. It is a removal to a different scheme of values and a different plane of action. When Natty actually leaves Templeton at the end of the book, his physical removal seems natural and inevitable, the outward manifestation of the essential change that has already occurred. Thus, the ending achieves resonance and a sense of closure despite the fact that, as Thomas argues, Natty's departure should represent Cooper's absolute failure to resolve the conflict between natural and civil law.

Cooper also hopes that Natty will carry with him the American Indian problem. The crucial moment occurs during the fire on Mount Vision. Elizabeth Temple has journeyed up the mountain to provide Natty with gunpowder so that he can continue to resist the forces of civil law. Instead of finding Natty, Elizabeth encounters Chingachgook, who has chosen the mountain as the spot where he will wait for death (from a mysterious injury he has received while illegally hunting the deer with Natty). While Chingachgook tells Elizabeth of the past and of the fall of his people, a forest fire makes its way up the mountain and eventually surrounds them. Oliver finds them but is unable to convince Chingachgook to flee. Just as they have given up any hope of escape, Natty arrives—but not before the fire has reached Chingachgook and ignited the gunpowder resting between his legs. Natty lifts the now castrated, dying Indian onto his own back and leads the way to safety. While this scene is perhaps no more improbable than many others in Cooper's novels, the seemingly gratuitous mutilation of Chingachgook is striking.[19] The dramatic scene creates a symbolic dimension and calls attention to Chingachgook as the dying Indian. The mutilation symbolically engenders the process of historical change, aligning the Indians' disappearance with their emasculation. The ultimate effect of such engendering of history is a question to which I shall return. For now it is enough to note how the scene upon Mount Vision re-envisions the history of Indian-white relations: the dying Indian is ultimately destroyed by his own (feminine) passivity, his refusal to flee the forces of destruction that encroach upon him; and Natty, the manly American hero, willingly takes upon his own shoulders the burden of the dying Indian.

Mourning the National Past

Cooper was not the first American to recognize the power of mourning as a means of expiating guilt and alleviating anxiety in the face of change. During the first half of the nineteenth century, mourning was often invoked in writings about Indians. In fact, from the Revolutionary era through the middle of the nineteenth century, writings lamenting the passing of the "Vanishing American" were so widespread and popular that they created what Brian W. Dippie has termed a national "habit of thought" (15). *The Last of the Mohicans: A Narrative of 1757* (1826), Cooper's next installment in the Leather-Stocking series, is one of the best-known works within this tradition. As indicated by its title, the novel represents the extinction of the Indians as an event accomplished in the past—a sad but inevitable fact that the reader can mourn but cannot resist. In the political realm, too, the attitude of mourning was commonly adopted as a response to the "Indian problem." The following passage from Andrew Jackson's "Second Annual Message to Congress" (1830) illustrates how mourning (and inheritance) could be invoked as a rationale for Indian removal:

> Humanity has often wept over the fate of the aborigines of this country, and Philanthropy has been long busily employed in devising means to avert it, but its progress has never for a moment been arrested, and one by one have many powerful tribes disappeared from the earth. To follow to the tomb the last of his race and to tread on the graves of extinct nations excite melancholy reflections. But true philanthropy reconciles itself to these vicissitudes as it does to the extinction of one generation to make room for another. (Richardson, 2:520–21)

Describing the dispossession of Indians in terms of generational change eliminated both violence and responsibility from the process. According to this model, removal became something "natural" and inevitable; the Americans who inherited the Indians' land need not resist but only mourn the passing of the generation whose "extinction" made room for their expansion. And while past generations might make claims upon the future, their demands, once defined as part of the past, would appear only as a spectral presence haunting the history to which they had been relegated.

Cooper further defines the object of mourning in *The Pioneers* when Natty speaks of his hut, now reduced to ashes. Elizabeth attempts to comfort Natty by suggesting that the hut can be rebuilt, but Natty replies, "Can you raise the dead, child? . . . can ye go into the place where you've laid your fathers, and mothers, and children, and gather together their ashes, and make the same men and women of them as afore? You do not know what 'tis to lay your head for more than forty years under the cover of the same logs, and to look on the same things for the better part of a man's life" (386). In mourning the loss of the hut, Natty mourns something he associates with a loss of family. The larger loss Natty alludes to becomes clear by the end of the novel, when the site of the hut has literally been transformed into a graveyard. Where the hut once stood now lie the graves of Major Effingham and Chingachgook, representatives of America's English and Indian origins, fated to become part of the new nation's past as it achieved independent political identity.

These two men had formed part of the odd "family" that had resided in Natty's hut, a family held together through a complex web of loyalties revolving around the aged Major Effingham, who, in addition to being the adopted son of Chingachgook, was once the benefactor of Natty. It is significant that these bonds are not determined by blood; rather, like the nation, this "family" is defined by voluntary bonds of loyalty among men. Major Effingham, Chingachgook, and Oliver—representatives of America's past and future—come together in Natty's hut, setting the scene for a transition between past and future envisioned in terms of continuity— of inheritance through an unbroken family lineage—rather than the discontinuity of dispossession and revolutionary rupture. But before he can affirm this new model of national origins, Cooper attempts one last time to lay to rest the guilt associated with more violent models of the nation founded upon acts of conquest and revolution.

Natty's hut (and later the cave), where the transition between past and future occurs, is associated in the minds of the townspeople with a vaguely defined guilt and the threat of social disorder. Imagining that Natty and his friends are conducting secret mining operations there, the sheriff is "burning with a desire to examine the hidden mysteries of the cave" (399). It comes to represent for the townspeople "a secret receptacle of guilt" where they locate all "that was wicked and dangerous to the peace of society" (425–26). When the contents of the cave are finally revealed, it becomes clear that the guilt associated with the cave is not Natty's but the nation's. Through a series of extended misunderstandings surrounding Judge Temple, Cooper has repeatedly raised questions regarding American injustice toward the Indians and betrayal of loyalty to England. At the moment of revelation before the cave (chapter 40) Cooper presents what would seem to be the most incriminating evidence of Judge Temple's (and the nation's) guilt. The reader discovers that the cave holds the corpse of Chingachgook, who was fatally injured during the recent forest fire, and the dying Major Effingham—the dispossessed and dishonored remnants of the past whose authority and property have been usurped by the Americans.

At this very moment, however, Cooper reveals the innocence of Judge Temple and thus clears the way for a vision of national origins based upon the legitimate transmission of authority through inheritance. Cooper exonerates the judge by demonstrating that his adherence to principles of personal loyalty transcends the disruptive power of revolutionary change. As the explanations pour forth, we discover that the judge, despite the misunderstandings caused by the Revolutionary War, did not betray the trust of his friend (Oliver's father) but instead has acted as a caretaker, preserving Oliver's inheritance for him. Cooper's strategy in this scene can be compared to what legal historian Thomas C. Shevory has described as Marshall's "interpretivist" approach to language and law. The key to Marshall's rhetorical mastery, according to Shevory, lies in locating a past point of reference from which legal intention is revealed unproblematically. Take, for example, Marshall's location of narrative perspective in *Johnson v. McIntosh* in a historical moment when violent conflict with warlike, "fierce savages" (Washburn, 4:2546) was necessary to national survival. Similarly, the rush of revelations before the cave, as Oliver discloses his true identity and Temple reads the will that justifies his actions, creates an unproblematic past point of reference from which intention is revealed as truth, and justice appears suddenly and unquestionably. The suddenness of revelation adds force to the resolution Cooper thus constructs. The Revolution becomes not a rupture with the past nor an occasion of betrayal but a test allowing the American to display the depth of his loyalty to and continuity with the past.

The cave, a place of secrets and suspicions, here becomes the site of national legitimation; grave becomes womb as the new order is born out of the death of the old. With the revelation of the dying Major Effingham, Oliver's true identity is established. As Oliver Edward Effingham, he assumes his proper station in society and claims his hereditary right to the land. This revelation eliminates the supposed differences in race and class which had complicated the developing romantic interest between Oliver and Elizabeth. With his marriage to Elizabeth, Oliver will unite (at least metaphorically) English, Indian, and American claims to the land to become the legitimate heir of all his fathers: his biological (grand)father Major Effingham, his adopted (great-grand)father Chingachgook, and his father-in-law Judge Temple. The union between Oliver and Elizabeth, then, marks the beginning of a new line of Americans whose legitimacy is beyond question.[20]

The role of Elizabeth in the project of national legitimation is worth examining. On the one hand, the marriage seems almost irrelevant. As the preceding analysis has suggested, legitimacy in *The Pioneers* is a matter to be established and conveyed among men. What the plot accomplishes through its complex machinations is a shift in how that legitimation is achieved. Instead of imagining legitimacy passing directly from father to son, Cooper downplays the role of fathers—Oliver's father is dead and there are no actual founding fathers in the novel—and locates legitimacy in a "family" constituted by bonds of loyalty. Translated into more abstract terms, Cooper enacts the transition from a patriarchal to a social-contract model of political authority and national legitimacy. In the words of Benedict Anderson, this is the modern nation imagined as "a deep, horizontal comradeship [or] fraternity" among men (7). As Carole Pateman has pointed out, from the beginning "the participants in the social contract are sons or brothers. . . . It is no accident that fraternity appears historically hand in hand with liberty and equality, nor that it means exactly what it says: brotherhood" (40).

With this in mind, I return to the question of Elizabeth's role in the novel. It is clear that Cooper considers her presence to be crucial.

Throughout the novel she is referred to as "our heroine," whereas no male character is referred to as "our hero." Nevertheless, she is not a compelling character. Both early reviewers and present critics declared Elizabeth to be wooden and unbelievable, like most of Cooper's heroines. She is marginal to the book's central action. Her position as heroine makes sense structurally, however, since her presence is necessary to both the resolution of the novel and the logic of modern nationhood. Pateman has argued that the social contract upon which the modern nation is founded depends not only upon the overthrow of the fathers but, even more crucially, upon the control of women. Through the subjugation of women and their relegation to a private world opposed to civil society—defined as a "universal sphere of freedom, equality, individualism, reason, contract, and impartial law" which is "the realm of men or 'individuals'"—the modern nation constructs a new, modern patriarchal order to replace the old (42–43).

In *The Pioneers* Elizabeth contributes to the construction of a patriarchal order neatly separated into feminine and masculine spheres. The clearest evidence of this order is the assertion of the woman's power (in her own sphere), which guarantees and legitimizes the man's power in his much wider sphere. Shortly after her marriage, Elizabeth announces the new order thus instituted: "You know, Effingham, that my father has told you that I ruled him, and that I shall rule you. I am now about to exert my power" (449). The power she proceeds to exert is completely conventional: she enlists her husband's help in tending to the emotional needs of those around her by providing marriage options for her friend, Louisa, and a home for Natty.

But Elizabeth's role in the book goes beyond this conventional affirmation of the patriarchal power structures upon which the modern nation rests. Cooper takes the conventional nineteenth-century association of women with feeling and injects troubling questions of race and morality which threaten to undermine American national legitimacy. In one of the many passages in the book to address the moral problem of Indian dispossession, Elizabeth expresses to Oliver the wish that she, too, were of Indian lineage:

> "It would be a great relief to my mind to think so, for I own that I grieve when I see old Mohegan walking about these lands, like the ghost of one of their ancient possessors, and feel how small is my own right to possess them."
>
> "Do you!" cried the youth, with a vehemence that startled the ladies.
>
> "I do, indeed," returned Elizabeth, after suffering a moment to pass in surprise; "but what can I do? what can my father do? Should we offer the old man a home and maintenance, his habits would compel him to refuse us.

Neither, were we so silly as to wish such a thing, could we convert these clearings and farms, again, into hunting-grounds, as the Leather-Stocking would wish to see them."

"You speak the truth, Miss Temple," said Edwards. "What can you do, indeed! But there is one thing that I am certain that you can and will do, when you become the mistress of these beautiful valleys—use your wealth with indulgence to the poor and charity to the needy;—indeed, you can do no more." (280)

In this passage Cooper employs a strategy that Harriet Beecher Stowe would apply three decades later to the moral dilemma posed by slavery. In answer to the question, "But what can any individual do?," Cooper responds with Stowe that one can "feel right" (Stowe 624). Or, as Cooper puts it, one can "feel how small is [one's] own right to possess them" (the lands taken from Indians) and grieve for the ghosts of those destroyed in the process of national growth. Unlike Stowe, who attaches radical transformative power to the act of feeling right, Cooper limits the effects of feeling to women's private sphere. Elizabeth's feeling of guilt over Indian dispossession is lumped together with other social concerns encompassed by the word "charity" and conventionally defined as women's business. The wish to do something about the history of injustice toward Indians—considered impossible according to the familiar argument that Indians are incapable of change—is replaced by the injunction to do something about economic inequality. Class supplants race as the focus of injustice and the arena in which a redemptive morality may be exercised. Because it remains circumscribed within a narrowly conceived feminine realm of feeling, this exercise of morality does not threaten the (masculine) business of national expansion. Cooper suggests how limited this power is when, just after Elizabeth and Oliver arrive at their solution, Louisa reminds them that women lose control of their property—and thus the ability to do good with that property—after marriage: Louisa quietly notes that "there will, doubtless, be one to take the direction of such things from her hands" (280).

The final solution to the moral problem posed by Indian dispossession is to be found in the realm of feeling—in the feminine feeling exhibited by Elizabeth and, even more powerfully, in the attitude of mourning that pervades the novel. The ending of *The Pioneers* emphasizes the importance of mourning in stabilizing the transition between past and future out of which the new nation has been born. In addition to assuaging guilt, mourning serves as an assurance of continuity in the face of change—an assertion that there are bonds (of love, loyalty, kinship) that remain despite loss, bonds strong enough to transcend the disruptive power of time. But even as it provides a sense of continuity with the past, the goal of mourning, ultimately, is to commit what is past to memory, to allow the mourner to move beyond it.

In his role as representative mourner, Natty remains always in the *process* of mourning. Although he performs the work of mourning for other characters in the novel as well as for the reader, helping others to commit the past to memory (as history) and to move beyond it into the future, he himself exists outside of time, embodying the site of emotional and historical transition itself. Natty is unable to move forward with history, while Oliver, although ostensibly committed to many of the same values as Natty, is free to move forward into the future. It is Oliver, after all, who oversees the dramatic evolution of Templeton described in the opening pages of the novel. Similarly, readers might identify with Natty in his attitude of mourning, thus affirming their respect for the past and denying any complicity in the process of change, without actually abandoning what Chief Justice Marshall described as the principles in which "the property of the great mass of the community originates" (Washburn, 4:2547) or changing the policies responsible for the very "losses" they mourn.

The final scene of the novel, appropriately set in the graveyard, helps to elucidate more precisely the meaning of Natty's role. When Elizabeth and Oliver discover Natty, he is lying on the ground above the graves of Major Effingham and Chingachgook. These two representatives of America's dual origins have found their final resting place, firmly located in the past, lying next to each other but pointing in opposite directions. Natty asks Oliver to read the inscriptions on the headstones, the histories into which their lives have been transformed.[21] On Major Effingham's headstone Natty finds himself described as the "servant" whose "enduring gratitude" and loyalty to his master will be remembered. Natty does not become part of the past with a headstone and historical meaning of his own; he is simply the "servant" who enables the history of others to be written. When Oliver reads Chingachgook's headstone, Natty detects a mistake in the spelling of Chingachgook's name—a serious matter since, as Natty notes, "an Indian's name has always some meaning in it" (452). As in the scene of mutilation, Cooper seems to acknowledge that the incorporation of Indians into American history inevitably entails a violation.

Natty, like those he mourns, serves as a marker of what the national narrative both depends upon and cannot accommodate. Lying above the graves, Natty is no more part of the present than those lying beneath the ground. With the burning of his hut and its subsequent transformation into a graveyard, he no longer has a place among the living in the present-day world of Templeton. But unlike those who are buried on the former site of his hut, he cannot be located firmly in the past as part of a national history.[22] Nor is he to be included in the nation's future (represented by the new order born of the union between Elizabeth and Oliver); he refuses their offer to build him a new home, choosing instead to drift ever farther west "towards the setting sun—the foremost in that band of pioneers who are opening the way for the march of the nation across the continent" (456). These concluding words express Natty's paradoxical role in national history. With his eyes fixed steadily on the past, Natty opens the way to the future, carrying forward the processes of historical change and national growth through his very efforts to escape them.[23] What Natty also carries is the reminder—and remainder—of all that cannot be contained in even the most intricately wrought narrative of legitimation, as well as all that will not remain buried in even the most carefully tended grave. Natty is the ghost that rises up from the graves where Cooper located the troubling history of American national origins.

In a 1991 revision of his influential work on the origin and spread of nationalism, Benedict Anderson added a final chapter entitled "Memory and Forgetting" which complicated his earlier reflections upon the role of history in national identity formation. Anderson reexamines why and how the nation is imagined "always [to] loom out of an immemorial past" (11). Anderson bases his argument upon the words of Ernest Renan cited at the head of chapter 1.[24] What every Frenchmen "is obliged to have forgotten" is the violence that, in the moment of national imagining, is rewritten as family history—the (now fraternal) conflicts by which the nation was forged and defined. The irony of Renan's statement lies in the fact that the injunction to have forgotten (in the past) itself serves to keep alive the memory (in the present and the future) by which all Frenchmen experience and define their common national identity.[25]

Anderson points to Natty and Chingachgook as prime examples of the attempt to incorporate into family history the violence of a national past. *The Pioneers* certainly points toward such conclusions—the "family" assembled in Natty's hut, the burial of Major Effingham and Chingachgook side by side—but Cooper consistently undermines the adequacy of such family history to account for the national past. Natty's "family" is destroyed by representatives of the law, and in the case of Chingachgook, the history meant to accommodate the violence of the past is acknowledged to be a lie. Much as Americans might wish to incorporate Indians into a legitimating national narrative—both Cooper and Marshall illustrate this desire—any attempt to do so was inevitably undermined by the fact that living Indians remained to challenge the narratives by which they were relegated to a place in the history of a nation not their own. The conclusion of *The Pioneers* offers its readers a way simultaneously to remember *and* forget what the national narrative cannot accommodate—

the Indians who will not remain buried because they are not dead, whose history, written upon their premature gravestones, must continually be reinscribed. Natty, the mourner who himself cannot be mourned and laid to rest, becomes a national hero for providing the means to confront and defer the national guilt that cannot be resolved.

Cooper's attempt to encompass the violence of conquest within the much less threatening (family) violence of revolution does not solve the American Indian problem. As the nineteenth century progressed, Indians continued to haunt the national conscience and to pose troubling challenges to national character and legitimacy. Many of the moral questions raised but not resolved in *Johnson v. McIntosh* were to resurface a few years later in legal and political debates over the forced removal of the Cherokee Indians from Georgia. In the face of these challenges, popular literature continued to provide an imaginative space in which Americans could reenvision the meaning of American history and attempt to resolve what Cooper saw as deep contradictions in American Indian policy and national identity. The next chapter will examine the popular stage as a site of national identity formation during the first half of the nineteenth century. In a series of popular melodramas about Pocahontas, nineteenth-century Americans again attempted to construct a myth of national origins that legitimated a nation founded upon acts of conquest.

THREE

DOMESTICATING THE DRAMA OF CONQUEST:

POCAHONTAS ON THE POPULAR STAGE

[H]aving feasted him after their best barbarous manner they
could, a long consultation was held, but the conclusion was,
two great stones were brought before Powhatan: then as
many as could layd hands on him, dragged him to them, and
thereon laid his head, and being ready with their clubs,
to beate out his braines, Pocahontas the King's dearest
daughter, when no intreaty could prevaile, got his head
in her armes, and laid her owne upon his to save him from
death. . . .
(*John Smith*, Generall Historie of Virginia)

IN THE THREE AND A HALF centuries since Captain John Smith
recorded these words and founded a national myth, the cultural
power of Pocohontas has not waned.[1] She has been the subject of
art, literature, drama, and film, yet little is actually known about
Pocahontas. She left no record of her own thoughts or experiences. Only
one portrait was made within her lifetime. What is known comes primarily from the writings of three contemporaries—John Smith, John Rolfe,
and Ralph Hamor—all of whom were outsiders to her culture. Even the
famous incident in which she saved Captain John Smith from execution
by her father, Chief Powhatan, remains a subject of controversy. Was it
the act of fearless generosity that Smith describes, or was it a culturally
scripted adoption ceremony that Smith misunderstood? Some cultural
historians wonder whether it happened at all.[2] More certain is the use
made of Pocahontas by Smith, who hoped to gain support for the Jamestown settlement, and by nineteenth-century Americans eager to define a
myth of national origins that would legitimate the acts of conquest that
continued to haunt American history.

This chapter examines two nineteenth-century plays about Pocahontas
that were both presented as national dramas and produced at a time
when the question of national character was of great concern to the
American public, which constituted the audiences for these performances. In terms of approach, I maintain a double focus, examining (1)
how these dramas reveal the interplay of race and gender in the dis-

courses of U.S. nationalism during the first half of the nineteenth century; and (2) how the popular theater served as a site where negotiations of power were enacted, cultural anxieties rehearsed, and challenges to national ideology confronted and eventually subsumed into a national drama whose culminating act was the idealized production (and re-production) of the American nation.

The Idea of a National Drama

> When the Revolution that has changed the social and political state of a people begins to penetrate its literature, it generally first manifests itself in the drama.
> (*Alexis de Tocqueville*, Democracy in America)

Calls for a national drama formed an important part of the project of American literary nationalism as it developed during the first half of the nineteenth century. In addition to the standard arguments applied to all types of literature produced by Americans—such as the need to assert cultural independence from England or the desire to display to the world what "the Genius of Liberty"[3] might produce—nineteenth-century discussions of national drama suggested a special connection between the drama's form and its function in a democratic society. In the conclusion to his *History of the American Theatre*, William Dunlap[4] described the power of the public theater in political terms:

> [I]f mankind are to govern themselves, as we know they ought to do, and as we believe they will—it is expedient that every source of knowledge should be opened to the governors, *the people*, every obstacle to their improvement removed, and every inducement held forth to qualify them for the high office they are destined to fill. If, in the progress to that high state of moral perfection enjoyed by the favored few who prefer the lessons of wisdom taught in the closet to those received in public assemblies, another state less refined must be passed through—a state in which the attractions of oratory or even scenic decorations are useful—let us give to theatres that purity, as well as power, which shall produce the high moral purpose here aimed at. (403–4)

Dunlap believed that the drama's immediacy and emotional power would reach the common man, whose intellect had not been cultivated or refined through the study of books.[5] He imagined the public theater as a space of democratic potential where good citizens might be produced, where "the mass of mankind [may be assisted] in rising to the level which republican governments make necessary for those who are henceforward to be self-guided and selfruled [*sic*]" (404).[6]

Not all Americans, however, saw the theater as a positive force. By 1786 all but two states—Maryland and New York—had passed statutes prohibiting theatrical productions. Antitheatrical sentiments remained quite strong in the United States well into the nineteenth century. One strain of antitheatricalism, illustrated by the Boston Anti-Theatrical Act of 1750, was informed by a lingering Puritan opposition to all "theatrical entertainments, which not only occasion great and unnecessary expences [*sic*], and discourage industry and frugality, but likewise tend generally to increase immorality, impiety and a contempt of religion."[7] Public theaters were also seen as potentially disruptive of the social order and class distinctions; until the 1830s, when the upper classes increasingly began to attend separate theaters featuring elite entertainments such as opera, the public theaters brought together all classes and races, including black and white workmen, shopkeepers and professional men, and genteel ladies and prostitutes. Behavior was often rowdy and riots were not uncommon, reinforcing fears of the dangerous effects of such promiscuous social mixing.[8] Antitheatrical critics were also suspicious of drama itself: How could a genre that appealed to and excited emotion be conducive to the cultivation of the rational self-government so necessary to a democracy?[9] Such fears suggest not only a suspicion of drama and the theater, but also deep anxieties regarding the nature and dangers of democracy itself: How were the uneducated and undisciplined masses to be made fit for self-government? How was order to be maintained in a society more mobile—economically, socially, geographically—than any that had gone before?[10]

The idea of a national drama answered some of these concerns. Writing in 1827, James K. Paulding defined national drama and its value as follows:

> By a national drama, we mean, not merely a class of dramatic productions written by Americans, but one appealing directly to the national feelings; founded upon domestic incidents—illustrating or satirizing domestic manners—and, above all, displaying a generous chivalry in the maintenance and vindication of those great and illustrious peculiarities of situation and character by which we are distinguished from all other nations. We do not hesitate to say, that next to the interests of eternal truth, there is no object more worthy the exercise of the highest attributes of the mind, than that of administering to the just pride of national character, inspiring a feeling for the national glory, and inculcating a love of country. (339)

According to Paulding, the theater was to serve as a space of social formation and reformation. The meaning of American identity was to be dramatized on the stage for all to see. The power of the drama to stir the emotions was to inspire patriotism, a feeling "worthy of the highest attributes of the *mind*." A national drama thus conceived would enlist (individual) feeling in the service of the (collective) nation, thus unifying the promiscuously mixed mass of theatergoers (and citizens) and limiting the dangerously individualistic tendencies of democracy.[11] For supporters of the national drama, the theater became a sacred space where "offerings on the altar of national pride" were imbued with the power to transform individuals into Americans.[12]

The very conditions identified as dangerous by some—such as the intermingling of classes—could also be seen as part of the particular power of the theater as a site of national formation. Early-nineteenth-century theater architecture reinforced this social function. In the typical theater, the upper classes sat in boxes, which surrounded the stage on three sides, while the lower classes occupied the gallery and the pit. Theater lighting of the house throughout the play meant that the lower-class audience would necessarily see the upper-class spectators as they watched the play. Nineteenth-century reviews suggest that the social function of the theater as a place to see and be seen was just as important as its function as a place of entertainment or enlightenment. One 1824 reviewer complained of "too much light on stage, and too little in the boxes," which made it hard to recognize those sitting across the house. Another, writing in 1828, explained that the boxes had been painted a color designed "to display the ladies to advantage."[13] By presenting upper-class spectators as models of propriety, the theater could be imagined as a site of social instruction. As the following anonymous critic, writing in 1819, explained,

> One great objection to theatrical exhibitions has been, that they occasion dissipation. In this allegation we do not concur. That the dissipated resort to theatres cannot be disputed. But the steady part of the audience are a great restraint upon them, and it may be a question well worthy of consideration by the enemies of these establishments, whether the contrast between the respectable and vicious portion of the visitors of the play-houses is not, itself, a corrective of considerable influence, outweighing all minor objections, and tending to reform profligates, whose habits had been previously and elsewhere formed, and who otherwise indulge their propensities in a more solitary and sequestered manner.[14]

According to this critic, as well as many proponents of a national drama, the public and social qualities of the theater served as a positive moral force to shape the American citizenry.

Of the plays describing themselves as national dramas, the most popular subjects were the Revolutionary War and American Indians. The former, however, was felt by some to be too recent and too familiar an event in the national history to lend itself to the drama. As one anonymous writer argued in 1828, "The mind would turn with disgust from any portion of fiction, intermingled with scenes, with every feature of which, all are familiar. . . . The wars of the early settlers with the fierce and unrelenting savages, are not liable to the same objection."[15] Because it was seen as distant and exotic enough to be romanticized, the history of Indian-white relations was available as a usable past that could be incorporated into the project of imagining the nation. And Americans did, indeed, make use of this history. During the first half of the nineteenth century, plays featuring Indian characters became extremely popular on the American stage.[16] As theater historian George Odell declared in his description of the 1820s, "Indians were everywhere."[17]

Pocahontas on the Popular Stage

The story of Pocahontas, including the celebrated incident in which she saved the life of Captain John Smith, was one of the most romantic and romanticized episodes of early American history; it was also the single most popular subject of Indian dramas during the nineteenth century.[18] In his *Generall Historie of Virginia* Smith recounted how he was captured by the Powhatan Indians late in 1607. After several weeks of captivity, preparations were made for Smith's execution (or so he thought): "[T]wo great stones were brought before Powhatan: then as many as could layd hands on him [Smith], dragged him to them, and thereon laid his head, and being ready with their clubs, to beate out his braines, Pocahontas, the King's dearest daughter, when no intreaty could prevaile, got his head in her armes, and laid her owne upon his to save him from death" (2:151). Smith went on to describe Pocahontas as the protectress of the Jamestown colony, bringing food in times of need and warning of attack. Pocahontas eventually converted to Christianity and married the Englishman John Rolfe in 1614, dying in London in 1617. By the beginning of the nineteenth century, the story of Pocahontas and her rescue of Smith had been retold several times by historians, poets, and novelists.[19] But it was during the first half of the nineteenth century—especially on the popular stage in the "numberless dramas that grew up around the character of Pocahontas" (Moses, 570)—that Smith's brief account assumed the status of foundational myth, with Pocahontas emerging as a popular national hero.

The first Pocahontas play—which was also the first American Indian drama to be performed in the United States—was James N. Barker's work entitled *The Indian Princess; or, La Belle Sauvage. An Operatic Melodrama in Three Acts.*[20] In his preface Barker emphasizes the fact that this is an *American* play. In requesting the indulgence of the audience,

Barker calls upon their national pride: "Dramatic genius, with genius of every other kind, is assuredly native of our soil, and there wants but the wholesome and kindly breath of favour to invigourate [*sic*] its delicate frame, and bid it rapidly arise from its cradle to blooming maturity" (Barker [1808] 1918, 576). At the same time, Barker reveals the insecurity of a young nation still uncertain of its cultural identity and power. He describes the "children of the American drama" as orphans "doomed to wander, without house or home, unknown and unregarded" (575). Like the American nation, born in an act of rebellion against king and mother country, the "orphan" play is an "independent urchin" (576). But even while proudly declaring its independence of parental authority, the orphan seeks the security of a new home and new sources of legitimacy.

In the final paragraph of the preface, Barker appeals to his female audience: "To your bosoms, ladies, sweet ladies! the little stranger flies with confidence for protection; shield it, I pray you, from the iron rod of rigour, and scold it yourselves, as much as you will, for on *your* smooth and polished brows it can never read wrinkled cruelty" (576). Barker sets up an opposition between feminine feelings (of sympathy) and the masculine "rod of rigour." If national drama is defined, as Paulding has suggested, by its ability to "inspir[e] a feeling for the national glory, and inculcat[e] a love of country," then Barker's preface implicitly raises questions regarding how such national feeling is to be (en)gendered.[21] Underlying this question is another, more fundamental one regarding the roles of feeling and reason in the constitution of an American citizenry. These issues, only hinted at in the preface, are developed more fully in the play itself. The request of the ladies to protect the "little stranger" anticipates the subject of the play that follows: the story of Pocahontas, who literally shields John Smith from injury and serves as a "foster mother" who protects the "infant colony" (623) of Jamestown from famine and Indian attack, thereby achieving mythic stature as heroic mother preserving and nurturing what will become the American nation. By means of this parallelism Barker makes the play and the nation metaphorically equivalent and links the survival and legitimacy of both to the domestic feelings and virtues of women.

Barker reworks the Pocahontas story in order to give women a central role, adding several female characters who, with Pocahontas, remain at the center of a romantic plot concerned with courtship and marriage. But he also interweaves the domestic themes with an equally well developed heroic drama of masculine adventure and conquest. This double structure enables him to examine troubling aspects of the nation's history of conquest—violence, greed, dispossession—while appealing to the narrative logic of the romantic plot to resolve (or displace) the causes of anxiety and guilt arising from the play's examination of national origins.

The opening scene of *The Indian Princess* introduces the play as a drama of masculine adventure. Upon landing in Virginia, Smith addresses his fellow "gallant cavalier adventurers," boldly announcing, "We have a noble stage, on which to act / A noble drama" (580). The "stage" upon which this drama is to be enacted is twofold. On the one hand, it is the feminized landscape of Virginia: "Is't not a goodly land? Along the bay, / How gay and lovely lie its skirting shores, / Fring'd with the summer's rich embroidery!" (579). It is a land receptive to masculine self-assertion, a land where "the bosom can dilate, the pulses play, / And man, erect, can walk a manly round" (580).[22] On the other hand, it is the stage of history where these adventurers will make their mark: "[F]or ye are men / Well worth the handing down; whose paged names / Will not disgrace posterity to read" (580). The play figures America—the "empty" land waiting to be filled by the heroic action of European settlers—and the theatrical stage upon which the colonial drama is reenacted before a nineteenth-century audience as imaginative spaces where history—and the nation—are made. The language of the play, including the preface, describes both of these spaces as feminized, metaphorically identified with or presided over by women.

In the second scene, immediately after he has defined the drama of conquest in unmistakably masculine terms, Barker introduces an alternative domestic drama of love, courtship, and marriage. As two of the colonists, Larry and Walter, are discussing Smith's previous (and quite violent) conquest of the Turks, Walter's wife, Alice, enters singing a love song in which she explains the motivation behind her own journey to this new land to build a home with the man she loves:

> Ah! what to me were cities gay;
>   Listen, listen, dear!
> If from me thou wert away,
>   Alas! how drear!
> Oh! still o'er sea, o'er land I'll rove,
>   Never, never weary;
> And follow on where leads my love,
>   Ever cheery.   (582)

Here the land is defined as wilderness not because it is unknown or because it is inhabited by "savages" but because it is undomesticated: "[T]his devil of a country, where there's never a girl nor a house" (583). In this domestic drama the wilderness will be conquered through romantic love and the assertion of feminine values.

By intertwining romantic and heroic plots, Barker translates conquest into terms of domesticity—love, courtship, marriage—thereby obscuring its violence. Romantic rather than colonial conquest ultimately takes center stage in Barker's play, but the deep connection between the two is never lost. Colonial conquest, in fact, is accomplished through the power of love, when Pocahontas becomes enamored of the Euro-American conqueror and his culture.

While the tendency to describe the colonial project of conquest and domination in sexual terms—with the body of the native woman metaphorically representing the colonized lands/peoples—has been studied in a wide variety of contexts, theories of colonialist discourse have seldom addressed the particular kind of rhetorical challenge faced by nineteenth-century Americans in their attempt to inscribe Pocahontas in the discourses of U.S. nationalism. The story of Pocahontas as first formulated by John Smith emerged in the context of British colonialism, but nineteenth-century American writers who retold this same story stood in a very different position from the British in relation to the colonial project. While the United States maintained a kind of internal colonialism in relation to American Indians—a position aligned with that of England in the original version of the Pocahontas narrative by Smith—this situation changed significantly when the story of Pocahontas was recast as a national drama. In terms of this nationalistic discourse, Americans found themselves in the position of the (formerly) colonized, attempting to assert their cultural independence from Britain and to define a distinctive American national identity. In nineteenth-century American versions of the story, the figure of Pocahontas was thus called upon to carry a heavy and rather unwieldy ideological burden: to represent and legitimate American colonialist *and* nationalistic projects; to serve as both the implicitly sexualized object of conquest who offers herself freely to the conqueror *and* the sanctified figure of the nation-as-mother who unites all her citizens/children in a unified "family." Barker's management of the play's domestic themes reveals most clearly his strategies for negotiating this complicated ideological field.

The third scene opens in the midst of preparations for Pocahontas's marriage to Susquehannock Prince Miami (584). The marriage is represented as a political act in which the daughter's will must bend to the father's authority: "The Susquehannocks are a powerful nation," Pocahontas explains to her friend Nima, "and my father would have them for his friends. He gives his daughter to their prince, but his daughter trembles to look upon the fierce Miami" (585). Pocahontas's marriage to John Rolfe later in the play is similarly described as a political act establishing ties between Powhatan and the English, but here it is an act that reinforces the power of the individual as agent of her own destiny:

Pocahontas is represented as freely choosing John Rolfe in an act of love, defying paternal authority in order to be true to her own heart. It would not be difficult for Americans of the early Republic to see in Pocahontas's act (as represented by Barker) a defense of American Revolutionary origins. Forcing a woman to marry against her will a man she does not love would be an unnatural violation of individual rights, just as England's taxation of the colonies without their vote was a violation. According to the conventions of melodrama, the actions of Powhatan, the tyrannical father, would have been recognized immediately as villainous. But a daughter's rebellion against such abuse of authority was, according to those same conventions, highly unusual. To make Pocahontas's actions seem not only justifiable but heroic, Barker adapted the melodramatic form to his own historical moment and nationalistic purposes.[23]

Peter Brooks has drawn a fundamental connection between revolution and melodrama. Brooks locates the origins of melodrama in the aftermath of the French Revolution: "It comes into being in a world where the traditional imperatives of truth and ethics have been violently thrown into question, yet where the promulgation of truth and ethics, their instauration as a way of life, is of immediate, daily, political concern" (15). Such a description applies not only to France but to post-Revolutionary America, where the uncertainties of establishing a new government and social order were complicated by the guilt of a patricidal revolution and moral questions surrounding American Indian policy. Because of the need to define national identity in terms consistent with the Enlightenment principles invoked to justify revolution, such questions of national morality were of immediate political concern. Following Brooks's argument, the moral complexity of the American nationalistic project, which coincided with efforts to define American Indian policy, would make the strategies of melodrama especially compelling to nineteenth-century Americans: "Precisely to the extent that they [authors of melodramas] feel themselves dealing in concepts and issues that have no certain status or justification, they have recourse to the demonstrative, heightened representations of melodrama" (21), in which all conflicts are reduced to "the confrontation of clearly identified antagonists and the expulsion of one of them" (16).

But the politics of national identity and Indian policy in the United States during the early nineteenth century were not easily assimilable to the simplifying strategies of melodrama. For example, the tyrannical father/king might be cast as the villain of the melodramatic plot, thus allowing the guilt of patricidal revolution to be purged dramatically in a patriotic ritual of national self-justification. But, as I have argued in chapter 2, post-Revolutionary Americans also wished to maintain a sense of continuity with the past; they were reluctant to completely sever their connection to England—nor could they, given the deep bonds of language and culture that still united them. Typical of this position was the response of James Fenimore Cooper, who imagined the War of Independence as an act of reformation rather than revolution. The first (rejected) design for the Great Seal of the United States of America—proposed by Benjamin Franklin, John Adams, and Thomas Jefferson on August 10, 1776—illustrates the deep sense of connection to England felt even by those most actively declaring America's independence. The design committee proposed that the seal should feature a shield divided into six sections. The first of these was to represent England, the others (in order) Scotland, Ireland, France, Germany, Holland, together representing "the countries from which these States have been peopled." The motto *e pluribus unum* was meant to include the European forefathers as much as the thirteen states, which were represented around the edge of the seal.[24]

The Indian problem, as it became intertwined with questions of national identity during the early nineteenth century, made post-Revolutionary American nationalism even more resistant to the kind of simple resolution offered by the melodrama. While Powhatan as tyrannical father/king could be cast as a villain, he simultaneously filled the role of victim, functioning as a representative of the American Indians' lost autonomy and claims to the land. Furthermore, the threat posed by the Indian problem could not be defined as an external one. Rather, it came from within, from the very moral center of the national drama: legal and political debates over American Indian policy called into question the morality—and thus the legitimacy—of a nation built upon a history of conquest. Such a threat could not simply be expelled like the villain of a melodrama.

Barker's solution to the ethical problems posed by American revolutionary origins and Indian-white relations is to make Pocahontas the moral center and active heroine of the melodrama.[25] While it was common for a woman to be the moral center of a melodrama, usually the heroine was passive and vulnerable: she displayed her virtue through filial piety and devotion rather than rebellion and served as the motive of others' heroic action rather than the agent of her own fate. By depicting Pocahontas herself as defying her father's authority, Barker simultaneously purifies and distances the violence of rebellion and conquest. If Smith or Rolfe, assuming the conventional role of the melodramatic hero, had rescued Pocahontas from her tyrannical father, the play would have represented all too realistically Euro-American violence at the center of the national drama. Instead, the act of rebellion against father/king and the Indians' loss of autonomy are both redeemed by their association with the unquestionable virtue of the melodramatic heroine. Pocahontas's goodness is signaled by her intuitive recognition of the superiority of the conquerors and their values. Her heroic rescue of Smith, for example, is seen as an instinctive response to the moral truth of European virtue. As dramatized by Barker Pocahontas simultaneously represents the Indians (as victims of conquest), the conquerors whose values she embraces, and the nation that will emerge from repeated acts of violence. Barker's play thus reconciles the motives of conquest with the values of the Enlightenment by bringing together American Indian policy and national identity in a single moral vision.

If Pocahontas's actions are to be viewed as models of universal principles, they must be motivated not by lust or even personal love but by humanity and virtue. In this Barker departs from seventeenth-century sources and earlier nineteenth-century popular versions of the Pocahontas story, both of which suggest that love for Smith played an important role in the rescue.[26] In Barker's play, before Pocahontas saves Smith or falls in love with John Rolfe, her attachment to Smith is defined as explicitly asexual. At the sight of Smith, the first European she has ever encountered, being led as a captive into the village, Pocahontas is immediately struck with awe. "O Nima!" she exclaims to her friend, "is it not a God!" (593). In Barker's rendition of the famous rescue, there is no suggestion that Pocahontas is motivated by romantic love. She pleads for Smith's life based on abstract principles: respect for his superior qualities, honor (her brother had declared Smith a brother and pledged his friendship), and mercy. When the execution is halted, she expresses her joy in chaste, sisterly terms, exclaiming "My brother!" (595).

Pocahontas's actions not only prove her goodness, they also prove her to be a true woman, according to Euro-American standards, and thus fit to serve as foster mother to the colony. Smith's first words upon being freed make clear the message Barker wants to convey to his audience:

> O woman! angel sex! where'er thou art,
> Still art thou heavenly. The rudest clime
> Robs not thy glowing bosom of its nature.   (595)

The universalized category of woman is here imagined as transcending that of race. This maneuver allows Pocahontas to occupy a double position of legitimacy: she is both child of the New World, embodying its innocence and its fruitfulness, and mother of the "infant colony," displaying all the feminine virtues associated with nineteenth-century American definitions of the true woman. Thus, Pocahontas as national hero offered Americans a doubly legitimized, alternative family lineage distinct from the Old World heritage they had rejected through patricidal rebellion.

Later, when Pocahontas meets and instantly falls in love with John Rolfe, the playwright identifies the European culture of which Rolfe is representative and conduit, rather than the man himself, as the ultimate object of Pocahontas's love:

> O! 'tis from thee that I have drawn my being:
> Thou'st ta'en me from the path of savage error,
> Blood-stain'd and rude where rove my countrymen,
> And taught me heavenly truths, and fill'd my heart
> With sentiments sublime and sweet and social . . .
> Hast thou not heaven-ward turn'd my dazzled sight,
> Where sing the spirits of the blessed good
> Around the bright throne of the Holy One?
> This thou hast done; and ah! what couldst thou more,
> Belov'd preceptor, but direct that ray,
> Which beams from Heaven to animate existence,
> And bid my swelling bosom beat with love!   (611–12)

Like her response to Smith, Pocahontas's relationship to Rolfe (her "Belov'd preceptor") is explicitly desexualized by Barker. Pocahontas's instant affinity with Euro-American values again illustrates her innate moral goodness and her suitability to serve as foster mother to the colony. The smooth, almost seamless shuttling of Pocahontas between men—from John Smith to John Rolfe—serves to reinforce the unity of the Euro-Americans, who emerge not simply as brothers in the colonial/national family but as virtually interchangeable in relation to Pocahontas.

The terms Pocahontas employs to describe her love for Rolfe also define an alternative economy of conquest which is crucial to the play's revision of Indian-white relations. Pocahontas describes civilization as a gift which is more than just recompense for whatever Indians might lose through their contact with Euro-Americans. "Thou art my life!" Pocahontas exclaims to Rolfe. "I lived not till I saw thee, love" (611). Earthly treasure for heavenly treasure, life for life: all that Pocahontas—here representing the ideal Indian of Euro-American fantasy—has given to the English has been repaid, and the idealized Indian responds with gratitude and love.[27]

The violence of conquest is not completely obscured, however, by the domestic plot and the language of love it employs. The third act opens with a telling exchange between Walter and his wife, Alice. Walter is describing the adventures he encountered on his recent "voyage of discovery" when Alice interrupts him to ask the crucial question, "But have you got their treasures?" (607). When, in the very next scene, Rolfe proposes to go to Pocahontas's father "to woo Powhatan to resign his treasure" (611), the echo is unmistakable. The treasures won through conquest have been conflated with the (supposedly emotional) treasures Rolfe hopes to gain through marriage to Pocahontas. While this ambiguity might be viewed as another attempt to cloak the motives of conquest in the language of love, it could just as easily be interpreted as accomplishing the opposite, coming dangerously close, it would seem, to disclosing and undermining its own strategies of repression.

A similarly revealing irony emerges in the subplot of the Indian suitor. When Miami discovers Pocahontas in the arms of Rolfe, he asks, "In what do the red yield to the white men?" (603). While the comment is motivated by the loss of Pocahontas, the audience could have replied to Miami's question by listing all that Indians had yielded to a rapidly expanding nation between the seventeenth-century setting and the nineteenth-century performance of the play. The scene thus invokes the broader implications of the Euro-American triumph over the Indians, again calling forth the troubling moral questions the play elsewhere seeks to evade.

When Miami seeks revenge for the injury he has received on the field of love, he initially directs his wrath not against the English but against Powhatan, who has permitted Pocahontas's marriage to Rolfe. Miami's tribe, the Susquehannocks, declares war against Powhatan's. Thus, the first manifestation of violence directed against Indians in the play is depicted as a conflict in which "bad" and "good" Indians destroy each other. The colonists participate in the violence only as loyal friends aiding their Indian allies. When Miami, who is eventually reconciled with Powhatan, convinces the chief to join forces against the English, violence erupts again. Here the violence is explicitly derealized through dramatization, as the stage directions indicate: "The English seize the uplifted arms of the Indians, and form a *tableau*" (625). The audience never sees the violence between Europeans and Indians carried out; instead they see the representation of violence "frozen" into art before their very eyes. While this staging technique seems to distance the violence of Indian-white relations through stylization, it is also true that tableaux vivants were popularly used in melodramas (especially at the ends of scenes) to provide a sort of visual commentary. Along with music and stylized gestures, tableaux vivants were among the most characteristic melodramatic strategies to illustrate and emphasize the meaning of the action, that is, to make meaning legible. Once again the same action that serves to repress troubling truths simultaneously reinforces them.

The subplot involving Miami concludes when the defeated warrior refuses Smith's offers to forgive him and incorporate him within the new colonial order. Claiming that he has been "wounded" beyond recovery, Miami stabs himself. Smith responds, "Rash youth, thou mightst have liv'd." "Liv'd! man, look there!" Miami cries, pointing to Pocahontas and Rolfe. The crucial moment of defeat is again displaced from the field of battle to that of love, and the Indian's destruction is represented as self-inflicted.

With the death of the Indian warrior Miami, the main obstacle to the resolution of the romantic plot has been removed. As Pocahontas and Rolfe embrace, Geraldine, an Englishwoman who has come to the New World disguised as a page to defend her virtue and reclaim her husband, reveals her true identity and flies to her husband's welcoming arms. At the same moment another settler named Robin declares that he plans to marry Pocahontas's friend and servant Nima. The courtship between Robin and Nima is described in highly sexual terms, contrasting with the desexualized nature of the Pocahontas-Rolfe union. This flurry of marriages incorporates upper and lower classes, sexual and desexualized relationships, and Indians and Euro-Americans in the new social order that Smith announces as he beckons all the couples to step forward and join in a dance:

> Wild Nature smooths apace her savage frown,
> Moulding her features to a social smile.
> Now flies my hope-wing'd fancy o'er the gulf
> That lies between us and the aftertime,
> When this fine portion of the globe shall teem
> With civilized society; when arts,
> And industry, and elegance shall reign,
> As the shrill war-cry of the savage man
> Yields to the jocund shepherd's roundelay.
> Oh, enviable country! thus disjoin'd
> From old licentious Europe! may'st thou rise,
> Free from those bonds which fraud and superstition
> In barbarous ages have enchain'd *her* with;—
> Bidding the antique world with wonder view
> A great, yet virtuous empire in the west! (627)

The new social order that Smith announces is described as distinctly American. Leaving behind the "shrill war-cry" of New World natives and the vices of "old licentious Europe," this "virtuous empire" is presented as the culmination of the play's action. Yet structurally the reference to Nature's "social smile" is an echo of Smith's words in the play's opening speech: "Mark / What cheery aspects look upon our landing: / The face of Nature dimples o'er with smiles" (579). The circularity makes this conclusion seem implicit from the beginning, preordained and approved by (smiling) Nature. The song that ends the play, a hymn to "Freedom," points to the American Revolution by means of which the United States would achieve its official status as a nation by declaring its political freedom from England. The moment of national origin, however, is articulated in what might be described as a past-perfect historical tense: from the imagined perspective of national prehistory, the nation is conceived as an idea projected onto the future, a prophecy to be fulfilled. The ease of the slippage between historical and mythical reveals the power of the stage as a site where the nation is "produced."[28]

In the play's concluding speech and song Barker incorporates history itself within the flexible bounds of dramatic time. Locating the roots of American freedom and distinctive national identity in its earliest colonial history makes the Revolution an inevitable, almost anticlimactic effect of a plot that has already unfolded and achieved resolution in the play. This, in itself, would serve to distance nineteenth-century Americans from the guilt and anxiety associated with the nation's Revolutionary origins. In addition, as the fulfillment of prophecy, the separation from "old licentious Europe" achieves the legitimacy of divine sanction.

The play's ending relies heavily upon the conventions of comedy to achieve a sense of closure. The greed, violence, and treachery which have characterized Indian and Euro-American relations throughout the play have not really been resolved. They are simply pushed aside to make way for the final, grand spectacle. In a dizzying rush of multiple marriages and unmaskings, all the characters are swept up into an elaborately choreographed social dance and harmonious chorus in praise of "Freedom!" Powhatan is lightheartedly forgiven his opposition to Rolfe and treachery against the settlers as he is included in the great marriage celebration at the end of the play. Only the jealous lover and rebellious warrior Miami is removed—by his own action. The rest, transcending differences of race and class, join in the final scene of social integration. The play thus substitutes structural closure for thematic resolution and provides simplified emotional responses to the complex moral problems it engages elsewhere.

The Question of Genre

Quite early in the play Barker self-consciously addresses the question of generic convention, as his characters reflect upon the same sort of generic slippage which his own play employs so brilliantly. In the first act, two of the colonists expand upon the metaphor according to which Smith has cast them as actors in a "noble drama":

ROBIN: But hark ye, master Larry, in this same drama that our captain spoke of, you and I act parts, do we not?
LARRY: Arrah, to be sure, we are men of parts.
ROBIN: Shall I tell you in earnest what we play in this merry comedy?
LARRY: Be doing it.

ROBIN: Then we play the parts of two fools, look you, to part with all at
home, and come to these savage parts, where, Heaven shield us, our heads
may be parted from our bodies. Think what a catastrophe, master Larry!
LARRY: So the merry comedy ends a doleful tragedy, and exit fool in the
character of a hero! That's glory, sirrah, a very feather in our caps!

(582–83)

If the history of conquest is conceived as domestic comedy, the men
imagine themselves as fools for willingly surrendering the stable domestic
arrangements of Old World society and entering into this New World,
where such social stability must be rebuilt in the face of great difficulties.
The motivation for such sacrifice lies in an alternative conception of conquest as a heroic drama which, even if it ends "tragically" in death, be-
stows glory. The men's playful exchange calls attention to the contin-
gency of history—and its justifications. Yet another shift in focus would
reveal the unfolding of an alternative drama not encompassed by either
comic or heroic emplotments of conquest.

The real tragedy is that of the Indians, whose lives and cultures were
destroyed by historical events, represented here through the conventions
of heroic melodrama. As Arnold Krupat has persuasively argued, the historical drama of Indian-white relations in the United States was alternately structured according to the generic conventions of either comedy
or tragedy. According to the "comic" version of American history, Indians were simply obstacles to be overcome in the course of the new
nation's inevitable drive toward cultural triumph and social integration.
But this comic rise was dependent upon the tragic downfall of the Indians, whose lands provided the ground for American expansion.[29] Following the conventions of tragedy, the hero/victim's fall was represented
as a manifestation of a higher order, a fate as inevitable as it was tragic. In
both comic and tragic emplotments of history the real human experience
of Indians was obscured to the same degree as the moral responsibility of
Euro-Americans was denied. The conventions of genre assert a logic and
power of their own.[30]

Barker's melodramatic version of the drama of conquest subsumes
both comic and tragic modes in a strategy of justification that moves
beyond mere denial. While the comic conventions seem to have the last
word, the play is not a comedy. It is true that the marriage plot, which is
typically the provenance of comedy, runs throughout the play, but it
functions primarily as a means of containing (especially in the final scene)
the moral ambiguities of the drama of conquest. The real center of interest lies in questions of morality that fall squarely in the realm of melodrama. But the moral structure of Barker's play is unusual. Here the
forces of good and evil are not presented as absolute in the Manichaean

terms typical of melodrama. There is no clear-cut villain to embody evil (conceived as an external threat) and then be expelled. This is due, in part, to the moral complexity of the subjects the play explores: the behavior of Pocahontas and the settlers, the project of conquest, and the idea of a nation founded upon (continuing) acts of violence.

Barker's strategies for adapting the conventions of melodrama to his subject can be seen in those instances when the play simultaneously reveals and represses a moral threat: when the equivalence between Pocahontas and other plundered "treasures" discloses the motives of conquest cloaked in the language of love; when Miami asks (rather pointedly for nineteenth-century audiences, who by 1808 would already have witnessed the widespread decimation and dispossession of Indian tribes), "In what do the red yield to the white men?" (603). Such moments occur frequently enough to suggest that they are not simply mistakes but rather create an imaginative space of judgment for the audience; they are encouraged to shift back and forth in their perception of the action or motive in question, interpreting it alternately in terms of the dramatic conventions and narrative logic of (historically distanced) melodrama or in the light of then contemporary political and moral questions that the play's subject, language, and historical trajectory clearly point toward. Given the ambiguity of this imaginative space, Barker's play confronts the audience directly with the acts of repression it performs.

This marks a significant departure from melodramatic conventions as they are usually understood. According to Brooks, melodrama is "the dramaturgy of virtue misprized and eventually recognized" (27), and "melodramatic rhetoric and the whole expressive enterprise of the genre is a victory over repression" (41). Melodrama is characterized by an exaggerated clarity in its definitions of good, evil, and the distinction between them. The moral center of the melodrama is the character whose virtue is questioned and eventually affirmed. Barker's play is unusual in that it ultimately makes each member of the audience and the American nation itself the moral center of the melodrama. Moments of apparent clumsiness, where the play seems to undermine its own strategies of repression, actually create the moral context in which the most compelling drama— "virtue misprized and eventually recognized"—is enacted by the audience itself. The popularity and power of melodramas about Indians, presented as national dramas, might be more clearly understood when interpreted in this light. During the first half of the nineteenth-century, when the morality of American Indian policy and the meaning of American national identity were both being questioned, melodramas such as Barker's provided an imaginative space for Americans to confront the moral principles that defined and, at times, threatened to undermine the legitimacy of national identity. Such melodramas might be described (to revise Brooks's formulation) as the dramaturgy of (national) guilt misrecognized as virtue.

Pocahontas, the Cherokees, and the "Removals" of Melodrama

On February 11, 1836, the Washington *Globe* advertised a special performance of "The National Drama of Pocahontas," a play by George Curtis entitled *Pocahontas, or The Settlers of Virginia, A National Drama*. On this night, during the second act of the play, "Ten Cherokee Chiefs" in Washington representing "the Delegation of the Tribe" would appear onstage. The advertisement went on to explain that the Indians, "having been much gratified by the performance of the National Drama, and anxious to give it full effect, have most liberally offered their services, and will this evening appear and perform their real INDIAN WAR DANCE, exhibiting Hate, Triumph, Revenge, etc., and go through the CEREMONY OF SCALPING."[31] The relatively large amount of space the ad devoted to the Cherokees suggested that they were to be the main attraction of the evening's entertainment. A notice in the *Globe* on February 13 indicated that the audience was not disappointed:

> The fifth representation of Mr. Custis' splendid melodrama *Pocahontas* brought together a very large audience, the interest of which was increased by the introduction of John Ross and his "merrie men," who performed their real Indian war dance, exhibiting hate, triumph, revenge, etc., and went through the agreeable ceremony of scalping, all of which seemed to give great satisfaction to a crowded house. The white men forming the *dramatis personae* were determined not to be outdone by their red allies, and their exertions were so effective that the whole went off with much *eclat*.

The February 15 issue of the *Globe* carried a news item which quoted a letter by John Ross insisting that no members of his delegation had appeared onstage:

> Among the theatrical communications thrust into our columns without our knowledge was one saying that "John Ross and his 'merrie men' performed their real Indian war dance," etc. We believe some such notice was also contained in the play bills. We have received a letter from Mr. Ross in which he says that "neither I nor any of my associates of the Cherokee delegation have appeared on the stage. We have been occupied with matters of graver import than to become the allies of white men forming the dramatis personae. We have too high a regard for ourselves—too deep an interest in the welfare of our people, to be merry-making under our misfortunes," etc.

The February 13 description of the performance suggests that some-one—Indians belonging to another tribe or white actors—had been en-listed to play the part of the Cherokee delegation performing "their real Indian war dance." The notion of white actors impersonating the Cher-okees and then staging a competition with the white actors portraying the Indians of Custis's play offers a glimpse into the complexity of and concern over questions of race, identity, and authenticity in mid-nineteenth-century American culture. The deception—and its apparent success—reveals the depth of the American public's desire to insert the Cherokees into the national drama. John Ross's letter reflects a sophis-ticated awareness of what is at stake when such desires are publicly enacted.[32]

To identify the Indians as the Cherokee delegation in Washington and to name John Ross specifically would be to call to mind the Cherokees' ongoing protest against American Indian policy. For almost a decade John Ross had led the Cherokees in a public campaign to resist removal. In December 1835 the conflict reached a turning point when a small pro-removal faction signed a treaty which the U.S. government hoped to impose upon all the Georgia Cherokees. In response, John Ross and the anti-removal faction increased their protest activities. The very delegation referred to by the *Globe* was just one of many who traveled to Washing-ton to appeal directly to Congress, the President, and the American peo-ple. Given the political events surrounding this performance of Custis's drama, one wonders exactly what part the Cherokees were thought to have played. What was the "full effect" that their participation was to produce? What was the appeal of the (imagined) scene of Indians watch-ing themselves cast as part of the American "National Drama?"

In the two decades between Barker's introduction of Pocahontas to the American stage (1808) and George Washington Parke Custis's revival of the subject (1830) questions about American Indian policy and the meaning of American national identity had become even more troubling. Changes enacted during the administration of Andrew Jackson—espe-cially the Removal Act of 1830—had become the occasion for intense public debate over national character. (The next two chapters will exam-ine in greater depth the cultural and political logic of American Indian policy during the 1820s and 1830s; here I will provide just a brief sum-mary of the events immediately surrounding this remarkable performance of *Pocahontas* in order to explore how the popular stage and the national myth of Pocahontas were enlisted to define American national identity in the face of the American Indian problem.) Custis's *Pocahontas, or The Settlers of Virginia, A National Drama* (1830) was the most successful of the many plays about Pocahontas produced in the first half of the nine-teenth century (until John Brougham's extremely popular burlesque of

Pocahontas came along in 1855). Part of the play's popularity arose from the ways Custis adapted the story of Pocahontas and the strategies of melodrama to address contemporary questions of American Indian policy and national identity.

Rather than rely upon misrecognition or repression, Custis seems to call attention to the moral problems associated with the U.S. government's ongoing dispossession of Indians. From the very beginning, Custis focuses much more openly and directly than Barker on the darker motives driving the drama of conquest. The play opens from the perspective of the Indians as they watch the English boats approach the shore: "They are called barques," Matacoran, a Powhatan prince and suitor of Pocahontas, explains to his companion, "and bear the adventurous English in search of their darling gold, the god they worship" (Custis [1830] 1925, 189). The reference to gold undoubtedly would have resonated deeply and disturbingly for Custis's audience: the discovery of gold on Cherokee lands in 1828 played a major role in Georgia's ongoing efforts to dispossess and remove the Cherokees. Custis does nothing to counter Matacoran's assessment of the Europeans' greed; in fact, the play repeatedly stresses the Indians' perception of the settlers' motives. Matacoran asks, "[I]f you English so love your own country, why cross the wide sea to deprive the poor Indian of his rude and savage forests?" (189). Chief Powhatan questions Smith directly: "[M]any do inform me that your coming hither is to invade my people, and oppress my country." Smith responds with an outright lie: "Great King, thou art falsely inform'd; we came not only to be friendly with thee, but to aid thee with our arms in thy wars with the Monecans" (195). But Powhatan clearly sees the truth that nineteenth-century audiences living in an era of unprecedented expansion must also have recognized: "They ask the lands from the mountains to the sea; but will they be content with part, when their object is to take the whole?" (198).

The colonial venture is immediately framed in terms of violence. In the play's opening scene Barclay, sole survivor of the ill-fated Roanoke settlement, greets Smith and describes how the earlier settlers "began to oppress and plunder the natives, who, in return, waylaid and slew them" (190). Undeterred, Smith replies, "For my part, having held warfare with wild Tartar and Hern, the savages of the Old World, I care not how soon I break a lance with his savage Majesty of the New. . . . [We will] demand, in behalf of our gracious sovereign, dominion in and over the countries from the mountains to the sea, and if denied us—why then— *Dieu et mon Droit*—for God and our right" (191). Whereas Barker, relying heavily upon the figure of Pocahontas as foster mother to the infant colony, took great pains to legitimize a distinctly American lineage freed both from the sins of "old licentious Europe" and the "savage" violence of the native inhabitants, Custis here places the New World in direct lineage from the Old, as the latest in a long series of violent European conquests. As for questions of legitimacy, Smith simply proclaims the legitimacy of conquest "for God and our right." Nowhere does Custis's Smith apologize for or attempt to minimize the violence of conquest.

In terms of the ideological work of the play, or even the plot itself, Pocahontas is not nearly as central to Custis's drama as she was to Barker's. The play is not about Pocahontas or the domestic activity of building a new society in America so much as it is about the violence of conquest and the ascendancy of capitalism, which is described in terms of masculine values and actions. Much more in keeping with the standard conventions of melodrama, Custis's Pocahontas, while still important as an emblem of virtue, is more passive and vulnerable than Barker's; she serves mainly as a motive force inspiring the actions of others and a foil by which to measure their moral worth.

Custis introduces Pocahontas only after the central dramatic conflict between opposing forces (Indians and settlers) has been well defined. Pocahontas's entry does nothing to advance the plot; indeed, her first words simply repeat what the audience has already seen, namely, the landing of the English upon the American shore: "Oh, 't was a rare sight to behold the chiefs as they leaped on shore, deck'd in all their braveries; their shining arms, their lofty carriage, and air of command, made them seem like beings from a higher world, sent here to amaze us with their glory" (191). Pocahontas here serves to reflect and define rather than advance the action.

Virtue is repeatedly revealed by Pocahontas's vision of characters or their actions toward her. With Pocahontas serving as the measure, good and evil, heroes and villains are quickly and sharply defined in the play. "Come good, come ill," Pocahontas summarily declares in the first act, "Pocahontas will be the friend of the English. I know not how it is, but my attachments became fixed upon the strangers the first moment I beheld them." A few lines later (with little concern for motive or dramatic development) Pocahontas announces that "Matacoran is the sworn enemy of the whites, and implacable in his hatred; but sooner shall the sun cease to shine, and the waters to flow, than Pocahontas be the wife of Matacoran" (191). Through Pocahontas's responses to them, European and Indian are designated as hero and villain, respectively.

In Barker's play, as in the historical record, Pocahontas's first encounter with the Europeans involves her dramatic rescue of Smith. Custis departs from history and his dramatic predecessor by having Pocahontas and Rolfe meet first.[33] Their initial encounter in the forest occurs by chance and is the occasion of nothing more than an exchange of civilities. Rolfe offers the princess his seat and his protection, insisting that "the duties of a Cavalier to your sex are the same whether in the Old World or the New" (193). Custis thus establishes the relationship between Pocahontas and the settlers on terms that emphasize the European's initial act of generosity rather than the Indian's. The encounter introduces the chivalric code that will prove crucial to the play's resolution. Whereas Barker's play appeals to the universal category of woman—and the domestic values associated with women during the nineteenth century—to transcend the boundaries of race and mask the motives of conquest, Custis's reference to Pocahontas's "sex" primarily serves to define a set of masculine values, including chivalry, that transcend the boundaries of race and subsume the motives of conquest.

Custis's play focuses upon the acts of men—protecting maidens, waging war, facing death with honor—that define them as men.[34] For example, when Matacoran goes into battle, it is not simply to defend his land from the intruders but to "uphold the fame and manhood of the Indian" (199). Smith refuses to leave behind "a distressed damsel" (Pocahontas) because "it would be but of ill savour to the fame of English cavaliers" (202). Indians and Europeans pause repeatedly during battle to "admire" each other's manhood. When Hugo, an English soldier, is captured, Matacoran frees him as a reward for his bravery, saying, "I like thee, old Warrior. Thou shalt return to thy chief, and tell him that Matacoran admires his valour and bids him to the combat" (203). Hugo repays the favor by saving Matacoran from death when he, in turn, is captured. The stage directions describe the incident as follows: "*English enter and attack* Matacoran, *who defends himself bravely—he is beaten down on one knee.* Hugo *enters and covers him with his buckler*" (204). Hugo's act and its staging parallel the famous episode (moved by Custis to the end of the play) when Pocahontas "*rushes down from the throne* [and] *throws herself on the body of* Smith" to save him from death (207). Thus, Pocahontas's heroic act of feminine virtue and self-sacrifice (as presented by Barker) is here anticipated and, in a sense, supplanted in significance by the soldier's chivalrous act of manly generosity on the field of battle.

The masculine values Custis places at the center of his play are precisely those associated with classical theories of republican virtue. In classical political theory the concept of *virtù* (the root of "virility") refers to that disinterested devotion to the state best illustrated by martial courage in the state's defense. It is, needless to say, a quality which only men can fully exhibit. J. G. A. Pocock, among others, has shown how this notion of republican virtue shaped American political thought during the Revolutionary era.[35] Competing and, ultimately, intertwined with the ideology of republican virtue were liberal values of individualism and competition, according to which the pursuit of self-interest was imagined to serve the public good. The ideology of liberalism became increasingly dominant as the American economy moved toward market capitalism in the nineteenth century.

The late eighteenth and early nineteenth centuries represented a period of transition in the political ideals of American nationhood and citizenship.[36] This period was characterized not only by the oscillation between republican and liberal values but by changes in the meaning of virtue itself. Under the influence of Scottish common-sense philosophy, virtue evolved from an essentially masculine attribute to a term denoting such feminine qualities as benevolence, gentility, moral sensibility, and (female) chastity.[37]

In Custis's *Pocahontas* we see the competing meanings of virtue at work. Classical notions of republican virtue are illustrated in the men's acts of chivalry and martial courage, while the liberal values of competition and individualism motivate the colonial enterprise. Pocahontas—chaste, benevolent, self-sacrificing—serves as a model of the feminized meanings of virtue. The self-consciously archaic terms (for example, of chivalry) which Custis uses to describe acts of republican virtue identify them with the past, yet the amount of time characters spend admiring each other's manliness affirms this older scheme of values. The masculine exchange of admiration in Custis's play both facilitates the transition in Euro-American values and rewrites the meaning of Indian-white relations by providing an alternative economy of values. Like the economy of love in Barker's play, the economy of admiration Custis constructs reconfigures conquest and the inequalities it produces as an equal exchange.

Pocahontas, too, is admired in the play, but in a manner that places her outside the system of exchange established among the men. Pocahontas's heroism (for example, when she braves a storm to warn the settlers of imminent attack, or when she risks her life to save Smith) falls squarely within the gender conventions of melodrama; Custis emphasizes Pocahontas's vulnerability and weakness and minimizes her own active agency. The scene in which Pocahontas decides to save the settlers is constructed as pure melodramatic spectacle:

> (*A flash of lightning.*) Ha! a storm is brewing, and how will these little hands, us'd only to guide the canoe in sportive race on a smooth and glassy surface, wage its struggling way, when raging billows uprear their foamy crests? Brave English, gallant, courteous Rolfe. (*Thunder.*) Night comes on apace—Oh, night of horror! (*Clasps her hands and looks up to heaven as if in prayer.*) Thank thee, good Spirit; I feel thy holy influence on my heart. (201)

Pocahontas assumes the role of the melodramatic heroine, less a hero than a victim of the violent weather, the night, and her own fears. She is not so much an actor as a conduit through which the "good Spirit" acts.

When Pocahontas saves Smith, Custis again deflects attention from her (heroic) action: "'t is his [God's] Almighty hand that sustains me, 't is his divine spirit that breathes in my soul, and prompts Pocahontas to a deed which future ages will admire" (207). Unlike the equal exchange of admiration among the men of the play, the admiration due Pocahontas establishes a debt to be paid in the future.

In the scene that follows the climactic rescue, Pocahontas receives the admiration of the Englishmen as each, in turn, kneels before her. The economy of admiration is projected into the future and reimagined as compensatory history: "Honor thanks thee, England will thank thee, while Virginians to remotest ages will venerate thy fame, and genius hand thee over to immortality" (207). This display of gratitude is immediately followed by Smith's bestowal of a gold chain upon Pocahontas. Another Englishman watching the scene associates freely from the symbolism of the chain to a proposal of marriage between Rolfe and Pocahontas: "And bind two in thy golden shackle, the good and gallant Master Rolfe, and thou wilt unite the hands of those whose hearts have long since been united." Pocahontas's response reveals the gesture of generosity to be simultaneously an act of domination: "She will most cheerfully submit to wear the chain which binds her to the honour'd master of her fate, even tho' the chain were of iron instead of gold" (207). Pocahontas's relationship to her English husband prefigures the subjugation of Indians by Euro-Americans. Pocahontas—the vulnerable, passive, and virtuous heroine of conventional melodrama who accepts the white man's mastery willingly and cheerfully—permitted nineteenth-century audiences to envision an idealized version of the drama of conquest. The Indian imagined as woman (as defined by the conventions of melodrama and feminized meanings of virtue), like the Indian imagined as child (the most popular metaphor informing nineteenth-century political rhetoric), required and justified the paternalistic control and "protection" that characterized nineteenth-century American Indian policy.[37]

The ritual of subjugation is followed immediately by the removal of chains from Matacoran, who is the embodiment of the Indians' resistance to Euro-American conquest. Through Pocahontas subjugation has been accomplished symbolically; the overt sign of violence, namely, the chains of captivity, must now be removed. Smith in effect proposes that they forget the past: "Let's in future be friends, and join in friendship those hands which lately wielded the weapons of enmity. Matacoran shall be of power and influence in the country which he hath so gallantly defended, and shall hold of the royal James posts of honour and trust in the newly acquired colony of Virginia" (208). Smith attempts to elide the fact of conquest, the fact that "the country which [Matacoran] hath so gallantly defended" has now become "the newly acquired colony of Virginia." He offers to return power to Matacoran—but now limited by and subsumed within Euro-American political structures.

Matacoran, however, will not surrender to the conqueror; rather than enter a future controlled by others, he instead chooses to consign himself to a past that remains his own:

> Now that he can no longer combat the invaders he will retire before them, even to where tradition says, there rolls a western wave. There on the utmost verge of the land which the Manitou gave to his fathers, when grown old by time, and his strength decay'd, Matacoran will erect his tumulus, crawl into it and die. But when, in a long distant future, posterity shall ask where rests that brave, who disdaining alliance with the usurpers of his country, nobly dar'd to be wild and free, the finger of renown will point to the grave of Matacoran. (*Matacoran rushes out.*) (208)

The irony of this speech grows out of the audience's awareness that the Indian's defiance is staged for, and even performed by, the white "enemy" he denounces. In fact, it is incorporated in the very national history the defiant (stage) Indian attempts to resist. The defeated but proudly defiant noble savage who futilely resists the advance of "civilization" was a particularly popular stereotype pervading American literature, history, and political rhetoric during the first half of the nineteenth century.[38] Custis's drama illustrates the power and appeal of this stereotype.

Whereas Pocahontas (the Indian as woman) represented one idealized resolution to the Indian problem, Matacoran provides another. Even as he refuses to submit to the conqueror, Matacoran essentially defines freedom for Indians as the freedom to remove and history as the record of extinction (the gravestone). Smith's approving response—"Brave, wild, and unconquerable spirit, go whither thou wilt, the esteem of the English goes with thee" (208)—illustrates the admiration and nostalgia that pervaded nineteenth-century rhetoric of "the dying Indian." Smith's farewell to Matacoran also incorporates the Indian in the play's alternative economy by offering history (the esteem of the conquerors) as compensation for the losses due to conquest.

This is not, however, the end of the play. The final words spoken are given to Powhatan, who, in Matacoran's absence, accepts the economy of compensatory history Smith has offered and Matacoran has rejected. Shifting attention to the future (the present of the play's nineteenth-century performance), Powhatan declares, "Let their [Pocahontas's and Rolfe's] union be a pledge of the future union between England and Virginia. . . . And may the fruits of this union of virtue and honour be a long line of descendents, inheriting those principles, gifted with rare talents, and the most exalted patriotism." Powhatan surrenders control of the future to the Euro-American conquerors, claiming for himself only

"the privilege of giving away the bride" and for his people the compensation of history: "Now it only remains for us to say, that looking thro' a
long vista of futurity, to the time when these wild regions shall become
the ancient and honored part of a great and glorious American Empire,
may we hope that when the tales of early days are told from the nursery,
the library or the stage, that kindly will be received the national story of
Pocahontas, or The Settlement of Virginia" (208). This final self-reflexive
gesture offers as promised compensation the very performance the audience has just witnessed. The applause that follows becomes the conclusion of the play and the fulfillment of history as the play has defined it.

But even as Powhatan explicitly embraces the symbolic economy of the
play, his final speech invokes Matacoran, the figure who rejects and thus
marks the limits of compensatory history. The inheritance Powhatan
imagines for future Americans is striking in that it emphasizes the one
virtue (patriotism) that is glaringly absent in the titular heroine.
Pocahontas turns her back upon her own people when she betrays their
plan to attack the English; she renounces her father and king, declaring
defiantly, "Cruel king, the ties of blood which bound me to thee are
dissever'd" (207). The settlers, while professing their patriotism, are repeatedly shown by Custis to be driven more by love of gold than love of
country. In fact, the only character who appears to be motivated solely by
patriotism is Matacoran.

From the outset Matacoran is identified as a passionate patriot. His
role as "sworn enemy of the whites" (191) is simply the complement and
manifestation of love for his own country: "[Matacoran] swears, by the
heroic fame of his fathers, eternal enmity to the invader, and devoted
fidelity to his king and country" (196). In a lengthy exchange with Powhatan before the war against the English begins, Matacoran describes
himself again as heroic patriot: "Since first I enter'd the ranks of men, I
have been in the service of my country; how faithfully, how daringly I
have serv'd her, the renown of thy arms, O king! will best declare. Yet of
all the spoils of war, what hath been the share of Matacoran? None—for
Matacoran fought not for wealth, but for glory and Pocahontas. Now he
must fight for glory and his country" (200). Matacoran clearly emerges as
the character who most perfectly illustrates (classical republican) virtue:
his patriotism is selfless and unwavering; his courage and honor are admired by all.

In the exchange that follows, Custis explores the competing principles
of self-interest and self-possession which underlie the definitions of virtue
and heroism in the play. Matacoran declares that he "must have done
with love. Glory and his country must return and possess his soul." Powhatan responds by insisting that Matacoran's "long and constant attachment deserves the possession of its object. Pocahontas shall be thine."

Again Matacoran refuses and struggles to regain self-possession: "Enough, enough—'t is the expiring struggle of love. Now Matacoran breathes alone of war, and pants for the combat. . . . Matacoran will deliver his country from her invaders, or soon exist only in his fame" (200). This exchange underscores the debate over personal versus national interest. Powhatan's offers of reward are based upon the liberal belief that self-interest, the urge to possess the object of one's desire, is the motive that drives the individual and ultimately serves the nation's good. Matacoran's actions, however, are motivated by the classical republican ideal of the individual giving himself over to the state, thereby allowing his country to "possess his soul."

Matacoran's heroism is dramatized most clearly in the war with the settlers, in particular the moment when he stands alone and confronts the enemy. Before the battle begins, Matacoran displays his selfless devotion to country by promising his men his own share of the spoils of battle. As they flee in fear before the superior weapons of the English, Matacoran calls out, "See, your prince advances first to meet the foe. Indians, place your trust in the spear, in courage, and Matacoran." Nevertheless his men desert him. "What remains now to face the foe," he asks, "nought but despair and Matacoran" (203). Matacoran's heroism is contrasted with the unworthiness of the common men who surround him.[39]

The heroism of the English is defined quite differently. When Smith falls into the enemy's hands almost immediately after Matacoran's fall, Mantea (wife of the Englishman Barclay) exclaims in despair, "Oh sad, sad day for us all!" Her husband responds reassuringly that "tho' a leader be slain, English soldiers are not long without another" (204). Pow-hatan, like Mantea, assumes that the fall of Smith means the downfall of all those he led: "How long," he asks, "before the remaining English are brought captive before my feet?" The Indian scout's answer confirms that among the English a leader is simply one among equals: "[T]ho' the leader is taken, the battle doth not abate. In truth, my King, there seem-eth to be many Smiths in the field; they fight as tho' they were all Smiths" (205). The Euro-Americans are presented as interchangeable parts in the whole (colonial/national) enterprise that unites them.

In his selfless devotion to country Matacoran remains a model of re-publican virtue, but as he stands alone, rising above his compatriots, he embodies the best hopes and the ultimate failure of the whole. The set-tlers, on the other hand, represent a democratic model of heroism in which equals united in a common purpose triumph. While their motiva-tion (greed) may be personal, their action is corporate, and the fortune of their country rises or falls with their personal fortunes. Custis here articu-lates the opposition between republican and liberal values in a way that produces a creative synthesis.[40] The individualism typically associated with liberalism is instead associated with the disinterested virtue of the republican hero as Matacoran stands alone against the enemy. Instead of leading to individual competition, the greed of the settlers produces equality and unity of purpose, with individuals working together like a well-oiled machine.

In his political writings Custis praised the ideal of civic virtue and expressed the fear—shared by many Americans of the day—that these republican virtues were disappearing in an era of acquisitive individualism. The alternative models of heroism presented in the play represent and, to some degree, resolve such fears. While Custis embraces the individual heroism of Matacoran—admired by all—he also consigns it to the past, as Matacoran disappears to erect his tomb in the West. The democratic hero, defined as a man of the crowd, is triumphant but (to use the play's own terminology) decidedly less "admirable." While the feminine virtue of Pocahontas is admired, it is associated with the powerlessness of the melodramatic heroine and consigned to a compensatory history. Her happy acceptance of the chain of friendship from Smith—and, by extension, the chain that binds wife to husband—represents the position of subjugation Pocahontas ultimately occupies in the play.

In bringing Pocahontas to the popular stage, Barker and Custis enlisted the conventions of melodrama to create morally simplified versions of American history and to define national identity in terms that reinforced a sense of social unity and cultural integrity. But the process of national identity formation was not as simple as the national dramas they produced, and the meanings that emerged from the performances of their plays ultimately circulated in ways not entirely predictable.

Barker, for example, resolved conflicts arising from an American history of conquest and revolution, but not without acknowledging the strategies of misrecognition upon which such resolution depended. He affirmed a vision of harmonious social integration—by bringing together Indian princess and English soldier, highborn characters and servants in one great wedding celebration at the end of the play—but the differences of race and class that are resolved so neatly in Barker's play remained a source of considerable anxiety for nineteenth-century Americans. Because of their mixed audiences, the popular theaters where *The Indian Princess* would have been performed actually became a locus of such anxiety. Despite his high hopes that the theater would hasten the triumph of democracy, even William Dunlap believed that it should be regulated by the government or men of taste in order that the "mass of men" might be guided on their path to virtue. The United States of the early nineteenth century was not the land of "jocund shepherd[s]" that John Smith imagines in the play's concluding speech. Unlike the resolution of Barker's melodrama, the kind of integration which the logic of democracy implies occurs in a social space not circumscribed by the generic conventions that Barker relied upon. Only in the safe space of the theater could the idea of the nation be enacted for and by citizens united in a shared vision transcending—at least for the duration of the performance—the differences that still divided them.

Similarly, Custis's *Pocahontas* called attention to the very questions of morality it hoped to resolve. Matacoran's shift from (melodramatic) villain to (tragic) hero implied a corresponding revision of the role of Euro-Americans in the drama of conquest. *Pocahontas* ultimately dramatizes Custis's genuine concern over the values of nineteenth-century American society—values implicit in an increasingly competitive market economy and the morality of American Indian policy. As the struggles of the Cherokees in Georgia revealed, Americans of the 1830s, still driven by a hunger for gold, defied federal law and seemed to come precariously close to betraying the principles upon which the nation, and its continued existence as a union, had been founded.

FOUR

MARY JEMISON AND THE DOMESTICATION

OF THE AMERICAN INDIANS

FOR THREE DAYS in November 1823 James E. Seaver, a retired physician living in Genesee County, New York, interviewed Mary Jemison, a white woman in her eighties who had spent much of her life among the Seneca Indians.[1] Captured in 1758, at age fifteen, she was adopted by the Seneca tribe and married two Indian husbands (in succession) with whom she raised seven children. At the time of the interview she lived near Genesee on her own farm, located between Indian and white towns, in a home she had built herself.[2] From his introductory comments, it is clear that Seaver believes he is presenting just another example of a genre he considers to be quite familiar to his readers—the Indian captivity narrative. Seaver places the Jemison narrative in the context of "the stories of Indian cruelties which were common in the new settlements" and hopes that, like most captivity narratives, it will reinforce the dominant values of nineteenth-century American culture by "increas[ing] our love of liberty [and] enlarg[ing] our views of the blessings that are derived from our liberal institutions" (vi–vii). But the narrative that follows, with its sympathetic account of Indian life and Jemison's willing accommodation to it, is hardly what Seaver's introduction would lead the reader to expect. Nevertheless, American readers clearly were ready for what the Jemison narrative offered. At a time when the captivity narrative was, according to its critic Roy Harvey Pearce, past its high point in popularity, the book became an immediate best-seller. First published by a small press in central New York as a piece of local history, the narrative was quickly reprinted in London and the United States. Within the first year over one hundred thousand copies were sold.[3]

In this chapter I will explore the implications of the Jemison narrative's remarkable popularity. Although it is impossible to enter into or reconstruct another's reading experience, it is possible to consider how a text was presented to readers, the reading practices and expectations they might have brought to it, and the literary precedents and historical issues with which it would have resonated. While the Seaver/Jemison text was not widely reviewed, Seaver and subsequent generations of editors did comment extensively upon the narrative, leaving a detailed record of one set of readers' responses.[4] These responses are especially important because they became part of the framework through which other readers would approach the text. Examining this extensive editorial apparatus in relation to the text itself reveals the Jemison narrative to be a textual site of dialogue and contestation over issues of central concern to American readers during the 1820s: the meaning and stability of racial and national identity; the limits and power of gender roles; the dichotomy between savagery and civilization; the history and future of Indian-white relations. By viewing these issues in the context of early-nineteenth-century political, social, and literary practices, one can better understand how the Jemison narrative engaged such issues and presented them to the readers who responded so enthusiastically to it.

(Re)defining the Conventions

In his introductory comments Seaver instructs the reader as to how to approach the text that follows. He suggests a wide range of uses for the narrative. The book is presented as a biography that will provide examples to "guide us through the world in paths of morality" (iv). Even more important, in terms of nineteenth-century conceptions of morality, is the opportunity the book offers readers to exercise their sympathies: "Here also may be learned, pity for the bereaved, benevolence for the destitute, and compassion for the helpless; and at the same time all the sympathies of the soul will be naturally excited to sigh at the unfavorable result, or to smile at the fortunate relief" (iv). The narrative is also represented by Seaver as a valuable record of national history. In fact, the "gentlemen of respectability" who employed Seaver to record Jemison's story did so "with a view not only to perpetuate the remembrance of the atrocities of the savages in former times, but to preserve some historical facts which they supposed to be intimately connected with her life, and which otherwise must be lost" (ix). Among these events are accounts of military conflict between U.S. soldiers and Indians which occurred before and during the Revolutionary War. The narrative calls special attention to the heroic activities of prominent Americans, including George Washington. Seaver's tendency to use Jemison's personal narrative as a window upon national history is illustrated by the fact that he begins his introduction to Jemison's story with reference to "The Peace of 1783" (vii), an event much more important to American national history than to the story Jemison recounts. Finally, Seaver suggests that on a more practical level the book may be utilized to "improve [the abilities of children] in the art of reading [since] books of this kind are sought and read with avidity, especially by children" (iv).

When he identifies the Jemison narrative as belonging to the well-known genre of the captivity narrative, Seaver again associates the narrative with children:

> It is presumed that at this time there are but few native Americans that have arrived to middle age, who cannot distinctly recollect of sitting in the chimney corner when children, all contracted with fear, and there listening to their parents or visitors, while they related stories of Indian conquests, and murders, that would make their flaxen hair nearly stand erect, and almost destroy the power of motion. (vii).

Seaver's relegation of such narratives to the past, along with his suggestion that they are especially appropriate for children, would seem to support what Pearce has argued in his influential study of the genre: "[I]t becomes apparent that towards the end of the eighteenth century American readers were not taking the captivity narrative very seriously. Even for a popular genre, it was quite old and quite tired" (1947, 12).

According to Pearce, there were three major phases in the development of the Indian captivity genre. The earliest examples were primarily religious documents, presenting the experience of captivity as parallel in several respects to religious conversion as envisioned by the Puritans. In the mid-eighteenth century, especially during the French and Indian wars, the captivity narrative served as a vehicle of propaganda. By the beginning of the nineteenth century, when Indian wars and the Puritan model of religious conversion were no longer pervasive concerns for most Americans, and when the genre had become quite formulaic and stylized, captivity narratives were no longer taken seriously as culturally significant or historically accurate documents. Most scholars of the captivity genre agree with Pearce's basic account of the changes in the form of captivity narratives. The genre, in general, did become increasingly stylized and sensationalized, eventually becoming overtly fictionalized. Edward Kimber's *History of the Life and Adventures of Mr. Anderson* (1754) and Ann Eliza Bleecker's *History of Maria Kittle* (1797) are two early examples of captivities refashioned as sentimental novels.[5]

While some recent scholars, such as Richard Van Der Beets, essentially agree with Pearce's dismissal of many late-eighteenth- and early-nineteenth-century narratives that were sensationalized and/or fictionalized, others argue that by the nineteenth century captivity narratives had simply changed their forms and functions in ways that Pearce failed to recognize as culturally significant.[6] Christopher Castiglia, for example, sees the generic instability of the captivity narrative as part of its cultural power rather than a sign of loss. Focusing on narratives written by women, Castiglia locates in this versatile genre "a basis for a female tradition in American culture" (15). Like Castiglia, Gary Ebersole stresses the capacity of the captivity narrative to accommodate changing concerns and values across a wide range of historical periods, settings, and literary styles. The subtitle of Ebersole's book, *Puritan to Postmodern Images of Indian Captivity*, indicates its wide scope. Ebersole identifies the shift toward sentimentalism in the captivity narrative not as a sign of decline but as one of the means by which the genre remained compelling and significant for an American public whose reading practices and moral beliefs had been shaped by eighteenth-century moral philosophy and sensational psychology (98–99). In the sentimental form of the captivity narrative, captivity provides an instance of "virtue in distress" that is significant to readers in its capacity to reveal the innate virtue of the sufferer and to stir sympathy, a morally loaded term in the eighteenth and nineteenth centuries (110–12).

Seaver's introduction to the Jemison narrative shows the influence of the sentimental tradition.[7] His hope that "all the sympathies of the soul will be naturally excited" (iv) by the narrative reveals a sentimental understanding of reading as moral exercise. Furthermore, Seaver makes a point of identifying Jemison as a woman of refined sensibilities, signifying that she is an appropriate heroine of a sentimental narrative: "Her passions are easily excited. At a number of periods in her narrative, tears trickled down her grief worn cheek, and at the same time a rising sigh would stop her utterance" (xi). When she refuses to provide the information Seaver desires regarding the wartime "atrocities" committed by her husband Hiokatoo, Seaver explains Jemison's reticence in terms consistent with the delicate character he has ascribed to her: "The thoughts of his deeds, probably chilled her old heart, and made her dread to rehearse them" (xii). But Seaver's attempt to inscribe Jemison as conventional heroine of the sentimental nineteenth-century captivity narrative stumbles over the fact that Jemison and her story refuse to conform to the generic, social, or historical conventions of such narratives. It is in the moments of conflict between Seaver's repeated struggles to impose narrative order and Jemison's persistence in telling her story that the significance and power of the text as a site of cultural contestation are revealed most clearly.

Seaver's difficulty in "placing" Jemison historically or narratively is revealed in the first sentence of the introduction: "The Peace of 1783 and the consequent cessation of hostilities and barbarities, returned to their friends those prisoners, who had escaped the tomahawk, the gauntlet, and the savage fire, after their having spent many years in captivity, and restored harmony to society" (vii). Such an introduction, which aligns the captivity experience with a peaceful state disrupted and then restored, is perfectly conventional. The problem is that Jemison's story does not fit this conventional structure. As the narrative's title page declares, Jemison "has continued to reside among [the Indians] to the present time." Only by conflating Jemison's history with national history (the Peace of 1783 did restore harmony to post-Revolutionary society) can Seaver force the conventional introduction to fit Jemison's unconventional story.

In so doing, Seaver simultaneously points to ways in which the narrative destabilizes the very structures he attempts to impose. Editors and critics, from Cotton Mather to Richard Slotkin, have read captivity narratives as cultural allegories in which the white (especially female) captive represents the community or nation as a whole.[8] To borrow a phrase from Lauren Berlant, the white female captive becomes a "national symbolic" in which the boundaries of the nation are aligned with the boundaries of the white female body. Joy S. Kasson, writing on the enormous popularity of Erastus Dow Palmer's sculpture *The White Captive* (1859), similarly identifies the white woman's body as symbolic of the body politic (72). Kasson argues that Palmer's statue, like conventional captivity narratives, shows the fragility of civilized culture by constructing parables of female vulnerability (76). The symbolic equation of woman/captive and nation performs its ideological work of affirming national identity and power only insofar as the woman/captive remains sexually and culturally intact and is eventually reincorporated within national boundaries. This is clearly not the case for Mary Jemison. While Seaver encourages readers to approach the narrative in conventional terms as a national allegory, the Jemison narrative actually undermines the nationalistic project by revealing (in ways I will subsequently explore) the boundaries of identity to be permeable and the ascendancy of Euro-American culture to be questionable.

Seaver attempts to locate Jemison more specifically in the context of American national history by identifying her with "the frontier" and the Euro-American progressivist narrative this term implies.[9] He writes: "Sometime had elapsed after [the Revolution] before the country about the lakes and on the Genesee river was visited, save by an occasional land speculator, or by defaulters who wished by retreating to what in those days was deemed almost the end of the earth, to escape the force of civil law" (viii). Seaver's account illustrates what Leslie Fiedler has described as a paradigmatically "American" scene of men fleeing civilization (and women) to the freedom of the frontier.[10] In this case, however, what the fugitives find is the last thing they expected: "'The White Woman,' as Mrs. Jemison is called" (viii), is already there waiting. A white woman was commonly represented in nineteenth-century national iconography as a symbol of American civilization diametrically opposed to the frontier.[11] By locating "The White Woman" on the frontier, while still describing it as the place beyond the reach of civilization, Seaver once again destabilizes the very conventions he employs to define it.

In the paragraph immediately following this second attempt to "place"

Jemison, Seaver's struggle is reflected in the language and rhetorical structure of the passage. He sets out to describe Jemison in terms that align her with the values of middle-class American culture, praising her hospitality and charity in language that clearly echoes the New Testament injunction to feed the hungry and clothe the naked:

> Although her bosom companion was an ancient Indian warrior, and notwith-
> standing her children and associates were all Indians, yet it was found she
> possessed an uncommon share of hospitality. . . . Her house was the stranger's
> home; from her table the hungry were refreshed;—she made the naked as
> comfortable as her means would admit of; . . . she became celebrated as the
> friend of the distressed. She was the protectress of the homeless fugitive, and
> made welcome the weary wanderer. Many still live to commemorate her be-
> nevolence towards them, when prisoners during the war, and to ascribe their
> deliverance to the mediation of "The White Woman." (viii–ix)

The repeated use of qualifying terms (although, yet) reveal Seaver's struggle to locate Jemison culturally, that is, to reconcile the Euro-American values he ascribes to her and the Indian world she inhabits. A few pages later Seaver points out traits which identify Jemison even more explicitly with Indians: "Her habits are those of the Indians—she sleeps on skins without a bedstead, sits upon the floor or on a bench, and holds her victuals on her lap, in her hands. Her ideas of religion, correspond in every respect with those of the great mass of the Senecas" (xiv). Seaver's confrontation with difference in the person of Mary Jemison produces rhetorical turbulence; he has difficulty incorporating Jemison within a smooth, consistent narrative. When he attempts to employ racial and cultural stereotypes to define—and thereby stabilize—Jemison and her experience, Seaver instead confronts and reveals the instability of those very categories of definition.

The problem that Jemison, with her ambivalent cultural identity, poses for Seaver is similar to that which Homi Bhabha associates with the colonial hybrid. "Hybridity," Bhabha explains, "is not a third term that resolves the tension between two cultures . . . in a dialectical play of 'recognition.' The displacement from symbol to sign creates a crisis for any concept of authority based on a system of recognition" (1994, 113–14). Seaver's difficulty with his subject is fundamentally a crisis of recognition: Jemison simply does not conform to the firmly established racial or cultural categories of identity he is capable of recognizing. While he repeatedly attempts to make Jemison a symbol of racial and cultural identity— "The White Woman"—she instead becomes a sign of difference that must be interpreted in order for these categories—or Seaver's narrative— to have meaning. Seaver ultimately fails to reconcile the conflicting elements in Jemison's character, or to establish a clear relationship between them, with one set of traits and values predominating over the other. Instead, the conflict remains unresolved, marking the text itself as a site of contestation that the reader must negotiate.

The question of textual authority in the Jemison narrative is extremely complex. It is clear that it is not strictly Jemison's, since Seaver shapes her oral account to create the written text the reader encounters. But neither is it entirely Seaver's, since he must work with the material Jemison provides, which does not always fit neatly into his own vision of her experience. In the preface Seaver insists that he is simply a faithful recorder of facts: "No circumstance has been intentionally exaggerated by the paintings of fancy, nor by fine flashes of rhetoric; . . . Without the aid of fiction, what was received as a matter of fact, only has been recorded" (v). It is apparent, however, that Seaver is not simply reporting the facts as Jemison presents them. For instance, when Seaver inserts a long account of the wartime exploits of Jemison's husband Hiokatoo— complete with stereotypical descriptions of the Indian warrior dashing out the brains of an infant and "thirst[ing] for the blood of innocent, unoffending, defenseless settlers" (108)—we know from Seaver's comments in the introduction that Jemison refused to provide such information. In a footnote near the end of the account, Seaver admits that he had to go to other sources for this information, which to him seemed crucial to Jemison's story. Elsewhere Seaver does not openly admit that he has shaped Jemison's account, but there are inconsistencies suggesting the presence of two very different voices. For example, near the end of the narrative Jemison is supposedly summarizing the meaning of her captivity experience:

> The bare loss of liberty is but a mere trifle when compared with the circumstances that necessarily attend, and are inseparably connected with it. It is the recollection of what we once were, of the friends, the home, the pleasures we have left or lost; the anticipation of misery, the appearance of wretchedness, the anxiety for freedom, the hope of release, the devising of means of escaping, and the vigilance with which we watch our keepers, that constitute the nauseous dregs of the bitter cup of slavery. (140)

This passage, with its conventional sentiments and phrasing, is hardly remarkable. It might have appeared in any number of nineteenth-century captivity narratives—except this one. Far from anxiously seeking to escape her captors, Mary Jemison actually praises her life among the Senecas and repeatedly refuses to return to white society—even when encouraged to do so by members of her adopted tribe.

The question of what to make of such a text, which is the product of collaboration and contestation, is important to a proper understanding of the Jemison narrative and its cultural meaning. It is also a question of some scholarly and pedagogical urgency as literary and cultural studies have expanded to include texts that engage differences—of race, gender, class, culture—which often translate into different levels of access to literary production. Scholars studying such early forms of African-American literary production as the slave narrative have struggled for years with the difficulties posed by the relationship between often nonliterate subjects and the literate and culturally more powerful amanuenses and/or editors who bring their stories into print. "As told to" autobiographies of nonliterate and ethnically diverse peoples, which have increasingly been made available to readers and scholars, pose similar challenges. In general, scholars faced with such texts have attempted to define as fully as possible the cultural perspectives and the motives (personal, political, economic) of all participants in the literary production so that the reader may be alerted to the textual "presence" of each or signs of conflict among them.[12]

In the case of the Jemison text, Seaver's editorial comments provide many clues to his cultural position, perspective, and motives. Information on Jemison is more scarce. While Seaver was not the only white man to interview her—there are also some local historical records relating to Jemison and her family—most of these accounts are quite brief.[13] Knowledge of Seneca social, historical, and narrative traditions provides some insight into Jemison's perspective as it was shaped by her adopted culture.[14] Still, the most complete source of knowledge about Jemison is to be found in the words of the Jemison text itself, if read with attention to signs of narrative dissonance, which may reveal Jemison's voice or motives in conflict with those of Seaver. But the significance of such moments of dissonance goes beyond the goal of recovering the "true" Jemison and her lived experience. Ultimately it is impossible to recover the originary subject—or author—of the text. Understanding the meaning of the Jemison narrative and its impact on nineteenth-century American culture requires more than simply identifying the different (authentic or inauthentic) narrative voices and strategies that produced it. The whole is indeed more than the sum of its parts. The contestation—between Seaver and Jemison, between Euro-American and Indian—inscribed in the Jemison narrative is itself crucial to the text's power and significance.

In order to clarify this power, I return to the notion of the hybrid. According to Bhabha, such texts arise from the margins of a culture, from the position of the minority, the colonized, the exile. The hybridity of the Jemison narrative is somewhat different. It arises from the confrontation with cultural difference which lies at the center of Jemison's experience and identity. The editor, representing the dominant culture, does not identify Jemison's position as marginal but instead tries to locate "The White Woman" within dominant cultural conventions and nationalist discourses. This illustrates the shifting boundaries of race and gender as they operated in relation to Indians in American discourses of nationalism during the early nineteenth century.[15]

Arnold Krupat's work on early as-told-to Native American autobiography is particularly relevant to the Jemison narrative. Krupat views such composite works produced by a "principle of original bicultural composition [as] the textual equivalent of the frontier," which he defines as "the reciprocal relationship between two cultures in contact" (1985, 33). The Jemison narrative may be considered a frontier text in this sense; however, it moves beyond this model to the extent that Jemison herself is not entirely identified with either culture. Seaver's introductory remarks reveal his difficulty in locating Jemison unambiguously in either Indian or Euro-American culture. Jemison's cultural identity remains complex throughout the narrative. While it is clear that in many ways Jemison identifies herself and lives as a Seneca woman, it is also true that she makes a self-conscious effort to retain a connection to the culture she was forced to abandon at age fifteen. For example, she describes how she practices her English in secret "in order that [she] might not forget [her] own language" (37). The fact that she names each of her children after a member of her white family also reveals a continuing attachment to the past. At several points—especially when Jemison is describing the attack and her early experiences among the Senecas—the narrative shifts between the perspective of a frightened and confused white child and the later, assimilated perspective of an insider in Seneca society who translates and explains the Indians' words, actions, and customs. For example, in her account of the Seneca adoption ceremony Jemison interjects a description of how she "sat motionless, nearly terrified to death at the appearance and actions of the company, expecting every moment to feel their vengeance, and suffer death on the spot" (36). Jemison's expression of love for her new Seneca sisters illustrates the extent to which past and present are intertwined for her: "The warmth of their feelings, the kind reception which I met with, and the continued favors that I received at their hands, riveted my affection for them so strongly that I am constrained to believe that I loved them as I should have loved my own sister had she lived, and I had been brought up with her" (54). Even in the most intense expression of love for her new family old attachments remain; loss and gain are sustained simultaneously as present affections are measured by thoughts of what might have been. Even when a double vision is not explicitly articulated in the text, its existence, illustrated in passages such as these, remains to inform the reader's perception of Jemison's experience. Thus the narrative perspective itself can be seen as a frontier where two cultures meet.[16]

The fact that Jemison, as represented in the narrative, remains geo-

graphically, culturally, and emotionally situated in a border region between Indian and Euro-American worlds marks an important departure
from the structure of most captivity narratives. Given Seaver's presentation of the text as a typical captivity narrative, failures to fit the familiar
model become significant for identifying gaps between reader expecta-
tion and experience. Such points of disjunction become textual openings
encouraging readers to re-envision the imaginative terrain of the captivity
narrative and the meanings it encompasses.

While it is difficult to speak of a "typical" captivity narrative, most do
share a three-part structure. The narrative necessarily begins with an act
of separation whereby the captive is forcibly removed from his or her
familiar world. This removal is followed by a "liminal" phase during
which the captive exists suspended between two worlds and belonging to
neither: having left the security and familiar customs of his or her own
culture, the captive lives for a time among the captors according to their
customs; yet to the extent that the captive continues to envision the
experience as captivity, he or she never fully belongs or locates self-iden-
tity in this world. The final phase of captivity is reincorporation or restoration, whereby the captive returns to his or her former world transformed by the captivity experience.[17]

Several critics have read captivity narratives, with their three-part structure, as accounts of initiation or rites of passage.[18] Early Puritan narratives
often explicitly align the experience of captivity with conversion, itself a
kind of initiation into a new awareness of one's identity in relation to
God. Richard Slotkin sees captivity as a form of initiation into American
experience in general, describing the Indian captivity narrative as "a vari-
ation on the great central myth of initiation into a new world and a new
life that is at the core of the American experience." Slotkin places the
emphasis upon the final step (restoration) that completes the initiation
process: "[T]he captive is not initiated into an entirely new way of life;
rather he is restored to his old life with newly opened eyes" (1973, 110,
179). While Alden Vaughan and Edward Clarke note the "danger in focusing too intently on the initiation ordeal and overlooking the significance of the much longer and equally profound captivity experience
itself," they similarly identify the defining structure of the captivity narrative as that of a three-part initiation or rite of passage (11–12).

In each of these interpretations, the ultimate meaning of the captivity
experience derives from the captive's reincorporation, since it is this step
that completes and gives value to the experience as a process of initiation.
The initiation imagined here is a conservative ritual, bringing the captive
back into the society he or she left, with a new (and firmer) understanding of his or her position in it. The captive's return is further emphasized
by the fact that, almost by definition, the narrative is told from the per-

spective of the reincorporated captive, since the captive must return in order to tell his or her story. The act of communication itself becomes part of the process of reintegration, for it involves an implicit assertion that the captive's experiences beyond the boundaries of his or her own culture and the transformations that have resulted from these experiences are meaningful and valuable to the culture to which the narrative is addressed.

The resolution of the Jemison narrative differs from this model in several important ways. Jemison is never reincorporated into the culture from which she was abducted. Nor is she absorbed completely—personally, culturally, or narratively—into the Seneca culture that adopts her. Instead, Mary Jemison remains permanently in what can be compared to the liminal stage of the initiation process, located between two well-defined cultural positions. Characterizations of the Jemison narrative as a typical captivity narrative overlook the fact that Jemison does not return to the society from which she was abducted. Likewise, critics such as Susan Walsh and Karen Oakes, who define the Jemison narrative as a Native American autobiography, miss the complexity and power that arise from Jemison's sustained border condition. Living between the Indian village and the white town, Mary Jemison has settled and made herself at home in a realm located geographically and culturally between white and Indian worlds. Even narratively Jemison does not enact the reintegration that usually occurs when the captive finally offers an account of his or her experience to the community being rejoined. Jemison does not offer her story to the white community; instead, Seaver approaches her to solicit and take the account from her.[19] Thus, the Jemison narrative, removed from the frontier she still inhabits, enters the white world without her, carrying with it the frontier textually inscribed in the narrative itself. Here the frontier is not a geographical or cultural boundary between opposed or conflicting worlds, nor is it simply a threshold (or *limina*) to be crossed in the process of initiation into a new position in the old social order. Rather, it is a space to be inhabited, a space that opens up the defining boundaries of cultures, in which readers can explore, test, and play with alternative conceptions of the frontier and its various meanings: the implications of cultural difference; the nature (and vulnerability) of cultural identity; the meaning of conceptual oppositions between society and wilderness, progress and loss; and the history and future of Indian-white relations.

The Jemison narrative does not provide a simple, straightforward account—historical or personal—of Mary Jemison and her experience; instead it presents a complex representation of the confrontation between Seneca and Euro-American cultures inscribed through the interaction of two narrative frameworks: Jemison's story of her experience and Seaver's notions of what kinds of stories can encompass such experience. The inevitable gaps between these two frameworks, apparent both in the introductory section and in the narrative itself, give the text a certain openness which contributes significantly to its power.[20] By creating within the text a discursive space where different cultural assumptions and narrative perspectives meet, this unusual narrative offers the white culture that appropriates it a way to imaginatively enter into the frontier that Jemison inhabits.

Comparing Jemison to James Fenimore Cooper's frontier hero Natty Bumppo helps illustrate the differences between the frontier inscribed in the Jemison narrative and the classic myth of the American frontier, defined predominantly by male writers as a site of masculine conflict and heroic activity. In her equivocal cultural identity Mary Jemison resembles Natty, the white man with the habits of an Indian. While Natty exhibits many Indian skills, his allegiance to his own race is uncompromised. In terms of Cooper's narrative, masculine identity is expressed largely through acts of violence: Natty never fights as an Indian (taking scalps) or with the Indians against Euro-Americans. Even though he often criticizes the ways of white men and spends his life trying to escape the encroachments of the latter's settlements, Natty remains a faithful servant of (Euro-American) civilization and progress. Thus, he partakes of both Indian and Euro-American worlds, embodying elements of each without belonging to either. Such a position gives him the unusual ability to negotiate between these two worlds without ever being defined as a threat to Euro-American values—either through his absolute opposition to them or by introducing into Euro-American society unacceptable attitudes or experiences resulting from his close association with Indians and the wilderness. His equivocal position between cultures allows readers to embrace and disavow selectively those aspects of American culture and history that affirm or trouble the identity they wish to cultivate.

Likewise, much of Jemison's power—as well as that of the narrative—arises from her simultaneous identification with the perspectives and values associated by nineteenth-century readers with Euro-Americans and Indians. Seaver seizes upon this in his introduction when he describes Jemison as a mediator: "Many still live to commemorate her benevolence toward them, when prisoners during the war, and to ascribe their deliverance to the mediation of 'The White Woman'" (ix).[21] Throughout the text Jemison also mediates between Euro-Americans and Indians as a cultural interpreter for her readers—mapping the geographic world the Senecas inhabit, describing their daily life, and explaining Seneca rituals and customs—providing knowledge, accessible only to one who has lived as part of the Indian world, from a perspective that her readers can trust and identify with. Seaver's inclusion of an appendix almost a third the length of the narrative itself—containing additional descriptions of Indian life and customs based "principally" on Jemison's testimony—suggests that he expects such information to be a significant source of interest to the readers.[22]

While Jemison's association with both Euro-American and Indian worlds is important, her power, like Natty Bumppo's, derives from the fact that she is represented by Seaver as not completely belonging in either world. If Jemison were seen as locating her loyalties and identity entirely in the Indian world, she would be considered either an outlaw, whose transference of racial allegiance would make her opposed to Euro-American values, or an outsider, whose severance of all ties to Euro-American culture would make her irrelevant to it. On the other hand, if she actually tried to reintegrate herself into American society, her experiences among the Indians—especially her violation of racial and sexual boundaries—might create difficulties.

Anxiety regarding sexual violation of women captives was a common feature of captivity narratives throughout the history of the genre. Although there was no ethnographic evidence that northeastern Indians raped prisoners, popular writing and art often focused upon the perceived sexual threat to women captives.[23] Cooper's account of captivity in *The Last of the Mohicans* (1826) is a prime example. Much of the plot is driven by the urgency of rescuing the Munro sisters from the threat of forced marriage to an Indian, which is described in the book as a fate worse than death. Cooper's anxiety regarding racial purity is also revealed through Natty's constant repetition of the fact that he is "a man without a cross" of Indian blood. Female authors of captivity narratives often felt the need to defend their sexual conduct to avoid suspicions that might prevent their full reacceptance into the white society to which they returned (Vaughan and Clarke, 14). At one point in the narrative Jemison expresses this fear of rejection to explain why she refused to return: "I had got a large family of Indian children, that I must take with me; and . . . if I should be so fortunate as to find my relatives, they would despise them, if not myself; and treat us as enemies; or, at least with a degree of cold indifference, which I thought I could not endure" (93). While this open acknowledgment within the text of Jemison's violation of cultural taboos might add to her interest as an outlaw figure, it makes even more remarkable Seaver's representation of Jemison in the preface and introduction as a model of conventional virtue and heroism.[24]

To better understand Jemison's status as heroine, it may be useful to compare her story with that of John Dunn Hunter, whose experiences were similar to Jemison's but whose cultural position and significance were perceived quite differently by nineteenth-century Americans. Like Jemison, Hunter was captured by Indians as a child and lived happily with the Osages, his adopted tribe, until a conflict broke out between the Osages and nearby settlers (he was nineteen at the time). After learning of his tribe's plan to attack a local trader, Hunter decided to warn the white trader and thus save him. Unable to face the Indians he had betrayed, Hunter (reluctantly) returned to white society. In 1823, just one year before the Jemison narrative, he published the story of his adventures.

Like Jemison, Hunter gives a sympathetic account of Indian life, rich in ethnographic information. Unlike Jemison, while living among the Osages Hunter locates his identity more firmly in the Indians' world. For example, whereas Jemison repeatedly expresses her memory of and fondness for her former life, even naming her children after her white family members, Hunter, who was younger when captured, remembers none of the details of his former life in white society. Hunter's position after leaving the Indians differs significantly from Jemison's. Jemison leaves her Seneca village to establish a life for herself suspended between the Indian and white worlds; Hunter, by contrast, returns to the center of white society, where his Indian loyalties are viewed as dangerous.

Upon his return, Hunter traveled to England, where he and his book attracted great attention and became the focus of ongoing debates concerning American Indian policy, debates which encompassed deep national rivalries. In this position of prominence, Hunter's narrative, expressing condemnation of the U.S. government's treatment of Indians, became a threat to the national image abroad. In defense, the United States enlisted its strongest forces to crush Hunter. Lewis Cass and Thomas McKenney, two of the nation's most respected and influential authorities on Indian affairs, published scathing attacks discrediting Hunter and his narrative, while English writers rallied to his defense. The narrative became the battleground between two nations, with American national character and pride at stake.[25] By assuming a position opposed to the national interest, Hunter, in effect, was fighting on the side of the enemy—one of the clearest and most abhorrent signs of "Indianization."

Even more threatening than his reentry into the white world—carrying his Indian loyalties with him—were Hunter's efforts to make the Indians themselves full and equal participants in white society. Hunter was not content simply to denounce the government's past treatment of Indians; he proceeded to devise a future plan that would genuinely and permanently integrate Indians into American social and economic life. After studying Robert Owen's model factory villages in England, Hunter developed a practical plan for saving and civilizing the Indians by building utopian farming communities on Indian land. But nineteenth-century Euro-Americans did not want such an alternative economic system, nor did they wish a new line of American yeomen within the boundaries of the United States; they wanted the bounty of the American "garden" for themselves, not the Indians. Hunter's efforts to test his model Indian community were doomed to fail, for he arrived in Arkansas after the Quapaw Indians had already ceded their lands to the U.S. government. He died in Mexico while still trying to find a place for the Quapaws and Cherokees to settle, his narrative discredited and largely forgotten.

While Hunter attempted to bring his Indian loyalties (and the Indians themselves) into American society, Mary Jemison offers no vehicle, practical or symbolic, to incorporate the Indians. On the contrary, she claimed that all efforts to assimilate the Indians were futile: "[T]he attempts which have been made to civilize and christianize them by the white people, ha[ve] constantly made them worse and worse; increased their vices, and robbed them of many of their virtues; and will ultimately produce their extermination" (48). Jemison's words echoed commonly held nineteenth-century attitudes regarding the "fate" of the Indians. According to Brian Dippie, the theory of the "Vanishing American" gained general acceptance as natural law during the second decade of the nineteenth century.[26] Even missionaries, who had been among the most adamant in their determination to "save" Indians, began to share the widespread conviction that their disappearance was inevitable. As one anonymous religious writer commented in 1830, "There seems to be a deep rooted superstition . . . that the Indians are really *destined*, as if there were some fatality in the case, never to be christianized, but gradually to decay till they become totally extinct" (quoted by Dippie, 10). Thus, while Indians had not yet quite faded into the past, they were allowed no place in the American future. Like the vision of Indian destiny presented in the Jemison narrative—and like Jemison herself—in this version of history Indians are suspended between two worlds, belonging to neither.

It is clear, then, that Jemison does not pose the kind of threat that a figure such as Hunter does; in fact, the Jemison narrative reassures nineteenth-century readers in some of their most cherished beliefs regarding the fate of Indians. Still, Jemison seems an unlikely candidate for the heroic role of harbinger of American values in which Seaver casts her. In spite of Seaver's insistence that the narrative will "enlarge [the white readers'] views of the blessings that are derived from our liberal institutions" (vi), it would instead seem to reinforce some of the deepest cultural fears represented by the captivity experience. Far from affirming the superiority of the white culture, Jemison openly enjoys her life among the Seneca and with her two Indian husbands, choosing to remain with them rather than return to the "blessings" of white civilization. The fact that Jemison's potentially threatening or unsettling qualities were not easily contained is suggested by the number of editors who "refashioned" the text over the years, attempting to reinscribe Jemison within an in-creasingly elaborate editorial apparatus, including new introductions, il-lustrations, additional chapters, notes, and appendixes.[27]

The most common strategy of containment was to reinforce Jemison's white cultural identification. For example, the editor of the second edi-tion (1842) added a rather dubious account of Jemison's deathbed con-version to Christianity. The introduction to the twenty-first edition again calls attention to Jemison's whiteness. Central to Jemison's "elevated character" and heroism, the editor of the twenty-first edition suggests, is the fact that "amidst the hardening surroundings of barbaric life, she preserved the sensibilities of a white woman" (h). The emphasis, I would argue, is on both "white" and "woman." The first edition implies what the twenty-first edition articulates more directly. In spite of the over-whelming evidence of Jemison's cultural identification with the Senecas, in his introduction Seaver strongly emphasizes those qualities that iden-tify Jemison with whiteness and the values nineteenth-century Americans associated with it. He notes that she speaks English well (with a slight Irish accent) and that "her complexion is very white for a woman of her age" (x).[28] The importance of Jemison's race *and* gender is perhaps indi-cated most clearly by her appellation as "The White Woman," which, beginning with the second edition, appeared in boldface on the title page of the book.[29] The most powerful means by which Jemison is identified with nineteenth-century, middle-class American conceptions of white womanhood is her association, throughout the text, with the values of domestic ideology.[30]

At Home on the Frontier

Both in the narrative and in the editorial apparatus that surrounds it, Jemison's story is presented in a way that emphasizes the significance of home and domestic values. Providing a wealth of biographical detail that is quite unusual for the genre, the narrative begins with a lengthy ac-count of Jemison's family history and childhood. The frontier home of Jemison's youth is described in terms that reflect popular nineteenth-century notions of the domestic ideal, calling forth the image of the home as the center of earthly bliss: "Health presided on every counte-nance, and vigor and strength characterized every exertion. Our mansion was a little paradise" (20). When a Shawnee and French raiding party intrude upon this "little paradise," breaking up the happy family and carrying Mary Jemison into the wilderness, we might expect the experi-ence of captivity to be described as a kind of hell (as the Puritans repre-sented it) in contradistinction to the "paradise" she left behind. What we find in the Jemison narrative, however, is not a vision of unremitting chaos and loss but rather the discovery of a new social order, the establishment of a new home and family.

With her adoption by the Seneca tribe, Jemison enters a new social order and begins to make herself at home. Immediately after her account of the adoption ceremony, Jemison goes on to describe her situation in terms of her new domestic role: "Being now settled and provided with a home, I was employed in nursing the children, and in doing light work about the house" (39). Soon Jemison's new family encourages her to marry a young Delaware named Sheninjee, a member of a friendly tribe living among the Senecas. By her fourth year with the Senecas, she seems to locate her social and personal identity firmly among them: "With them was my home; my family was there and there I had many friends to whom I was warmly attached in consideration of the favors, friendship and affection with which they had uniformly treated me from the time of my adoption" (46).

This transformation of cultural identity, and the radical shift in perceptions of cultural difference/relativity that it implies, are marked in the text by moments of dialogical play between different narrative perspectives. For example, just after the report of her marriage, Jemison begins to describe her husband Sheninjee in culturally neutral terms by referring to him simply as "a noble *man* [emphasis added]; large in stature; elegant in his appearance; generous in his conduct; courageous in war; a friend to peace, and a great lover of justice." Suddenly, in the middle of this account, the narrative shifts to a Euro-American cultural perspective: "Yet, Sheninjee was an Indian. The idea of spending my days with him, at first seemed perfectly irreconcilable to my feelings." The description resumes and concludes by acknowledging the "strangeness" it incorporates and thus to some degree, deconstructs: "[B]ut his good nature, generosity, tenderness, and friendship towards me, soon gained my affection; and, strange as it may seem, I loved him!—To me he was ever kind in sickness, and always treated me with gentleness; in fact, he was an agreeable husband, and a comfortable companion" (44). Whether the shifts in perspective come from Jemison's own double vision of her experience, from Seaver's response to the story Jemison tells him, or from Jemison's anticipation of Seaver's response, they are attributed to Jemison and as such shape the meaning and experience of the text for its readers. The passage offers a vision of cultural difference redefined through the eyes of "The White Woman" as Sheninjee the man becomes Sheninjee the Indian, who in turn becomes Sheninjee the good husband. Thus, the strangeness of racial and cultural difference is accommodated within the familiar structures of nineteenth-century conceptions of women's identity constituted primarily by family relations.

Jemison's account of her Seneca mother and sisters works in a similar way to familiarize difference. The narrative devotes much more space to the female members of Jemison's new family than to her Seneca brothers. Jemison consistently describes them in terms compatible with prevailing nineteenth-century, middle-class notions of a woman's proper character and role: "I was very fortunate in falling into their hands," Jemison notes early in the narrative, "for they were kind, good natured women; peaceable and mild in their dispositions; temperate and decent in their habits, and very tender and gentle towards me" (41). A later anecdote portrays Jemison's Seneca mother in a situation that illustrates even more dramatically sensibilities and values that a nineteenth-century American audience would have associated with a woman's proper sphere. When she discovers that her Seneca daughters plan to take their sister (Jemison) to witness the torture of a white captive, the Seneca mother intervenes. "In the most feeling terms," Jemison reports, "[she] remonstrated against a step at once so rash and unbecoming the true dignity of our sex" (56). The mother goes on to give her daughters further instruction regarding the proper roles and feelings of women:

> How, my daughter, (said she, addressing my sister,) how can you even think of attending the feast and seeing the unspeakable torments that those poor, unfortunate prisoners must inevitably suffer from the hands of our warriors? . . .—Our task is quite easy at home, and our business needs our attention. With war we have nothing to do: our husbands and brothers are proud to defend us, and their hearts beat with ardor to meet our proud foes. Oh! stay then, my daughter; let our warriors alone perform on their victims their customs of war. (56–57)

What the Seneca mother teaches her daughters about the proper role of women is a lesson that would have sounded familiar to most (white, middle-class) nineteenth-century readers: war is a man's business, whereas a woman's place is in the home; necessity may make men heartless, but women should feel for and empathize with others. Given the power of women in matrilineal Seneca society at this time—including deciding the life and death of prisoners, choosing male members of the war council, and removing them if they did not comply with the wishes of the clan mothers—the echoes of nineteenth-century domestic ideology here seem to represent the editor's universalizing vision, his assertion that the "bonds of womanhood" transcend the boundaries of race. Thus, the radical challenge the Jemison narrative poses to the stability of American cultural identity and superiority is stabilized by a vision of "true" womanhood that in effect erases Seneca culture as it imperialistically universalizes and imposes nineteenth-century, middle-class American social norms.[31]

An important turning point in the narrative occurs when Jemison's home among the Senecas, like her childhood home, is destroyed—this time by Euro-American violence. During the Revolutionary War American soldiers destroy her tribe's winter provisions. Mary Jemison "immediately resolve[s] to take my children and look out for myself" (74). Thus, she sets out to find yet another home for herself and her family. The land that Jemison settles upon, Gardow Flats, would have been identified by her white nineteenth-century readers as "the frontier": it is not part of the "wilderness," defined from a Euro-American perspective as the realm inhabited by Indians; but the fact that two runaway slaves are farming this land places it beyond the legal and social controls that characterize "civilization."

Jemison describes her frontier home with reference to Seneca tradition, which taught that this land was cleared neither by blacks nor by Indians but by a mysterious race whose bones were occasionally uncovered there. Such theories of a vanished race supplanted by the Indians were embraced by early Americans as a means of justifying the Indians' own supplantation by whites, making it part of a larger, natural cycle of the rise and fall of civilizations. Such theories also served to root American national history in a mythic past, while assigning Indians a liminal position in the historical narrative of nationhood. An anonymous essay entitled "American Antiquities," which was published in 1828, illustrates this point. The author contends that America, far from lacking historical depth in terms of its national identity, exhibits "a perfect union of the past and present; the rigor of a nation just born walking over the hallowed ashes of a race whose history is too early for a record, and surrounded by the living forms of a people hovering between the two" (quoted in Dippie, 17). According to this formulation, Indians have no natural place in America's vision of itself and thus become less than real—mere "forms" of a race "hovering" between worlds.

Jemison comes to the frontier as a mother motivated by the need to protect her children from starvation, and she succeeds in building a new home there with her own hands. As a mother Jemison achieves heroic stature: when a statue is erected in her honor in 1910, it is no surprise that she is portrayed carrying a child upon her back.[32] The nearly seventy pages that describe Jemison's life after she leaves her tribe focus on her efforts to support and raise her family on the frontier. Jemison's Seneca husband, who lives with her for much of this time, is hardly mentioned; the domestic drama, as the narrative represents it, centers upon mother and children.

Most critics locate the significance of the Jemison narrative in the fact that it is a woman's story. Karen Oakes analyzes the narrative as a Seneca woman's autobiography. June Namias argues that readers were free to place the emphasis where they wished—on *white* woman or white *woman*. In either case, she maintains that the narrative's popularity is due, at least in part, to its appeal to women readers: "[T]his 'true' story of struggle in a woman's life in a strange world allowed its female readers to identify with a heroic figure who was small and appeared weak yet who accomplished much, both in dealing with others and in summoning her own strength" (1993, 178). Annette Kolodny suggests that the Jemison narrative is revolutionary because it is the first to depict a woman's willing accommodation to the wilderness, to bring "the baggage of communal and familial domesticity [into] the wilderness preserve of the male hunter-adventurers" (1984, 80). She locates Jemison at the beginning of a female tradition of reenvisioning the frontier as garden. However, Kolodny concludes that Jemison was ultimately unacceptable as an American hero because her "Indianized" behavior veered too far from dominant nineteenth-century conceptions of ideal womanhood. In their discussions of the Jemison narrative as a woman's story, each of these critics refers to gender and race as if they were well-defined, stable categories, as if the "baggage" of cultural assumptions could be carried intact into a radically new field of experience and meaning. Seaver's difficulty in the face of Jemison's hybrid cultural/racial identity and the fact that Jemison's "Indianization" did not prevent nineteenth-century editors from depicting her as "The White Woman" or as an American cultural hero suggests the complexity of nineteenth-century attitudes concerning the interplay of race, gender, and identity.

The domestic drama Jemison enacts on the frontier is marked by struggle. One by one, Jemison's sons fall prey to alcoholism and cultural conflict as fights break out between those living by Seneca values and those adopting the ways of Euro-Americans. Eventually all three sons die violently, two killed by their own brother. But the ending of the narrative smooths over the violence, which is uncannily prophetic of social problems faced by Indians after removal. The narrative concludes with a vision of the family (comprising thirty-nine grandchildren and fourteen great-grandchildren) united around the mother: "Thus situated in the midst of my children, I expect I shall soon leave the world, and make room for the rising generation" (144). As Richard Slotkin has noted, this final picture of Jemison as matriarch surrounded by her children plays off the popular image of Daniel Boone as patriarchal hero of the frontier (450).

There is, however, a significant difference between Boone and Jemison which Slotkin does not mention: whereas Boone was father to a new line of American frontiersmen, Jemison's mixed-race children are defined in the text as Indians.[33] This perception of Jemison as white mother to Indian children lends the Jemison narrative tremendous cultural force, for it allows readers to encompass and explore within the narrative one of the central problems facing the United States in the nineteenth century: how to locate American Indians in the nation's vision of its history, its future, and its national character. The discourse of domestic ideology which pervades the Jemison narrative contributes to its capacity to stabilize such troubling racial and moral conflicts for its nineteenth-century readers.

The Domestication of the American Indians

By the time the Jemison narrative was published, the disappearance of Indians was considered by most Americans to be a foregone conclusion, a mere footnote in America's already "manifest" destiny. After the War of 1812, with the American claim to virtually all land east of the Mississippi secured, fears of a significant Indian threat to American sovereignty had diminished. Once Indians were no longer seen as a threat, they increasingly came to be viewed as powerless. In a report to the Speaker of the House in 1818, Secretary of War John C. Calhoun noted that "helplessness has succeeded independence" among the tribes on the western frontier. "The time seems to have arrived," he continued, "when our policy toward them should undergo an important change. They neither are, in fact, nor ought to be, considered as independent nations. Our views of their interest, and not their own, ought to govern them" (quoted in Dippie, 8). Such thinking formed the basis of Jacksonian Indian policy, with the U.S. government assuming the role of the "Great Father" firmly insisting that his Indian "children" remove to lands west of the Mississippi "for their own good."

Interpreting the rhetoric of nineteenth-century American Indian policy in psychoanalytic terms, Michael Rogin argues that this paternalistic model of Indian-white relations tends to include an element of violent, forceful domination which arises, in part, from the dynamics of the relationship among father, child, and mother. Francis Parkman, writing in 1851, reflects the popular nineteenth-century vision of Indians as children of nature who resist growing up (becoming "civilized") because of excessive attachment to their mother (nature). According to Parkman, the Indian is the "irreclaimable son of the wilderness, the child who will not be weaned from the breast of his rugged mother."[34] In Rogin's analysis, white civilization, imagined as the "Great Father," was completely excluded from and threatened by this intense mother-child relationship. From the perspective of the excluded father, then, efforts to "civilize" Indians required the often forcible intervention of paternal authority to sever the Indians' excessive, even unnatural, ties to their mother (1975, 208). This formulation quite accurately describes the course that Jacksonian policy ultimately followed with respect to the forced removal of Indians from their lands.

Although it is not the story line Jemison herself would apply to her experience, it is possible to see in her narrative an alternative account of Indian-white relations and Indian removal. In the story of Mary Jemison, portrayed as a white mother struggling to raise her Indian children, readers might see certain parallels to the U.S. government's attempts to "civilize" its Indian "children." Such a representation of a mother figure as a civilizing force was quite consistent with nineteenth-century domestic ideology. Nancy Cott's summary of dominant nineteenth-century conceptions of the social role of women concludes that "the purpose of women's vocation was to stabilize society by generating and regenerating moral character" (97). By instilling American values in her children, the argument went, it was the mother's responsibility to produce good citizens and to reproduce cultural norms.[35] Because of Jemison's unusual position, which is defined in the text as white mother to Indian children, nineteenth-century readers might envision her performing a similar role in relation to Indians. Regenerating Indian character in accordance with middle-class American values, Mary Jemison, "The White Woman," could be imagined as providing an alternative model to "civilize" the Indians—conceivably without the element of violent domination implicit in the paternalistic model. According to this maternalistic model, white civilization, represented by the figure of the White Mother, could be envisioned as stepping in gently to replace the Indians' "natural" mother. Americans could then hope that Indians would willingly accept their new mother and learn how to act in accordance with the values and goals of white civilization.

When the Jemison narrative was first published in 1824, the U.S. government, under the authority of President James Monroe and the direction of Secretary of War John C. Calhoun, was in the process of formulating the first official, comprehensive Indian removal policy. Whereas by 1824 the state of Georgia was already demanding that the Cherokees be removed forcibly from the state, most Americans still believed that the Indians could be persuaded to exchange their lands in the East for new lands in the West. In a special message to the Senate and House delivered on 27 January 1825 President Monroe summarized his hopes for the success of voluntary removal:

> [Removal] would not only shield them [the Indians] from impending ruin, but promote their welfare and happiness. Experience has clearly demonstrated that in their present state it is impossible to incorporate them in such masses, in any form whatever, into our system. It has also demonstrated with equal certainty that without a timely anticipation of and provision against the

dangers to which they are exposed, under causes which it will be difficult, if not impossible, to control, their degradation and extermination will be inevitable.[36]

According to this philanthropic justification of Indian removal, Indians must be shielded from the vices of (white) civilization while they gradually acquire its virtues. Removal is thus imagined as one step in a larger process af cultural and historical initiation, a temporary stage of protective isolation to be followed by the eventual integration of fully "civilized" Indians into American society.

Monroe's optimistic vision of removal extends even further as he envisions the policy providing a perfect resolution to all conflicts—past, present, and future—between whites and Indians:

> The relation of conflicting interests which has heretofore existed between them and our frontier settlements will cease. There will be no more wars between them and the United States. Adopting such a government, their movement will be in harmony with us, and its good effect will be felt throughout the whole extent of our territory to the Pacific.

Given the picture of removal he paints, it is no wonder Monroe believes "that the advantages attending it to the Indians may be made so apparent to them that all the tribes, even those most opposed, may be induced to accede to it at no very distant day" (Richardson, 2:281–82). Just as Monroe imagines that the Indians will certainly consent to removal once they understand the benevolent aims of the policy, the Jemison narrative, as construed by the book's editors, represents the Indians as willingly and naturally accepting the values and goals of white America—including the goal of Indian removal—thanks to the benevolent influence of a white mother.

Even after the forced removals of the 1830s revealed the failure of the fantasy that mild persuasion would bring willing compliance, the idea of the White Mother and her benevolent influence still remained central to the 1842 edition's representation of Jemison. The editors, Seaver's brother William and local land speculator and lawyer Ebenezer Mix, emphasize this point by adding material tracing the civilizing influence of Jemison upon her Indian descendants. The editors note that "several of the grandchildren of Mrs. Jemison, now living, are highly respected in their nation. . . . They have acquired the use of the English language sufficiently to speak it fluently, and have adopted the dress, habits, and manners of civilized society." The editors go on to express the hope that the Indian descendents of Mary Jemison "will, undoubtedly, ere long, take their departure from the land of their fathers, and assume important positions in legislative and judicial stations in the new Indian territory west of the Mississippi" (197). Envisioning removal as a simple shift in the Indians' filial loyalties—from the lands of their Indian fathers to the civilized values and policies associated (by the editors) with their white mother—tended to mask the radical violence and violation inflicted by removal.

The 1877 editor, iron magnate William Pryor Letchworth, makes even more explicit the significance of Jemison's maternal role as a civilizing force by adding a long chapter describing her grandson Buffalo Tom as the ideal of the civilized Indian. He is honest, industrious, thrifty, and the owner of a prosperous farm and home that "differs little from the ordinary abode of well-to-do farmers in the New England or Middle States". Tom's white grandmother is imagined as the direct source of his civilized virtues: "In fact, it would seem that the virtues which adorned the character of the grandmother, after lying dormant for one generation, had blossomed into rarer beauty in the next" (204). Like his grandmother, Tom became famous for his hospitality. While Mary Jemison provided food and shelter for whites who ventured into the wilderness, her grandson provided hospitality to the wave of westward emigrants who flowed steadily past his home. According to the editor, his home became "a vision of beauty to the wayward pilgrims passing by, on whom it beamed a smile of welcome" (203). The values and interpretive structures of domesticity are applied to the (male) Indian: his inward character is revealed by the outward appearance of his home. Just as the 1842 editors ended their account of Jemison's civilizing influence with an appealingly positive vision of Indian removal, the 1877 editor ends with a similarly positive vision of the Indian in the context of the policy of allotment and the continued westward expansion which it facilitated.

In 1876 the Commissioner of Indian Affairs proposed the first comprehensive plan for the allotment of Indian lands in severalty. According to the logic of allotment, the bestowal of private property was to instill in Indians the values and attributes associated with American citizenship—attributes which in 1876 were still explicitly defined as masculine. The plan was warmly received by President Hayes, by Indian advocacy groups such as the Indian Rights Association, by eastern philanthropists and by western settlers eager to gain access to the vast reservation lands that would remain after each adult male Indian had received his allotment. Still, there was much debate about the specific terms of land allotment and the linked question of Indian citizenship. The policy was finally implemented through the Dawes Severalty Act of 1887.[37] Senator Joseph E. Brown of Georgia, speaking before Congress in 1881, summarized the popular philanthropic arguments favoring allotment:

Under the benign influence of the Christian denominations, we shall see
Sunday schools and churches planted among them; and instead of roving
bands without fixed habitations, goaded to desperation by injustice and
wrong, spreading death and destruction in their pathway, we shall find them
in the comfortable homes of civilized man, not only a Christian people but
many of them cultivated and honorable citizens.[38]

Brown's optimistic account of the effects of allotment echoes the image
of Buffalo Tom presented by the 1877 editor of the Jemison narrative: a
vision of the Indian at home on his own farm, embracing the values of
white civilization, offering a smile of welcome to the settlers as they move
farther west to claim what was recently Indian land. In describing civilized Indians, both emphasize feminine, domestic values rather than the
masculine attributes nineteenth-century Americans associated with land
ownership and citizenship. Like the Jemison narrative, Brown's rhetoric
reveals basic inconsistencies in the logic of "civilizing" Indians.

The actual effects of allotment were quite different from those imagined by philanthropic supporters of the policy. Between its implementation in 1887 and its abandonment in 1934, Indian lands had shrunk from
137 million to 47 million acres, almost half of which was desert or semi-
arid land.[39] Similarly, idealized constructions of Mary Jemison as White
Mother leading her Indian children on the path to civilization were sadly
inconsistent with the historical reality of Indian-white relations during
the nineteenth century. There are clues within the editors' optimistic accounts that betray a truer picture. The fact that the editors consistently
refer to Jemison's descendents as Indians and locate their sphere of influence entirely within the "Indian territory west of the Mississippi" or that
the success of the civilizing process seems to be measured by the Indians'
acceptance of the need for their physical exclusion from white society
suggest that the influence of the White Mother was not meant to lead
the Indians toward genuine integration; the final step in America's benevolent plan to "civilize" the Indians was never meant to occur.[40]

While the maternalistic model of Indian relations might have been
more palatable to nineteenth-century Americans than the paternalistic
model, both entailed the cultural destruction of Indians. Both defined
the Indians as children; according to the logic of this metaphor, childhood, which is a temporary stage, must be left behind by all who continue to live and grow. To grow up, according to the symbolic system
nineteenth-century Americans employed, is to become white. As Michael
Rogin has concluded in his study of Jacksonian Indian policy, "In the
white scheme, civilization meant, no less than death, the disappearance of
the Indians. They could not remain Indians and grow up" (1987, 153).

To grow up, one should add, was also to be male. Nineteenth-century women, like Indians, were defined as children in terms of their social and economic dependency upon men and their lack of political rights. Self-possession and republican virtue, attributes considered constitutive of citizenship, were denied women and Indians by their very natures. It is therefore not surprising that when nineteenth-century Americans imagined Indians as "civilized," they described them in terms more feminine than masculine. William Gilmore Simms, writing in 1845, illustrates this tendency to feminize the "civilized" Indian: "This, in fact was the secret cause of the moral improvement of the Cherokees. The Creeks boasted to have made women of them. They had whipt [*sic*] them into close limits, where they were compelled to labour,—and labour,—a blessing born of a penalty,—is the fruitful mother of all the nobler exercises of humanity" (138). Thus, Pocahontas could readily be incorporated into American national narratives, while her noble suitor, with his manly resistance to subjugation, must be expelled. In Cooper's *Pioneers*, Chingachgook's final acceptance of defeat is marked by his castration. Whereas women were endowed with significant social and symbolic power in the separate sphere of the domestic, the "noble savage" was admired for his manly courage and independence as long as he remained in the separate sphere of history.

Rather than honestly attempting to civilize and assimilate Indians *or* engaging in an open campaign of extermination, nineteenth-century Americans relegated Indians to a position of social, political, and historical liminality: forever in the process of being civilized; ghosts hovering between the past—where Americans were anxious to embrace them as relics of the national history they longed for—and the present—where they could be located neither entirely within nor outside of American society. The U.S. government would not permit Indians to achieve their independence—whether as a potentially threatening force opposing American destiny or even as separate, sovereign nations following their own destiny within the boundaries of the United States. At the same time, the government would not grant Indians full membership in American society, with the rights of American citizens. The 1831 Supreme Court decision *Cherokee Nation v. Georgia* (which chapter 5 considers at greater length) made clear the Indians' liminal position in American society: Chief Justice Marshall ruled that the Cherokees should be considered neither as subjects of the United States nor as a separate sovereign nation, but as "domestic dependent nations" (Washburn, 4:2556). The exact definition—and legal rights—of this (implicitly feminized) entity remained vague. The policy of Indian removal translated into historical fact the inherent meaning of the Indians' position. In 1824 Secretary of War John C. Calhoun developed a plan for a "permanent Indian frontier." Removal to this permanent frontier would disrupt the integrity of native cultures by breaking ties to ancestral lands, altering traditional sources of livelihood, and subjecting Indians to Euro-American laws and policies. At the same time, it would keep Indians "permanently" on the fringes of American society.

Like the frontier which Mary Jemison embodies, the "permanent Indian frontier" is neither a line nor a threshold meant to be crossed but rather a space to be inhabited; it is a transitional phase in a rite of passage (from a savage to a civilized condition) never meant to be completed. The story of Mary Jemison struggling to raise her Indian children on her farm located midway between Indian village and white town symbolically situates the Indians precisely where Americans wanted them to remain: suspended between two worlds and belonging to neither. Jemison achieves cultural significance and heroic stature through her capacity to embody symbolically within a stabilizing narrative and ideological framework the contradictory meanings of removal policy.

Representing the transformation of Indians from members of independent social orders to disempowered, liminal figures in American society in terms of a frontier mother's struggle to find a home for herself and her children makes "familiar" what is actually a complex and potentially disturbing process of change. Similarly, the narrative conventions of the Indian captivity genre stabilize this process of change by making what is radically new appear as a restoration of the old order. Like more conventional captivity narratives, the Jemison narrative ends with a vision of the family united around the captive who is once again at home. On the surface it seems as if the standard resolution through the process of restoration has occurred. But here the social unit that was disrupted by captivity has not been restored. Instead the original family has been replaced by an entirely new kind of family configuration, one that now includes American Indians. The very conventionality of the concluding scene serves structurally to close down the conflicts the narrative has opened up and to subvert the reader's questions about just what kind of family configuration this is and what, precisely, is the nature of the Indians' new position in the American family. Thus, potentially disturbing elements of the new vision could be accommodated without necessarily being acknowledged.

Popular literature in particular has been characterized by its power to "make familiar" new or disturbing features of social experience.[41] To understand the power of the Jemison narrative, one must examine the double meaning of "familiar." Jemison's maternal relationship to Indians, stressed by the book's editors, functions like the metaphors of family relation that pervaded nineteenth-century rhetoric about Indians intended to naturalize the political subordination of Indians to the U.S. government. It simultaneously contains within the stabilizing structures of nineteenth-century domestic ideology what is potentially subversive in the Jemison narrative itself. But gaps remain between conventional notions of domesticity and female character—which the editors attempt to impose upon the Jemison narrative—and the elements of Jemison's story and experiences which reach beyond the boundaries of such conventions. This disjuncture threatens to reveal the merely conventional status of social roles and power relations which had been lent authority by their supposed status as "universal" and "natural." In the case of the Jemison narrative, a genre defined by a conservative movement to re-form a temporarily disrupted family structure and aimed at reinforcing nineteenth-century American social norms and cultural ascendancy actually reforms notions of racial boundaries, gender roles, and the stability of cultural identity.

Like the fictional frontier hero Natty Bumppo, who moves ever farther west, carrying with him the very civilization he seeks to escape, Mary Jemison represents a contradiction. Like Natty, she falls victim to the very forces of civilization she symbolically serves. As "The White Woman" Jemison could be presented to nineteenth-century readers as a heroine carrying the values of white civilization into the border region she inhabits. The 1842 editor, however, informs the reader that when the advance of white settlers led the Senecas to sell their land and move to the Buffalo Creek Reservation in 1825, Mary Jemison found herself "surrounded by whites in every direction" (194). In a radical inversion of the captivity tradition, Mary Jemison is again made captive. In 1831 she finally abandons the middle ground between the white town and the Indian village, where she had built her home and spent most of her life, to find yet another home among her "kindred and friends" on the reservation. Ironically, the final act of this heroine who provided nineteenth-century Americans the means to imagine a positive vision of Indian removal is to enact her own removal.

This final move completes the cultural work performed by the Jemison narrative. Operating within the conventions of "an old and tired genre," the narrative makes the new and troubling seem natural and familiar. But it does more than that. In ways unaccountable in official rational stories, Jemison's decision to remove, like Natty's decision to burn his hut in *The Pioneers*, reveals the meaning of the larger historical events (of Indian removal and westward expansion) against which Jemison's story unfolds. The Jemison narrative is an account of initiation into marginality, not society. Ultimately the narrative gives readers exactly what they want: it makes the Indian problem literally go away by simultaneously enacting and denying the hoped-for outcome and presenting it as being the conscious choice of the victim. In effect, the very language and form of the captivity narrative and initiation rite accomplish the removal of the Indians—but not without a trace. Each attempt by editors to claim Jemison as a "symbol of national authority" simply accentuates the signs of difference that mark the text as a site of contestation. The gaps in the narrative remain to unsettle even its own conclusions.

The Jemison narrative, published just as the official policy of removal was being formulated and before it had actually been tested, offered readers a discursive space in which to project a vision of removal as they wished to see it. Black Hawk's *Life* (1833), the subject of chapter 5, was written at a very different moment in the history of Indian-white relations, in the wake of the famous Cherokee Supreme Court cases that placed the moral complexities of the "Indian problem" under intense public scrutiny. Although it does not deal directly with the Cherokees or with removal policy, this text offered readers preoccupied with these issues an opportunity to conceptualize the meaning of removal as it actually occurred, in the face of Indian resistance, an act marked by violence and coercion.

FIVE

BLACK HAWK'S *LIFE*: THE INDIAN
AS SUBJECT OF HISTORY

I N THE SPRING of 1832, Black Hawk, a Sauk war chief in his sixties, led a group of several hundred men, women, and children across the Mississippi River to reclaim their ancestral village along the Rock River in Illinois. These lands had been ceded in 1804 under highly questionable circumstances. Four members of the tribe had gone to St. Louis to negotiate the release of a Sauk prisoner. By the time they returned home, they had signed a treaty surrendering all tribal lands east of the Mississippi. They could not remember the exact details of the transaction since, as they reported, they had been drunk most of the time. Not surprisingly, a large part of the tribe, including Black Hawk, considered this treaty invalid. When, in 1829, white settlers actually began to take possession of the ceded lands and drive the Indians from their village, Black Hawk led the resistance.

As an act of protest, Black Hawk's group planned to return home to plant corn in what they still considered their own fields and to remain there until driven out by force.[1] When it seemed that this was about to happen, Black Hawk sent three warriors with a white flag to meet the approaching army. But before the Indians could communicate their message, they were fired upon. This was the beginning of the Black Hawk War. Within fifteen weeks it had ended, with the majority of Black Hawk's band killed—many while trying to retreat across the Mississippi—and additional land ceded to the United States as reparation for the war.

During the months that Black Hawk and eleven of his supporters were imprisoned, a steady stream of visitors came to interview, sketch, or simply gaze upon the defeated warriors. In the summer of 1833 the prisoners were sent by President Jackson on "tour" through the eastern United States. Public enthusiasm was enormous. Throughout the East Black Hawk was received as a celebrity—even a hero, according to one reporter.[2] At the conclusion of this tour in August 1833, the prisoners were released at the Rock Island Indian Agency. Here Black Hawk dictated the story of his life to the agency's translator, Antoine LeClaire (who was part Potawatami, part French). Within a few months, the *Life of Ma-ka-tai-me-she-kia-kiak, or Black Hawk* was published under the

editorship of John B. Patterson, a local newspaperman.³ Once again
Black Hawk stirred considerable interest—enough to warrant five editions of the *Life* within the first year of publication.

This chapter examines the conditions and implications of Black Hawk's
popularity, both as he was presented to the American public during his
imprisonment and subsequent tour in the East and as he was represented
in the text of Black Hawk's *Life*. It is significant that this representation
of an Indian as autobiographical subject occurred during the same period
that the nation was embroiled in debates over the policy of Indian removal, which ultimately defined the status of Indians within the United
States as subject peoples without sovereignty or citizenship. The process
by which Black Hawk's subject status (as both autobiographical and political subject) was constructed—through the interplay of presentation
and representation, theatricality and textuality—sheds light upon the
larger question of how Americans attempted to construct a sense of national identity and legitimacy in the face of the challenges posed by the
"Indian problem" during the second quarter of the nineteenth century.

The Cherokees, the Law, and the Nation

During the nine years separating the publication of Mary Jemison's narrative (1824) and Black Hawk's autobiography (1833), the American political climate—and the politics of Indian removal in particular—had un-
dergone significant changes. Although removal had been discussed ever
since the Louisiana Purchase of 1803 made it a plausible solution to the
"Indian problem," it remained a hypothetical solution throughout the
first half century of U.S. history: no official policy of removal or legal
framework for its large-scale implementation yet existed. By the time
Black Hawk rose to national prominence in 1832, removal had ceased to
be hypothetical and had become a very real and often troubling fact of
American Indian policy. The election of Andrew Jackson as president in
1828 significantly changed the political context and meaning of removal.
While Americans had never slackened in their efforts to obtain Indian
lands since the beginning of the nation's history, official justifications of
the process had been premised upon an implicit acknowledgment of Indian independence and sovereignty. The signing of treaties, which usually
accompanied the transfer of land—whether that land was acquired
through purchase or in reparation for a "just war"—was a testimony to
the fact that Americans considered Indian consent crucial to legitimate
their acquisition of Indian lands. Even when it was not an expression of
the Indians' will but simply an empty gesture obtained through trickery

or coercion, considerable effort was expended to secure at least an out-ward show of consent.

At treaty ceremonies such displays of consent literally resembled shows. Constance Rourke, among others, has proposed that Indian treaties should be considered the first American plays.[4] Benjamin Drake's 1838 description of a council with the Sauk and Fox and the Sioux Indians in Washington makes clear that he viewed the event in terms of its theatrical qualities. The Indians stood on a platform while "spectators" sat in sur-rounding pews. Drake criticized the Sioux for speaking with their backs to the audience and praised Keokuk for his fine "performance" (135).

At such performances Indians and whites enacted before an audience of onlookers (and readers of the frequently published transcripts) one of the central dramas of early American history: the transfer of land and power from Indians to whites, the crucial action that underlay the found-ing and continued growth of the American nation. Upon the "stage" of the treaty ceremony, a process that was historically complex and violent became a well-defined, orderly, and dignified event. Indians, whose real power weakened with the signing of each treaty, assumed a certain illu-sion of power within the context of the performance. The ceremony itself was often modeled upon native traditions, suggesting an acknowledg-ment of the Indians' cultural integrity. More significant, the very exis-tence of the ceremony implied reciprocal power relations. If the Indians had no power, if they were entirely dependent upon the U.S. govern-ment and had no sovereignty over their lands, why would it be necessary to expend such effort to commemorate their consent to Euro-American demands?

It was precisely upon this point that Andrew Jackson differed sharply from his predecessors. As early as 1817, while serving as military com-mander in the South, Jackson voiced his opinion that the Indians were subject peoples to be governed rather than treated as sovereign. Accord-ing to Jackson, "Congress ha[d] full power, by law, to regulate all the concerns of the Indians," including the right to occupy and possess their lands whenever national interest, broadly defined, made this necessary. Jackson denounced the treaty process, which implied that Indian "na-tions" possessed a large measure of independence and the rights of sover-eignty and domain, and in his capacity as military commander he repeat-edly advised President Monroe to abolish it.[5]

Given Jackson's well-known views, those who supported the Indians' rights to remain upon their lands responded with alarm when, shortly after his election, in the midst of rising tensions between the Cherokee nation and the state of Georgia, Jackson began to lobby for the passage of a removal bill. On the surface, the Removal Act of 1830 seemed harm-less enough. It simply provided the framework and funding necessary to implement a large-scale voluntary exchange of Indian lands in the East for unincorporated lands west of the Mississippi. The act did not, in itself, do away with the treaty process. In fact, in its final version it included the specific guarantee that "nothing in this act contained shall be construed as authorizing or directing the violation of any existing treaty between the United States and any of the Indian tribes."[6] However historian Francis P. Prucha has pointed out that "those who knew the policy and practice of Jackson and the Georgians understood that force would be inevitable" (1962, 239). Thus, it is not surprising that the Removal Act of 1830 became the occasion for an intense (and widely publicized) reexamination of the nation's relationship to the American Indian.[7] Politicians, especially those opposed to Jackson, encouraged the public to become actively engaged in the debate. Before the bill was officially introduced, petitions had already begun to pour into Congress, and even after its passage expressions of opposition continued.

The legal conflict between the Cherokee nation and the state of Georgia became a central focus of the continuing debate over American Indian policy in general and removal in particular. This conflict had begun to escalate when, on 4 July 1827, the Cherokees held a constitutional convention and asserted their right to self-government. The state of Georgia responded by enacting a series of repressive laws intended to encourage removal by systematically undermining the personal and political rights of those Cherokees who chose to remain in Georgia. In December 1828 the Georgia legislature announced that after 1 June 1830 the laws governing Georgia would be extended to encompass the territory claimed by the Cherokees, and that all "laws, usages, customs" of the Cherokees would be "declared null and void." The surveying of Indian lands was to begin immediately. In addition, the state legislature stipulated that no Indian "shall be deemed a competent witness or party to any suit . . . to which a white man may be a party." When gold was discovered on Cherokee territory in the spring of 1829, the legislature added a resolution claiming all mineral resources the property of Georgia and forbidding any Indian from mining gold. In response to this attack upon their rights, the Cherokees launched a massive campaign of protest, writing letters to philanthropists, editorials to newspapers, and memorials to Congress.[8] In *Cherokee Nation v. Georgia* (1831) and *Worcester v. Georgia* (1832) the Cherokees carried their struggle for justice to the Supreme Court. They challenged the constitutionality of Georgia's new laws on the basis that they violated provisions of federal treaties and the Trade and Intercourse Acts.[9] These cases were followed closely by the public: excerpts from and commentary upon the legal arguments were extensively reprinted in periodicals and pamphlets; the Cherokees published several appeals to the American people and went on speaking tours in the East in an effort to stir up support for their cause; Jackson's political opponents did all in their power to keep the issue before the public, hoping that it would damage Jackson's chances for reelection in 1832.[10]

The Cherokee controversy called into question many of the basic premises underlying American Indian policy. For example, if, as Jackson claimed, the Indians were being removed to the West for their own good so that they could "advance in the arts of civilization" without interference from hostile or corrupt whites, how did one explain the need to remove the Cherokees, who were already quite civilized by Euro-American standards, possessing extensive farms, a written language, and a government modeled upon that of the United States? In addition, the Cherokees' determination to assert and protect their national existence in Georgia challenged the popular illusion that removal could be accomplished without violence or coercion.

The Cherokee cases focused attention on these contradictions. But the impact of the cases reached beyond American Indian policy to questions of national morality and the meaning of American national identity. Central to the Supreme Court's consideration of the first case, for instance, was the fundamental question of what defines a nation. The Court's decision in *Cherokee Nation v. Georgia* turned upon whether the Cherokees could be considered a foreign nation for the purposes of bringing a suit in the U.S. Supreme Court. Such a question was of great import for a people still defining their own character and identity.

Writing for the majority, Chief Justice John Marshall admitted that "the acts of our government plainly recognize the Cherokee nation as a state" if the latter is defined as "a distinct political society, separated from others, capable of managing its own affairs and governing itself" (Washburn, 4:2555). However, Justice Marshall went on to qualify this political definition of a state by introducing geographic and economic considerations:

> The Indian territory is admitted to compose a part of the United States. In all our maps, geographical treatises, histories, and laws, it is so considered. In all our intercourse with foreign nations, in our commercial regulations, in any attempt at intercourse between Indians and foreign nations, they are considered as within the jurisdictional limits of the United States, subject to many of those restraints which are imposed upon our own citizens.

Marshall's solution to the problem of the Cherokee "nation" was to create an entirely new political category:

> The condition of the Indians in relation to the United States is perhaps unlike that of any other two people in existence. . . . Though the Indians are

acknowledged to have an unquestionable, and, heretofore, unquestioned right to the lands they occupy, until that right shall be extinguished by a voluntary cession to our government; yet it may well be doubted whether those tribes which reside within the acknowledged boundaries of the United States can, with strict accuracy, be denominated foreign nations. They may, more correctly, perhaps, be denominated domestic dependent nations. They occupy a territory to which we assert a title independent of their will, which must take effect in point of possession when their right of possession ceases. Meanwhile, they are in a state of pupilage. Their relation to the United States resembles that of a ward to his guardian. (Washburn, 4:2555–56)

While Justice Marshall was sympathetic to the Cherokees and hoped to protect them from dispossession, his solution to the problem of Indian-white relations reinforced stereotypical nineteenth-century notions of primitive peoples as representing the childhood of the human race. These are the same stereotypes that so readily allowed readers to imagine Mary Jemison as White Mother to America's Indian children. Though the Court appeared to have settled the question of nationhood for Indians, issues arising in connection with this conclusion—such as the precise nature of the nation Americans had formed and the type of power relations existing among citizens, states, and the national government—were not so easily answered.

In his dissenting opinion, Justice Smith Thompson returned to the question of what defines a nation and offered a somewhat different answer from Marshall's. According to Thompson, a nation consists of "a body of men, united together, to procure their mutual safety and advantage by means of their union" (Washburn, 4:2583). Thompson's definition echoes social contract theory, according to which a legitimate government exists through the consent of the governed. This is the same theory that formed the basis of a national identity authorized by the mutual consent of "We the People." To establish the foreign status of the Cherokee nation Thompson again applied strictly political criteria: "It is the political relation in which one government or country stands to another, which constitutes it foreign to the other. The Cherokee territory being within the chartered limits of Georgia, does not affect the question" (Washburn, 4:2584). Thompson drove home his point with an analogy between Cherokees and Americans that undermined the majority's attempt to claim the exceptional status—and therefore unequal treatment—of Indians under the Constitution. "It is manifest from these cases that a foreign state, judicially considered, consists in its being under a different jurisdiction or government, without any reference to its territorial position. . . . So far as these states are subject to the laws of the union, they are not foreign to each other. But so far as they are subject to their own respective state laws and government, they are foreign to each other" (Washburn, 4:2585). In other words, if states can maintain a limited sovereignty in relation to the United States, why can't the Cherokee nation do so in relation to the states and the United States? The fact that the Cherokees chose July 4 to announce their new constitution and government, modeled directly upon those of the United States, reveals their strategic effort to claim parallel status and rights. Thompson recognized the parallels and held up the Cherokees as a mirror to Americans.[11] Not only did this gesture collapse the sense of difference necessary to justify unequal treatment of the Cherokees, it also revealed to Americans deep divisions within their own nation regarding the meaning and government of the Union.

When the Cherokees returned to the Supreme Court in 1832 with the case of *Worcester v. Georgia*, the plaintiff was a white missionary imprisoned after defying Georgia's extension of state law governing Cherokee territory. This time the Supreme Court could not deny that there was a legal (white) plaintiff, and it ruled five to one that Georgia's statutes were "unconstitutional, void, and of no effect." The Cherokees were declared "a sovereign nation, authorised to govern themselves, and all persons who have settled within their territory" (Washburn, 4:2606). The Cherokees, it seemed, had triumphed. The Court had denied the power of the states to violate agreements between Indians and the federal government and seemed more willing than in *Cherokee Nation v. Georgia* to acknowledge the tribes' autonomy. But this autonomy was severely limited: Indian nations were still defined as "domestic dependent nations" under the guardianship of the U.S. government. In his concurring opinion Justice John McLean located the Cherokees' rights in immutable principles: "Nations differ from each other in condition, and that of the same nation may change by the revolutions of time, but the principles of justice are the same. They rest upon a base which will remain beyond the endurance of time" (Washburn, 4:2638). The majority opinion was not based upon principles of natural law or immutable justice; Marshall argued instead from "the actual state of things" as revealed through history (Washburn, 4:2609). Seventeen pages in a twenty-six-page opinion are devoted to a survey of history. The history Marshall recounts is a tale of conquest: the Indians' natural rights, possessed "from time immemorial" yielded to the conquerors' "irresistible power," which conferred rights "conceded by the world." As in the case of *Johnson v. McIntosh* (1823), the immutable principles of natural law yield to the contingent actions of particular governments recorded in the pages of history.[12] And, as the Cherokees were to be reminded repeatedly during the next decade, history ultimately belongs to the conqueror.

Whatever sense of victory the Cherokees derived from *Worcester v.*

Georgia was quickly dampened by Georgia's refusal to obey and Jackson's failure to enforce the Supreme Court's ruling. This phase in the Cherokee controversy called into question some of the most basic (and sacred) premises underlying the national character of the United States. The president's refusal to uphold the Court's decision was viewed by many as undermining the division of power (among the executive, legislative, and judicial branches) so fundamental to the basic structure of the government.[13] Jackson's unwillingness to honor treaties established by previous presidents was presented by his critics as a betrayal of the principles of the founding fathers. Those who argued for the Cherokees on the basis of natural rights implicitly questioned the nation's adherence to the very ideals that had legitimated the Revolution and authorized the present government. The Cherokees' attorney, William Wirt, framed the issue in terms that were widely quoted, reprinted, and discussed. According to Wirt, the principles underlying the conflict in Georgia were extremely far-reaching. Wirt argued that if Georgia were allowed to violate treaties made and guaranteed by the federal government, "then we have no nation. Our constitution, laws, and treaties are empty pageants, that but mock us with a show of national existence. And it were well for us if we could persuade the world of this fact; far better, far better would it be for us to be no nation than to be a nation without faith and honor."[14]

The nullification crisis of 1832 brought these divisions into even clearer focus and threatened to make prophetic Wirt's "we have no nation." By imposing state law upon the Cherokees and defying the Court's decision, Georgia in effect nullified federal law. Georgia's actions were similar in principle to South Carolina's 1832 nullification of the federally imposed tariff of 1828. Both South Carolina and Georgia claimed that the federal government had overstepped its bounds and threatened to secede from the Union, if necessary, to protect what they defined as their states' rights. According to Wirt, a nation unable or unwilling to enforce its own federal laws and treaties could no longer consider itself a nation in political or moral terms. According to the secessionists, if the federal government enforced laws and treaties the states opposed, even the "mere show of national existence" as a union would come to an end.

It is in this context that Black Hawk's War and his subsequent popularity must be viewed. The conflict began in May 1832, just two months after Chief Justice Marshall delivered the *Worcester v. Georgia* decision, and ended in August 1832, three months before the 1832 election. By the time Black Hawk embarked upon his tour of the East, in June 1833, many of the questions that had occupied Americans during the preceding year seemed to have been settled. Andrew Jackson had been reelected. The missionaries Samuel Worcester and Elizur Butler, who had gone to prison in order to challenge Georgia's repressive laws governing the

Cherokees, had withdrawn their suit for fear that further resistance might lead Georgia and other southern states to join South Carolina in nullification and secession. Two days after the missionaries left prison, Jackson presented Congress with the Force Bill, which was quickly passed into law; a few days later, on January 21, South Carolina suspended its nullification proclamation. The crisis seemed to have been averted. As William McLoughlin has stated, "The nation, Whigs and Democrats alike, united in praise of the strong executive who had saved the Union from secession and civil war" (446).[15]

Despite this resolution, many of the questions raised by the removal debate had not been settled. While Jackson may have cleared the way for the large-scale removal of Indians residing east of the Mississippi, it still was not clear, from the vantage point of the early 1830s, how to bring about Indian removal without seeming to abandon the moral and legal principles which historically had governed U.S. relations with the Indians and which formed the basis of national character and legitimacy as traditionally articulated. If, as the Marshall Court's opinions suggested, the law and its legitimacy were to be based upon history, then the history of Indian-white relations required further revision. Americans needed to find ways to envision the Indians, and American policies toward them, in terms consistent with the idea of the United States as a moral nation.

The Subject of History

When President Jackson determined to send Black Hawk and his party on a tour of eastern cities before allowing them to return home, his ostensible purpose was to exhibit to the Indians the power and prosperity of the American nation in order to convince them that any future resistance would be pointless.[16] One wonders whether Jackson actually expected that Black Hawk—already in his late sixties and demoralized after the near destruction of his band of followers in the recent war—needed this display of power to discourage him, which seems highly unlikely. Another, perhaps more important, effect of the tour was to exhibit the Indians to the American people. At every stop large crowds gathered to see the famous warrior. In Albany so many people lined the shore to await Black Hawk's arrival that it was an hour before the steamboat could land, and even then he had to be smuggled ashore incognito. In Baltimore the size of the crowd outside Black Hawk's hotel made it necessary for his party to move to Fort McHenry.[17]

This was not the first time that Indians had visited the East. Chiefs often came to Washington to speak with the president or to sign treaties. A delegation of Cherokees had recently toured the East in an attempt to enlist public support in their fight against removal. By displaying to the American people the progress achieved by the Cherokee nation, the delegation hoped to convince the U.S. government that the Cherokees should be allowed to remain where they were while they continued on the path toward "civilization."[18] These other Indians, however, did not stir the same kind of response that Black Hawk did.

But these Indians had not just waged a war against the United States at a moment when Indian wars were not common occurrences. As the following review of Black Hawk's autobiography indicates, by the 1830s Indian wars—and warriors—were associated with the distant (and therefore romantic) past:

> The war (though it scarcely deserves the name) which, not long since, attracted so much interest, and excited such alarm on our western frontier . . . will, probably, be the last regular conflict with the unfortunate aborigines of this continent. The name of Indian was, at one period, identified with war, slaughter, devastation and blood; and the horrors of Indian warfare, and the dread of Indian irruptions, in former times, blanched many a cheek, and made the heart of the stoutest warrior to quail. But these are mementos of years that are past; the lingering records of once powerful, numerous and formidable tribes, the masters of the field, the mountains and the floods which we now possess. . . . The struggle to which we have alluded, was the expiring throe of a fast-fading, yet, even in decay, a fearless and independent people.[19]

This passage helps to clarify what, exactly, people "saw" in the figure of Black Hawk. At the most obvious level, Black Hawk represented the former threat that had "excited such alarm on our western frontier" and was now contained. But in the preceding quotation Black Hawk himself is not identified as a real threat. Black Hawk's War, the reviewer claims, "scarcely deserves the name." Instead, Black Hawk serves as a reminder of "former times" when the Indian did pose a real threat and stir real terror. Black Hawk is more a source of pity than terror, more a subject for history than news. His vanquished resistance to the policies of the U.S. government merely becomes the evidence that defines the Indians' place in the past. In his role as the last savage warrior, Black Hawk represents the "Vanishing American" of the popular imagination, noble though—or, rather, because—conquered. He also serves metonymically as a reminder of an important chapter in Americans' own national history—the history of "the field[s], the mountains and the floods which we now possess."[20] It would appear, then, that when Americans viewed Black Hawk, they also saw a vision of themselves.

When considered in the context of the tour, it becomes clear how Black Hawk, as spectacle, served as a mirror in which Americans could see a positive reflection of themselves and the meaning of their history. The exhibition of a conquered enemy might be expected to reflect back upon the conqueror a vision of his own strength, given that the former threat has become a measure of the power that has triumphed over it. The tradition of parading captives in chains through the streets can be understood in this light. But Black Hawk was not exhibited in chains, nor was he executed so that his head might be mounted upon a post, as was the head of the Wampanoag chief Philip after King Philip's War of 1675–76. Instead, Black Hawk was entertained and celebrated, invited to dine with "leading citizens" and to preside as guest of honor at society balls. The different treatment received by Philip and Black Hawk clarifies the differences in their historical and symbolic roles.

When Philip united several northeastern tribes to mount a large-scale war against the whites, his actions were seen by the colonists as a very real physical threat to their still tenuous survival in America. By mutilating Philip's body—parading his head through the colony and mounting it upon a pole in Plymouth, where it remained for the next twenty years, serving (in the words of Increase Mather) "as a monument of revenging Justice"—the colonists were able to assert and repeatedly reinforce their sense of triumph.[21] By the 1830s, however, Indians were generally seen as the last remnants of a vanishing race, hardly a serious physical threat. History itself completed the work of containment. Black Hawk's mere identification as representative of a "once powerful" but now "fast-fading" people inscribes him in an existing historical narrative to which every American already knows the conclusion. The more serious threat posed by Indians at this point in American history was moral rather than physical, a threat to the nation's self-image rather than its survival.

The presentation of Black Hawk on tour addressed this moral threat. News coverage of Black Hawk's tour emphasized his role as defiant warrior in the recent war. This is not surprising, given that the war was the basis of his fame, but the tone of the reports reveals that the meaning of Black Hawk's "role" as warrior was being redefined by the audiences that viewed him after the war had ended. Accounts of Black Hawk's travels and public appearances were regularly featured by many newspapers with columns bearing titles such as *BLACKHAWKIANA*. These entertaining reports tended to exaggerate the primitive attributes of the Indian. The following account is typical:

> Being invited to a ball at Philadelphia, Black Hawk was pressed to join in the dance, whereupon he sent for his dancing dress, consisting of a Buffaloes hide with the horns and tails on. In this costume, he commenced such an outrageous system of capering accompanied with such hideous yells as he uses in his own native forests, that the admirers of nature and simplicity

became greatly alarmed. . . . Among the admiring women was one who presented him with a tomahawk. Black Hawk patted her on the head and observed to his son, "what a beautiful head for scalping." How must the female bosom shudder at such an expression from him (though at the time a prisoner) who have scalped of the most promising youths, among whom where [*sic*] not only many interesting young ladies, but even the lovely infant upon its mothers breast has shared the same merciless fate.[22]

The pleasure of such scenes derives from their enactment of the taming of Black Hawk: the once fierce scalper is now reduced to an exotic guest at a ball.

But such representations of Black Hawk as warrior served other purposes beyond titillation or containment. By virtue of his role as a warrior, Black Hawk helped justify American Indian policy; the Indian himself made necessary the violent military response by means of which order was maintained and additional Indian lands acquired. Black Hawk, the doomed chief—noble in his wish to die fighting, unchangeable in his primitive violence, pathetic in his hopeless resistance to his inevitable fate—was precisely the kind of Indian Americans needed to see as representative in order to justify American Indian policy. In *Johnson v. McIntosh* (1823), for example, Chief Justice Marshall appealed to such a vision of Indians as inveterate warriors in order to justify American claims to the land:

> [T]he tribes of Indians inhabiting this country were fierce savages, whose occupation was war, and whose subsistence was drawn chiefly from the forest. To leave them in possession of their country, was to leave the country a wilderness; to govern them as a distinct people, was impossible, because they were as brave and as high spirited as they were fierce, and were ready to repel by arms every attempt on their independence. (Washburn, 4:2546)

According to Marshall, the policies first adopted by the Europeans and then inherited by the Americans were "the inevitable consequence of this state of things."[23] In accounts of Black Hawk on tour, such as the one just quoted, the Indian's role as warrior was both reinforced and trivialized. Even as the idea of the Indian as warrior continued to serve American political purposes, responses to Black Hawk show that "the Indian warrior" had, in the minds of most Americans, ceased to be a real threat and had become simply a role in a harmless performance. The tragedy of the Indians' defeat was obliterated, with Black Hawk recast as a comical figure. A good time, the reports suggest, was had by all.

Black Hawk's tour addressed in yet another way the national guilt regarding American Indian policy. In his frequent and widely circulated speeches, Black Hawk admitted that he was wrong to resist the whites, expressed regret for his past actions, and professed his determination never to fight again. According to one report, Black Hawk even "wished that all the tribes were collected on the fine lands west of the Mississippi."[24] Whether or not these were actually Black Hawk's words is impossible to know. Black Hawk does complain in the autobiography about the skills of the translator employed during the tour; this could simply be one of the "misrepresentations" Black Hawk hoped to correct by writing his autobiography. On the other hand, they could represent Black Hawk's efforts to tell the whites what he thought they wanted to hear, to assure them that he was no longer a threat, so that they would allow him to return home. Whether fact or fiction, such statements of capitulation were reported and read (one assumes) as if they were true. At a time when the Cherokee conflict in Georgia brought to public attention troubling questions regarding national honor and the justice of American Indian policy, such affirmations must have been welcome. Black Hawk, the defeated warrior presented to Americans on his tour, offered a reassuringly simple version of Indian-white relations. In contrast to the legal ambiguities and moral contradictions associated with the Cherokee controversy, Indian wars could—and must—be settled definitively and clearly through force. Black Hawk's statements during the tour reaffirmed the justice and success of American policies.

One thing that Americans saw when they looked upon Black Hawk was a vision of themselves framed by his perspective. As a spectator carried from city to city in order that he might gaze upon and acknowledge the power of the whites, Black Hawk offered Americans an opportunity to measure their own power through his eyes. As a representative of an era that had passed, Black Hawk helped Americans to situate themselves within a historical framework that defined the present as a triumph over the past.[25] In his comic performances, no less than in his public admissions of error, Black Hawk provided a reassuring commentary upon that history.

Textual Justice

When, at the end of the tour, Black Hawk was finally released at the Rock Island Indian Agency, he reportedly approached the agency interpreter and "express[ed] a great desire to have a History of his Life written and published, in order, (as he said) 'that the people of the United States, (among whom he had been travelling, and by whom he had been treated with great respect, friendship and hospitality,) might know the *causes* that had impelled him to act as he has done, and the *principles* by which he was governed.'"[26] According to this account of its production, the autobiography was a direct response to the tour, an expression of Black Hawk's desire to re-present from his own perspective, the figure who had already been presented to the American people during the tour.

The balance of this chapter focuses on the nature of the intimate connection between Black Hawk's story and Euro-Americans' vision of their own history and character. I am concerned less with the events recounted by Black Hawk—which help to define, in factual terms, a particular moment in American history—than with the way in which those events and Black Hawk himself are represented textually as history. The representation of Black Hawk as speaking subject, telling his story to a white man, contributes significantly to the way in which the *Life* serves as a textual site upon which (white) American readers could reenvision the meaning of their history and moral character as defined in relationship to "the Indian."

What Americans saw when they opened the pages of Black Hawk's autobiography was in many ways similar to what they would have seen during the tour. In the book's dedication, addressed to General Henry Atkinson, who was in charge of the campaign, Black Hawk presents himself in familiar terms as the conquered warrior:

> Sir,—The changes of fortune, and vicissitudes of war, made you my conqueror. When my last resources were exhausted, my warriors worn down with long and toilsome marches, we yielded, and I became your prisoner.
>
> The story of my life is told in the following pages; it is intimately connected, and in some measure, identified with a part of your own: I have, therefore, dedicated it to you.
>
> The changes of many years have brought old age upon me,—and I cannot expect to survive many moons. Before I set out on my journey to the land of my fathers, I have determined to give my motives and reasons for my former hostilities to the whites, and to vindicate my character from misrepresentation. (37)

Here, as in the tour, Black Hawk appears as the "Vanishing American" of the popular imagination: the fallen chief, the representative of a dying race, speaking from the edge of the grave, accepting his conquered status. Here, too, the conquered Indian serves as a mirror for the conquering white man. But the kind of mirroring offered in the text is quite different from that provided by the tour. The closing paragraph of the dedication illuminates the complexity of the "intimate connection" proposed between Indian and white:

> I am now an obscure member of a nation, that formerly honored and respected my opinions. The path to glory is rough and many gloomy hours obscure it. May the Great Spirit shed light on yours—and that you may

never experience the humility that the power of the American government
has reduced me to, is the wish of him, who, in his native forests, was once as
proud and as bold as yourself. (37)

This is not the relation between Other and Self, defined oppositionally,
but a relation among equals made unequal only by the "vicissitudes of
war." Black Hawk speaks with defiance even as he acquiesces in defeat
and makes claims for equality even as he confirms his status as a humbled, vanquished foe. Whether these are Black Hawk's sentiments is un-
determinable since his words were mediated by interpreter and editor
before they found their way into print. For the purposes of this study it is
sufficient that they are the words of the "Black Hawk" nineteenth-century readers encountered in the pages of the autobiography.

The editorial apparatus emphasizes Black Hawk's agency and presence
as speaking subject. The translator specifically states that Black Hawk
sought him out and expressed his own desire to publish his story. At the
end of his "Advertisement" for the *Life*, the editor insists that the contents of the book are entirely Black Hawk's creation (and responsibility):
"The Editor has written this work according to the dictation of Black
Hawk. . . . He does not, therefore, consider himself responsible for any
of the facts, or views, contained in it—and leaves the old Chief and his
story with the public, whilst he neither asks, nor expects, any fame for his
services as an amanuensis" (39). The dedication, introducing the book as
Black Hawk's attempt "to vindicate [his] character from misrepresentation," lends it a sense of authenticity by distinguishing it from acts of
false representation (which presumably occurred or were called to Black
Hawk's attention during the tour). The cumulative effect of the introductory material is to suggest that Black Hawk is actually "presented"
within the pages of the text rather than represented from a white
perspective.

As if further to underscore the authenticity of Black Hawk's "voice" in
the text, the dedication first appears in the Sauk language (transliterated),
followed by an English translation. The transliteration, an attempt to represent the actual words Black Hawk spoke before the work of translation
and transcription transformed them into the English text of the *Life*,
would seem to bring the reader closer to Black Hawk as speaking subject.
The exotic language, however, conveys a sense of mystery and inacces-
sibility to that which is being represented. It also calls attention to the act
of translation, which belies any pretensions to the Indian's simple or immediate self-presentation in the text. It serves as a reminder that only
through the mediation of whites (the translator and editor) does the
reader gain access to Black Hawk's "own" words.

From the nineteenth century to the present, there has been much discussion regarding the role of the translator and editor in the production of Black Hawk's *Life*. While early critics argued about whether the autobiography might be a hoax, produced entirely by the "editor" for profit, more recent debate has focused upon questions of textual authority and cultural authenticity.[27] As in the case of the Jemison narrative, it is ultimately impossible to separate the contributions of Euro-American and Indian coauthors or to establish the authenticity of Black Hawk's voice. I intend to examine Black Hawk's autobiography as its nineteenth-century readers encountered it in order to understand how notions of "the real" (or history), the figure of "the Indian," and authenticity itself—as constructed and deployed within the text—helped nineteenth-century Americans to manage the "Indian problem" and the challenges it posed to American national identity.

The editor's "Advertisement," which directly follows Black Hawk's dedication, suggests some of the implications of representing Black Hawk and his life as text:

> It is presumed no apology will be required for presenting to the public, the life of a Hero who has lately taken such high rank among the distinguished individuals of America. In the following pages he will be seen in the characters of a Warrior, a Patriot and a State-prisoner—in every situation he is still the Chief of his Band, asserting their rights with dignity, firmness and courage. Several accounts of the late war having been published, in which he thinks justice is not done to himself or nation, he determined to make known to the world, the injuries his people have received from the whites—the causes which brought on the war on the part of his nation, and a general history of it throughout the campaign. In his opinion, this is the only method now left him, to rescue his little Band—the remnant of those who fought bravely with him—from the effect of the statements that have already gone forth. (38)

The description of Black Hawk as warrior and prisoner simply repeats the characterization already established in news accounts of the tour and in Black Hawk's dedication of the book. However, the insistence that Black Hawk is "in every situation," whether as warrior or as prisoner, "still the Chief of his Band" suggests the text's capacity to exploit this characterization in new ways. Viewing Black Hawk on tour as the defeated warrior would have reinforced the fact that the conflict had ended, and that Black Hawk had passed from warrior to prisoner to demoted chief. Yet, as a figure constructed within the text, Black Hawk simultaneously remains warrior, prisoner, and chief, still fighting a battle for justice that will never be concluded, a conflict in which the Indian no longer fights for a place in the land of his fathers but rather for his place in the history of (white) America. With the writing of Black Hawk's autobiography, then, the drama of conflict and containment moves from the realm of action to the realm of language, from the ephemerality of presentation to the permanence of textual representation.

At first glance the text seems to enhance rather than contain the moral threat posed by the Indian. In the text Black Hawk does accept his status as conquered enemy, but he does not admit that he was wrong, as he did during the tour; instead, he justifies himself and denounces the actions and policies of the whites. Black Hawk's account of the war's commencement, for example, is highly critical:

> [I had] sent a *flag of peace* to the American war chief—expecting as a matter of right, reason and justice, that our *flag would be respected*, (I have always seen it so in war among the whites) and a council convened, that we might explain our grievances, having been driven from our village the year before, without being permitted to gather the corn and provisions which our women had labored hard to cultivate, and ask for permission to return—thereby giving up all idea of going to war against the whites. Yet, instead of this *honorable course* which *I* have always practised in war, I was *forced* into WAR, with about *five hundred* warriors, to contend against *three* or *four thousand*! (126–27)

Far from the humbled, conquered chief of the tour, Black Hawk here appears as a fierce warrior in a war of words, defiantly hurling accusations at the whites, attempting to shape history by presenting his own account of events.

By the 1830s, when actual wars between the Indians and whites were no longer frequent, it was primarily within the arena of language that the Indians' fate was being determined: written treaties and laws defined Indians' rights; debates within the pages of periodicals and the halls of Congress helped shape public opinion and official policy toward Indians; and the historical writings that proliferated during this period of intense nationalism inscribed the meaning and role of Indians in American history. By allowing Black Hawk's account of his experience to reach the American public, the text of the *Life* ushered Black Hawk into the arena of language in which such power was exercised. But what happened when Black Hawk entered this arena is by no means a simple matter. The conditions under which Black Hawk's "own" story was transformed into text, attitudes toward the Indians and their relationship to language, Black Hawk's own attitude toward written language as expressed in the text, the particular historical controversies and concerns that preoccupied readers as they encountered the text, and the dynamics of the reading process itself—all these issues influenced the way in which Black Hawk's account of events shaped Americans' vision of the history the autobiography records.

Responses to the *Life*, as exemplified by the comments of the editor and reviewers, betray no attempt to deny Black Hawk's accusations or justify Americans' actions in the face of these grievances. In fact, in the "Advertisement," the editor acknowledges and even reinforces Black Hawk's criticism of white policies: "[T]he Indians might well question the right of Government to dispossess them, when such violation [as occurred during the treaty of 1804] was made the basis of its right" (39). This is quite different from the emphasis upon Black Hawk's remorse and admission of error in accounts of the tour.[28] When one considers how the textual representation of Black Hawk functions as a whole, however, it becomes clear that Black Hawk's accusations against the whites play an important role in the mechanism by which the text eventually works to contain the moral threat posed by the "Indian problem."

Within the context of the tour—representing an official, public display of national power—Black Hawk's accusations might indeed seem to threaten the national self-image, for such accusations would undermine American power (over Indians) at the very moment this power was being asserted and displayed. Within the private space of the text, however, such accusations function differently. Because Black Hawk's battle for justice is transformed in the text from an accomplished fact to an ongoing struggle that is represented in the text over and over again, final or "official" conclusions regarding the meaning and ultimate justice of Indian-white relations are deferred. By participating in the war of words being waged within the text, each reader is, in fact, able to contribute personally to its outcome. Black Hawk's accusations undoubtedly would have raised unsettling issues in the minds of white readers. The editor's own comments on the immorality of white actions toward the Indians suggest that Black Hawk's attacks hit their mark. But by reading and accepting Black Hawk's account of Indian-white relations, readers might see themselves as actually assisting Black Hawk in "rescu[ing] his little Band" and "asserting their rights" by "the only method now left him." This textual act of justice accomplished within the private space of reading might appear to redress, or at least displace, the injustices that have already occurred within the public space of official policy, thus giving each reader a personal sense of absolution from complicity in those public actions, which, in spite of each individual act of textual justice, remain the same.[29]

An 1835 review of Black Hawk's *Life* that appeared in the *North American Review* illustrates more specifically how the text could be perceived as a means of doing justice to the Indians. In the review, past injustices are viewed as the result of the Indians' exclusion from the language of Euro-Americans: "They have no historians to record their grievances"; "The Indians have no advocates, know not how to plead their own cause, and would not be regarded if they did"; "We are persuaded that, could Black Hawk and his counsellors have been permitted to plead their cause on the floor of Congress, attended with a proper interpreter, all the misery, expense, and bloodshed which ensued, might have been prevented." In the pages of the autobiography Black Hawk *is* permitted to "plead [his] cause" with the help of a "proper interpreter"; he is able to "record [his] grievances"; and, the reviewer suggests, he is able to obtain justice: "Let the result show and the reader judge, which was the right side."[30] Black Hawk's *Life*, as described by the reviewer, gives the Indian access to written language and the structures of power within Euro-American society based upon the written word. It thus becomes an act of textual justice offsetting historical injustices born of the Indians' exclusion from (the white man's) language.

According to Arnold Krupat, much of the writing about Indians produced in the East after 1830 was motivated, by a desire for "historical justice." However, Krupat maintains that those works about Indians written by a white man could not succeed in the textual redress of injustice since they "never went so far as to grant the Indian the right to speak for himself. Whatever the wrongs and injuries [the white author] protested, he was not yet able to protest in the actual form of his work what Gilles Deleuze has called the indignity of speaking for others" (1985, 50–52). Krupat believes that by allowing the Indian to speak in his own voice Black Hawk's *Life* succeeds in achieving a kind of textual justice ("in the actual form of his work"):

> Admitting an Indian to the ranks of the self-represented . . . questioned progressive expansionism. For the production of an Indian's own statement of his inevitable disappearance required that the Indian be represented as speaking in his own voice. . . . And it is in its presentation of an Indian voice not as vanished and silent but as still living and able to be heard that the oppositional potential of Indian autobiography resides. (34–35)

Neil Schmitz, essentially in agreement with Krupat's analysis, attempts to carry the investigation a step further by recovering within Patterson's text "the substance of Black Hawk's resisting text, its contrary logic, its contestation" (2). Schmitz argues that "Black Hawk's text is everywhere barbed, reproachful, scathing in its irony" (3). He then identifies every "barbed" criticism of white policy as an authentic expression of Black Hawk's voice speaking in resistance to Patterson's text. Schmitz seems to forget that Patterson, too, expressed harsh criticism of U.S. policy in his introductory remarks. In fact, he reads the text exactly as Patterson encouraged nineteenth-century (Euro-)Americans to read it: "It is just as Patterson advertises it," Schmitz proclaims, "a text that operates, 'the only method now left it to rescue his little Band'" (5). Like the 1835 review of the autobiography, these twentieth-century interpretations do indeed suggest that the representation of Black Hawk as an independent subject telling his own story allows readers to feel that they are engaging in an act of justice—an act undoubtedly more personal and immediate than could be experienced through reading a white author's defense of the Indians. I am less willing than Krupat and Schmitz to align the reader's feeling and the actual achievement of justice, or to accept the equation between "voice" and power upon which their interpretations rest. The production of such "feelings" within the reader is precisely the text's most powerful strategy of (false) justification.

David Murray has noted that the Indian "voice" is frequently invoked in works that claim to represent Indians in order to assert the authenticity of the representation. He goes on to argue that authenticity itself is not a neutral term but rather a textual category produced by and implicated in the problematic of text and "voice" (1988, 31). Murray explores a variety of ways in which this category is deployed within texts. The specific conclusions he draws are less important, for the purposes of my argument, than the premise they rest upon, namely, that once the "voice" enters a text it becomes something new, no longer fully belonging to or controlled by the original speaker. This is not to say that it inevitably belongs to or is controlled by the editor who constructs the text but simply to emphasize the fact that the textualized "voice" speaks its meaning through the text, mediated by the structures of the text and the practices of the reading act. Any attempt to understand Black Hawk's "voice" must take into account the processes of textualization and reading that form the basis of the "passage" back and forth between the text and "the world beyond the text" (Krupat 1985, 33).

Black Hawk's explicit comments on language within the *Life* suggest a fairly sophisticated awareness on his part of the ambiguities of the written word and the complexities of his relationship to it. Although the text is introduced by both Black Hawk and the editor as the means by which Black Hawk will save himself from misrepresentation and injustice, written language is repeatedly characterized within the text as leading to misunderstanding and betrayal. All of Black Hawk's troubles began in 1804 when a few Indians visiting St. Louis unknowingly signed away a large portion of the tribal lands, including Saukenuk, Black Hawk's home. His first personal experience with writing occurred when he signed the treaty of 1816.[31] Once again writing is associated with misunderstanding and the loss of land: "Here, for the first time," he later wrote in the *Life*, "I touched the goose quill to the treaty—not knowing, however, that, by that act, I consented to give away my village. Had that been explained to me, I would have opposed it, and never would have signed their treaty, as my recent conduct will clearly prove" (87). But Black Hawk very quickly learned how written treaties operate and attempted to employ the strategies of textual interpretation they rely upon for himself and his people. When the U.S. government insisted that the Sauk and Fox Indians remove west of the Mississippi, based upon the provisions of the 1804 treaty, Black Hawk turned the language of the treaty to his own purposes:

> I was told that, according to the treaty, we had no *right* to remain upon the lands *sold*, and that the government would *force* us to leave them. There was but a small portion, however, that *had been sold*; the balance remaining in the hands of the government, we claimed the right (if we had no other) to "live and hunt upon, as long as it remained the property of the government," by a stipulation in the same treaty that required us to evacuate it *after* it had been sold. (105)

While this attempt to wield the power of textual interpretation ultimately failed to achieve its goal, the incident is important in revealing Black Hawk's savvy understanding of the power and dangers of the written word.

The first time Black Hawk attempts to employ writing for his own purposes he is also unsuccessful. Wishing to communicate with the settlers who have moved into his village in order to explain his desire to return and to ask them to leave, Black Hawk approaches the interpreter at the Rock Island agency and asks him to write down his message: "The interpreter wrote me a paper, and I went back to the village, and showed it to the intruders, but could not understand their reply" (99–100). This last incident in many ways echoes the conditions under which the text of the autobiography was created: Black Hawk, wishing to plead his cause before the whites, must employ the written word to convey his meaning. The success or failure of this strategy, as described within the text, remains ambiguous: Black Hawk cannot determine whether the interpreter misrepresented his message or if the settlers misunderstood or simply ignored his plea. Similarly, even if the translator and editor of Black Hawk's autobiography accurately conveyed his meaning, it is impossible to control white readers' understanding or response.

The example of the Cherokees' struggle against removal serves to illustrate what Black Hawk's *Life* suggests: the relationship among language, power, and justice is not as simple as many readers—from nineteenth-century reviewers to twentieth-century critics—might wish to believe. While Black Hawk's autobiography offered one Indian the opportunity to "plead his cause" and obtain justice within the pages of a text, the Cherokees were engaged in what historian Brian Dippie has termed "their paper war against removal" (71). Publishing appeals to the American people and presenting memorials to Congress, the Cherokees employed the written word as a weapon in their battle for justice. Pleading their case before the Supreme Court, the Cherokees staked their future on a belief in the power and permanence of the written laws and treaties which were to define their rights. However, as their struggle to avoid removal progressed, the Cherokees discovered that writing was far from a stable repository of meaning since the meaning of writing ultimately depends upon an act of interpretation.

The Supreme Court's decisions in the Cherokee cases fundamentally rested upon the Court's exercise of textual interpretation. From a twentieth-century perspective this statement seems self-evident, but during the 1830s the role, meaning, and basis of interpretation in American law were still being defined.[32] The perceived significance of the Cherokee cases and the deep political and moral implications of the subject placed particular pressure on questions of interpretation. Marshall's rejection of the Cherokees' status as a foreign nation in *Cherokee Nation v. Georgia* rested upon his interpretation of the words of Section 8, Article 3 of the U.S. Constitution,

> which empowers congress to "regulate commerce with foreign nations, and among the several states, and with the Indian tribes."
>
> In this clause they are as clearly contradistinguished by a name appropriate to themselves, from foreign nations, as from the several states composing the union. They are designated by a distinct appellation; and as this appellation can be applied to neither of the others, neither can the appellation distinguishing either of the others be in fair construction applied to them. The objects, to which the power of regulating commerce might be directed, are divided into three distinct classes—foreign nations, the several states, and Indian tribes. (Washburn, 4:2557)

Judge Smith Thompson rejected Marshall's conclusions as "mere verbal criticism" and went on to show that the same passage could just as easily be construed to support a position diametrically opposite to Marshall's:

> The argument [of the majority] is, that if the Indian tribes are foreign nations, they would have been included without being specially named, and being so named imports something different from the previous term "foreign nations." . . . But the clause affords, irresistibly, the conclusion, that the Indian tribes are not there understood as included within the description, of the "several states"; or there could have been no fitness in immediately thereafter particularizing "the Indian tribes." (Washburn, 4:2589)

The game of "verbal criticism," Thompson implicitly argues, can be played from both sides.

In a nation founded upon an act of writing, whose structuring principles were delineated in a written constitution, to question the stability of interpretation was to question the stability of the nation itself.[33] In his concurring opinion, Justice Henry Baldwin counters Thompson's vision of radical instability with one of absolute truths and transparent meaning. Baldwin avoids the question of interpretation altogether by declaring the Constitution a "book of prophecy" beyond interpretation: "In taking out, putting in, or varying the plain meaning of a word or expression, to meet the results of my poor judgment, as to the meaning and intention of the great charter, which alone imparts to me my power to act as a judge of its supreme injunctions, I should feel myself acting upon it by judicial amendments, and not as one of its executors" (Washburn, 4:2573–74). Baldwin then turns his attention to Article 1 of the Constitution, which forms the basis of his single dissent from the majority opinion. Baldwin interprets or, rather, announces the Constitution to mean that Indian tribes have no sovereignty whatsoever, not even the ambiguous sovereignty of a domestic dependent nation. "The meaning of this section," Baldwin proclaims, is stated "too plainly to require illustration or argument" (4:2575). To rule out interpretation, Baldwin's statement makes clear, is simply to declare that one's own interpretation rules and thus to undermine the democratic principles that inform and authorize the judicial system.

The question of interpretation reappeared as a central issue in the case of *Worcester v. Georgia* (1832), which called into question the language of the treaties by which the Cherokees claimed their basic rights in relation to the United States. Returning to the Treaty of Hopewell, the first between the Cherokees and the United States, Marshall takes on those attempting to turn the language of the treaty against the Cherokees:

> The fourth article draws the boundary between the Indians and the citizens of the United States. But, in describing this boundary, the term "allotted" and the term "hunting ground" are used.
>
> Is it reasonable to suppose, that the Indians, who could not write, and most probably could not read, who certainly were not critical judges of our language, should distinguish the word "allotted" from the words "marked out." The actual subject of contract was the dividing line between the two nations, and their attention may very well supposed to have been confined to that subject. When, in fact, they were ceding lands to the United States, and describing the extent of their cession, it may very well be supposed that they might not understand that, instead of granting, they were receiving lands. If the term would admit of no other signification, which is not conceded, its being misunderstood is so apparent, results so necessarily from the whole transaction; that it must, we think, be taken in the sense in which it was most obviously used. (Washburn, 4:2616)

Against the instability of interpretation that Thompson's accusation of "verbal criticism" pointed to, Marshall argues that it is possible to return to the "community" that formed the original act of communication, to recover the primary and "obvious" meaning of the written word. Marshall thus denies one of the essential characteristics and powers of the written word, namely, its capacity to move beyond the speech community to express meaning in new contexts. This conclusion is particularly ironic given the fact that during the nineteenth century this capacity of the written word was commonly considered to be a necessary and defining condition of civilization. The Indians' lack of a written language was often cited as proof of their primitive status and their inability to change.[34]

Even when the Cherokees finally succeeded in stirring the conscience of the nation and moving the Court to a favorable interpretation of the law, they discovered that justice still remained elusive; the gap between judgment and action remained wide. When President Jackson refused to enforce the Supreme Court's decision in *Worcester v. Georgia*, he defended his inaction by insisting upon his "sacred duty" to interpret the Constitution according to his own conscience, regardless of how the Supreme Court or Congress might interpret it. The question of interpretation thus threatened to undermine the very structure of the American government and its division of power. While Jackson proclaimed his right to interpret the Constitution, southern states insisted upon their right to do the same, and the Supreme Court was powerless to enforce their own. The words spoken by Henry Storrs, the representative from New York State, during the House debate on removal in May 1830 seem relevant here: "[T]his was to be a government of law, and not prerogative, and especially not of executive prerogative. . . . The states may destroy the Union themselves by open force, but the concentration of the power in the hands of the Executive leads to despotism, which is worse" (Washburn, 2:1032, 1036). Storrs ends his speech with an appeal to history as the final arbiter of justice: "Our country will be brought by the historian—*custodia fidelis rerum*—to that standard of universal morality which will guide the judgment and fix the sentence of posterity. It will be pronounced by the impartial judgment of mankind, and stand forever irreversible" (2:1069).

Whereas Storrs speaks of history as providing a stable and objective moral perspective, Black Hawk's *Life* reveals the extent to which history and the sense of justice it provides are simply contingent textual effects. Rather than making up for past injustices, the textual justice produced by Black Hawk's *Life* simply seems to stand in for injustices that are still occurring. While the Cherokees' "paper war" posed a complex moral dilemma with very real political and economic repercussions, Black Hawk's war of words posed a moral challenge circumscribed within the pages of a text. While the Cherokees demanded corrective action within the public space of politics and law, the justice Black Hawk's *Life* asked of its readers required only proper feeling regarding actions that were past, exercised in the private space of reading.

In order to permit readers to enact textual justice, the text must actually seem to "present" Black Hawk within the pages of the *Life* as controlling narrator, telling his story from his own perspective, so that justice may be done and the Indian's place in history, at least, may be faithfully established. Ironically, one of the means by which the editor reinforces a sense of Black Hawk's presence is to stage his exit. Near the end of the *Life* Black Hawk suddenly breaks out of narrative time and returns to the real: "I have not time now, nor is it necessary, to enter more into detail about my travels through the United States. . . . [M]y people have started to their hunting grounds and I am anxious to follow them" (153). This sudden shift to real time impresses upon the reader the fact that "Black Hawk," the character constructed and represented through written language within the autobiography, is also Black Hawk the living Indian, sitting in a room at the Rock Island Indian agency in August 1833, presenting his story to a translator and white editor; it also reinforces an image of Black Hawk as the restless Indian impatient to be on the move once again.

The act of self-presentation, as the text describes it, occurs only once. The Indian speaks his story and then disappears. The white editor produces the textual representation of Black Hawk that will remain long after the Indian himself has gone. It is not surprising that the editor should choose hunting to mark the exit of Black Hawk from the text. It is consistent with nineteenth-century characterizations of Indians as quintessentially hunters, which persisted even in the face of clear evidence of substantial agricultural activity among many tribes. Just as hunting (supposedly) leads Black Hawk out of the permanent realm of written representation, so the stereotype of the Indian as hunter served as a popular nineteenth-century rationale for denying Indians a permanent place on the American land or within American society. For example, in 1829 Andrew Jackson appealed to this stereotype to justify removal. It is "visionary," according to Jackson, that Indians should assert a permanent claim to lands "on which they have neither dwelt nor made improvements, merely because they have seen them from the mountain or passed them in the chase"[35] It is in keeping with this vision of "the Indian" that the place finally assigned to Black Hawk in the autobiography is the realm of the ephemeral: speaking rather than writing; hunting rather than farming.

In his study of the relationship between speech and writing in Native American texts, David Murray notes that "it is striking how often the issue of the Indian voice comes up as a way of characterizing authenticity in a text" (1988, 30). I would add that for the nineteenth-century readers of the *Life*, the Indian's "voice" served not simply figuratively as a metaphor for authenticity, but rather literally in the sense that the Indian's voice was a defining condition of authenticity. As the following 1835 review indicates, Black Hawk's autobiography was considered authentic only because here the Indian told his story to a white man rather than presenting it directly to the reader through his own writing:

> This book is a curiosity; an anomaly in literature. It is the only autobiography of an Indian extant, for we do not consider Mr. Apes and a few other persons of unmixed Indian blood, who have written books, to be Indians. . . . But here is an autobiography of a wild, unadulterated savage, gall yet fermenting in his veins, his heart still burning with the sense of wrong, the words of wrath and scorn yet scarce cold upon his lips, ("If you wish to fight us, come on,") and his hands still reeking with recent slaughter.[36]

Following the logic of this argument, the real "unadulterated" Indian is a wild Indian, and by definition wild Indians do not write. For an Indian, then, the only way the "real" can be recorded and history preserved is through an act of representation performed by a white. The authenticity of this history is measured not by its correspondence to the experience, thoughts, or voice of a real Indian—one would expect the unmediated words of an Indian written by himself to reproduce most faithfully his actual voice and experience—but by the extent to which the text produces the illusion of a performance in which a wild Indian speaks before a white man.[37] Authenticity, as defined here, is not simply dependent upon the primacy of the spoken word but upon the conditions under which the originary speech act is imagined to occur and the process by which it enters into print.[38] The white audience, in relation to the Indian, forms the community in which the truth is at once spoken into being and authorized. Such a conception of history—and of the "real" Indian who is its subject—presents the Indian as a speaking subject at the same time that it subjects the Indian to white control. Indians themselves remain associated with the ephemeral; only through the agency of whites do they enter into the permanent realm of textual and historical representation.[39]

The Indian is granted subject status only as he becomes subject to white representation. Indians, such as the Cherokees, who establish their own representative government or Indians, such as William Apes, who represent themselves through writing cannot be tolerated *as* Indians. The Cherokees were offered an opportunity to stay in Georgia, but only if they renounced their tribal identity and became individual American citizens. "The Indian," as represented by whites, was essential to nineteenth-century efforts to construct national identity not only because he provided the national history Americans desperately wanted but because the process of representation offered Americans the chance to purge that history of its moral taint by enacting textual (or artistic) justice. Thus, textual justice does not simply replace or displace historical injustice but rather creates the imaginative space that allows subjugation to be recast as subjectification. The persistence of real Indians and their resistance to the historical script Americans attempted to force upon them often threatened to expose the "act" for what it was—or, in the words of William Wirt, to reveal "our constitution, laws, and treaties [as] empty pageants, that but mock us with a show of national existence."

It is fitting that Black Hawk tells his story from the perspective of one who is facing death, for as he is transformed from speaking subject to the subject of white history he becomes the Vanishing American. Benjamin Drake's 1838 history of Black Hawk describes this transformation quite aptly: "Black Hawk may die, his name be forgotten, and the smoke of his wigwam be seen no more, but the "Black Hawk war" will long form a page of deep interest, in the history of this country" (75–76). Black Hawk the individual is as ephemeral as the smoke billowing forth from his wigwam. The history that will remain as the permanent record of his life is not even his own but rather the history of those who have taken his land and subordinated his nation. Black Hawk, as represented textually, provided the authentic material out of which Americans could construct an account of their own history and the occasion by means of which they could redefine the historical meaning of Indian-white relations by granting Black Hawk textual justice.

A year after his tour through the East, Black Hawk returned for a brief visit. While he was not the celebrity he had been during his earlier tour, Black Hawk was not forgotten. In fact, in New York he was invited to preside as guest of honor at a performance of a new drama based on Black Hawk's War.[40] Thus, Black Hawk's life had literally become a performance produced by whites, a performance from which Black Hawk as independent "actor" was entirely excluded. Through a series of performances—the treaty ceremonies that obscured the Indians' loss of power at the very moment that it was being taken away; the laws that were shown to be "empty pageants"; the display of Black Hawk as defeated warrior; Black Hawk's performance as he recounted to a white audience the story of his own subjugation—the meaning and strategies of Indian-white relations were revealed. If plays about Pocahontas domesticated the drama of conquest, Black Hawk marks the site at which that drama is inscribed as history that simultaneously compensates for and reenacts conquest. Sitting passively in the theater—the honored guest whose silent gaze authorized the performance that alienated him from the events of his own life—Black Hawk again took part in a spectacle that displayed, even more clearly than his tour five years earlier, the complex act of mirroring by which both conquered and conqueror were mutually constituted in popular representations of Indians during the nineteenth century.

SIX

A GUIDE TO REMEMBRANCE:
THE CAPITOL TOUR AND THE CONSTRUCTION
OF A U.S. CITIZENRY

> Nowhere else do the citizens seem smaller than in a demo-
> cratic nation, and nowhere else does the nation itself seem
> greater, so that it is easily conceived as a great picture. Imag-
> ination shrinks at the thought of themselves as individuals
> and expands beyond all limits at the thought of the state.
> Hence people living cramped lives in tiny houses often con-
> ceive of their public monuments on a gigantic scale.
> (*Tocqueville*, Democracy in America)

> The miniature is considered . . . as a metaphor for the inte-
> rior space and time of the bourgeois subject. Analogously, the
> gigantic is considered a metaphor for the abstract authority of
> the state and the collective, public, life.
> (*Susan Stewart*)

WHEN Alexis de Tocqueville traveled to the United States in
the mid-1830s to investigate the American democratic "exper-
iment," he included a visit to the nation's capital on his tour.
As the epigraph suggests, this visit inspired reflection upon the nature of
democracy itself. If, following Susan Stewart, we read metaphors of scale
as representative of relations between private and public, which are crucial to the formation of the modern subject, then Tocqueville's comments suggest the extent to which the meaning of democracy inheres in
the relationship between individual citizens and the nation—a relationship revealed in the way that citizens imagine national monuments.

This chapter explores how guidebooks to the U.S. Capitol spanning
the 1830s to the 1860s participated in the project of national formation.
They taught American citizens how to "read" the meanings of the Capitol and how to position themselves *as citizens* in relation to the stories it
told. In a nation beset by ever-deepening political divisions during the
years leading up to the Civil War, guidebooks promoted the Capitol as a

means of unifying the citizenry through shared participation in a common national past.

The rebuilding of the U.S. Capitol in 1825 after its destruction in the War of 1812 became a charged symbol of national destiny. The American victory in the war (while somewhat ambiguous militarily) had affirmed the nation's political power and expanded its territory. But, as we have seen, postwar calls for a national literature and art revealed a need to confirm imaginatively what had been achieved politically. It was in this climate that the first guidebooks to the U.S. Capitol appeared during the 1830s.

The introductions to these early guidebooks show their authors groping toward a new genre, the shape and purpose of which was still in flux. While some authors describe their goals in practical terms—providing an aid "for those doing business with the Capitol" (Mills, "Introduction")—most attach a broader significance to their projects. Jonathan Elliot opens his 1830 guidebook with the following declaration: "From the rising destinies of this District it is evident that a sketch of its history and a description of the City, and the Public Buildings, may be acceptable to the citizens, as well as sojourners, at the Metropolis" ("Preface"). Elliot envisions travel to Washington not simply occurring as part of necessary business but also accruing value in itself through association with a certain idea of the Capitol's—and the nation's—meaning. In directing the book to citizens *and* sojourners, Elliot defines the category of the citizen in contrast to the sojourner. If the sojourner is one who passes through a (typically foreign) place only briefly, the citizen is, implicitly and conversely, one who is at home even when traveling.

In his 1839 guide to the Capitol Philip Haas explicitly defines his project as nationalistic and directs his book to the American citizenry at large. His goal is "to bring home to everyone throughout the United States the localities of that spot so interesting to all, the capital of this great republic" ("Preface"). While Elliot encourages citizens to travel to the Capitol, noting that his "pocket size" guide may be carried while on a tour, Haas addresses his book to all Americans, including citizens who do not travel.

Both Elliot and Haas propose a way of imagining the category of the citizen in terms of touristic experience. But their introductory pages make clear that the kind of tourism they envision is something new, something very different from the grand tour of Europe or the tour of natural wonders, the most common form of domestic tourism of the day.[1] Instead of expanding the self through exposure to the foreign or exotic, travel to the Capitol is designed to bring Americans home or, rather, "to bring home to" Americans a new vision of national identity and citizenship, a vision structured by the dynamics of the Capitol tour they describe.

To understand what it is that these guidebooks wanted to "bring home" to citizens, one must look to the guidebooks themselves, to the vision of American history they presented and how they positioned the American citizen-tourist in relation to it. This vision of history is revealed most clearly in the guidebooks' accounts of the Capitol's commemorative artwork. These works of art are described in dramatic terms that encourage readers to complete imaginatively the larger action the artwork implies. The guidebooks thus provide a prompter's cue, turning the Capitol into a site of civic ritual where symbolically charged moments from the national past were to be staged again and again within the minds of the "imagined community" of citizens who had come to tour the Capitol. Making these works of commemorative public art the occasion for national imaginings, guidebooks to the Capitol nostalgically constructed a past that never was and a citizenry that emerged through the very act of (guided) interpretation, in which "the citizen" was cast as audience and actor in an ongoing national drama.[2]

Race, Removal, and the (Re)construction of a National Past

The history of contact between Euro-Americans and Indians is a dominant theme of the Capitol's commemorative artwork. The appeal of this subject to nineteenth-century Americans can be understood in several ways. Most obviously, it allowed a young nation to locate its origins in a (relatively) distant past. Benedict Anderson's argument that the idea of the nation is imagined to be rooted in time immemorial and to extend into the immeasurable future is particularly apt in connection with the Capitol, where past and future meet to create its meaning as symbol of the nation. The representations of Indians in the Capitol artworks also brought into sharper focus such themes as the debate over Indian policy, encompassing this debate within a vision of national destiny that justified the means to the end the Capitol celebrated. By defining the citizen in relation to the implicit discourse of race they represented, the Capitol artworks made the continued political exclusion of Indians seem natural and necessary.[3]

Jonathan Elliot's 1830 guidebook begins by linking the rise of the United States with the history of Indian decline. As Elliot informs the reader, the Capitol is built upon the same land "where councils were held among various tribes" (12). He goes on to direct the reader's response to this fact: "The coincidence of the location of the National Legislature, so near the scite [sic] of the council house of an Indian nation, cannot fail to excite interesting reflections in the mind of an intelligent reader" (12). Thus, Elliot presents a vision of one nation superseding another, with

Indians consequently removed both from the land where the Capitol now visibly stands and from history ("we have a very imperfect account") except insofar as they form the foundation of the rising American nation.

With the reader-tourist thus prepared, Elliot proceeds to describe the four Rotunda sculptures by Antonio Capellano, Enrico Causici, and Nicholas Gevelot. All feature contact between Euro-Americans and Indians. Elliot criticizes Capellano's *Preservation of Captain John Smith by Pocahontas* (figure 1) for "want of truth": Pocahontas is described as "Grecian" and Powhatan is "less like an Indian than a European" (115). He dismisses Gevelot's relief sculpture *Penn's Treaty with the Indians* (figure 2) as "dull" (120). Clearly, these representations of peaceful coexistence between Euro-Americans and Indians are inconsistent with the national history Elliot wishes to present.

The two relief sculptures Elliot praises most strongly both represent Indians in positions of inferiority and/or conflict in relation to Euro-Americans. Elliot's account of Causici's *Landing of the Pilgrims* (figure 3) begins with a description of the Indian, who "kneels, offering corn" to the European. While Elliot asserts that the Pilgrim is the best executed figure, he suggests that "the Indian may, by many, be viewed with the most gratification" because of "his brawny form and peculiar position on the rock" (116). Elliot does not elaborate further. If the viewer were to examine the Indian's position to determine what is "peculiar" about it, what would stand out most markedly, in contrast to the rest of the group, would be his passivity. The Indian is the only seated figure. While one hand is extended toward the Pilgrim in a gesture of friendship, the Indian offering to share with him the bounty of the land, the other hand hangs limply, pointing as if by chance at the boot of the Pilgrim. Unlike the passive Indian, the Pilgrim is shown in motion as he sets foot upon the very rock that supports the Indian. The Indian's own casual gesture thus points to the key event that gives meaning to the sculpture, namely, the historic landing upon Plymouth Rock. The hands of the Pilgrim and his wife, raised in benediction, provide the gloss: the sense of providential destiny implicit in this moment but made fully manifest only from the perspective of the viewer, who, two centuries later, stands within the Capitol of a nation that is defined, within this historical vision, as the inevitable culmination of this act. Thus, the space of the Capitol itself contributes to the meaning of the drama that unfolds in the minds of citizen-tourists.

Elliot concludes his discussion of the relief sculpture by informing the reader that the very rock upon which the Indian sits (now renamed "Forefathers' Rock") has been removed to the center of Plymouth, "where New Englanders visit it with veneration" (116). This final anecdote serves to reinforce the meaning of the sculpture: the story it tells is

Figure 1. Antonio Capellano, *Preservation of Captain Smith by Pocahontas* (1825), sandstone. U.S. Capitol Rotunda, above west door. Courtesy of the Architect of the Capitol.

Figure 2. Nicholas
Gevelot, *William Penn's
Treaty with the Indians*
(1827), sandstone. U.S.
Capitol Rotunda, above
north door. Courtesy of
the Architect of the
Capitol.

Figure 3. Enrico Causici, *Landing of the Pilgrims* (1825), sandstone. U.S. Capitol Rotunda, above east door. Courtesy of the Architect of the Capitol.

about Euro-Americans laying claim to the American land. The Indian, who appears almost one with the rock he straddles, has been removed from the land and denied control of its ultimate historical meaning as he is transformed into a monument to the nation that has displaced his own. Elliot's description of the sculpture both averts and embraces the deep and divisive debates over the policy of Indian removal during the 1830s. He offers no explanation of the particular—and often troubling—historical actions that occurred between the Indian's offering of corn and the Euro-American's taking of Indian lands. The pilgrim's first step seems to set into motion the whole history of Indian-white relations. To venerate this moment (and the Forefathers' Rock associated with it) is to embrace all that followed from it.

Elliot's reference to Plymouth Rock also serves to instruct citizens as to how to position themselves in relation to this commemorative artwork and the national story it represents. If the rock represented in the sculpture has become a site "New Englanders visit . . . with veneration" (in other words, if it has become a tourist attraction), then the citizen is defined, quite explicitly in this moment, as tourist. Dean MacCannell defines the basic structure of a tourist attraction as constituted by "an empirical relationship between a *tourist*, a *sight* and a *marker* (a piece of information about a sight)" (41). He explains that "markers may take many different forms: guidebooks, . . . slide shows"—and paintings, we might presume. By concluding his discussion of Causici's relief sculpture with the anecdote about Plymouth Rock, Elliot prompts the reader to see the sculpture not simply as a representation of an important moment in the nation's history but also as the marker of a tourist attraction. On one level the guidebook is the marker defining the Capitol as tourist attraction. On another level the guidebook suggests that the Capitol and its artwork are themselves simply markers for another attraction that achieves its status by virtue of being more authentic and immediate—a "real" piece of history, as in the case of Plymouth Rock, or the nation and its history, which the commemorative artwork within the Capitol represents. Thus, Elliot's guidebook implicitly problematizes the citizen's relationship to the nation by highlighting the extent to which that relationship is mediated by representation. The guidebook posits national history as the object of the touristic gaze, but it is a gaze that is "marked" over and over again, ever receding from its object. The guidebook defines the Capitol as the site of a public ritual of nationhood, but it is a ritual that remains uncompleted, leaving the participants to reflect upon the ritual act itself. It offers citizen-tourists guidance in the ritual behavior appropriate to the sacralized site while maintaining a certain openness as to the final object of the ritual. The role of the citizen, Elliot's guidebook suggests, is to gaze ("with veneration") upon the nation and its history. By virtue of the ability to recognize and interpret a variety of objects, representations, or events as historical markers, the citizen-tourist lays claim to and inscribes himself within the national history thus marked, thereby affirming his own authenticity as citizen.

The only other artwork in the Rotunda to receive Elliot's high praise is Causici's *Conflict of Daniel Boone and the Indians* (figure 4). Guidebooks of the 1830s (including Elliot's) commonly referred to this piece as the best artwork in the Rotunda. Like Causici's *Landing of the Pilgrims*, the relief sculpture is described not only as a representation of national history but as a lesson instructing the citizen as to how (and by whom) national history is to be viewed. Here the bodies of Euro-American and Indian are locked in battle, both grasping the rifle that rises between them, each poised (with knife and tomahawk, respectively) to kill his enemy. An Indian lies dead upon the ground, visually uniting the two contesting figures (both rest a foot upon the body of the fallen Indian). Causici chooses to represent the combatants just before the outcome of the battle is clear, thus drawing the viewer into the drama at its very climax and leaving the latter imaginatively to complete the action that will produce a sense of resolution. In other words, ultimately it is the historical perspective of the viewer, for whom the outcome of the contest between cultures has already been decided, that authoritatively completes and determines the meaning of the episode.

To grasp the ideological work the relief sculpture performs, one need only recall what it suppresses: it actually refers to a battle in which a group of Indians triumphed over Boone and his followers, killing six men and causing the party to retreat forty miles.[4] Despite its specific historical reference (indicated by the date 1773 carved upon the tree), the artwork was interpreted by guidebook authors and reviewers alike as the triumph of Euro-Americans over Indians. The disjuncture reinforces the extent to which this historical artwork is much more about the present than the past; it is the viewer's perception of the present and future destiny of the United States rather than the factual truth of the event recorded that provides—and, with each act of interpretation, continually reaffirms—the meaning of this commemorative art.

Haas concludes his discussion of Causici's relief sculpture with an anecdote describing the artwork from the perspective of Indians as he imagines them:

> Formerly, some Winnebago Indians, wild and savage as those represented in this plate, were on a visit to the seat of government, and upon one occasion, they visited the Capitol. Standing beneath this representation of a fierce fight, they seemed to understand who was the victor, and they uttered a warlike shout of defiance, and ran across the rotunda, disappearing by the door over which is the figure of the beautiful Pocahontas. (Haas, n.p.)

Figure 4. Enrico Causici. *Conflict of Daniel Boone and the Indians* (1826–27), sandstone. U.S. Capitol Rotunda, above south door. Courtesy of the Architect of the Capitol.

Living Indians are recreated in the image of the artwork. The Winnebagos are excluded from the ongoing movement of history. Indians, according to Haas, do not change; the contemporary Winnebagos are "wild and savage as those represented in this plate."

History, as it is imagined in relation to Euro-Americans, makes this image of battle—even a battle which the settlers lost—simply one act in a larger drama of the growth and development of a nation. It is this historical perspective that makes the viewing of the relief sculpture by the American citizen-tourist an experience of national affirmation and patriotic pride. The fact that the Indians, as Haas imagines them, do not move forward in time turns the viewing of the artwork into a kind of nightmarish mirror scene for the Winnebagos of the anecdote. According to Haas, the Indians recognize themselves in the same glance that simultaneously reveals the inescapable law that excludes them from the American national destiny. It is a scene of recognition that erases rather than affirms identity. Their exit from the Capitol building beneath the figure of Pocahontas is a reminder that the only terms under which Indians have ever been offered inclusion are those of complete assimilation and virtual erasure of tribal identity. Without ever mentioning contemporary politics, Haas rearticulates a message implicit in 1830s American Indian policy: assimilate or remove.

Elliot's 1830 guide to Causici's relief sculpture of Boone offers no historical information about the event pictured, instead focusing upon the two combatants' expressions. The significance of the work, according to Elliot, is to be found in "finely contrasting the cool intrepidity of the hero with the ferocity of the savage" (119). Similarly, Robert Mills's 1834 guidebook contrasts the "cool resolution and self-possession" of Boone with "the ferocity and recklessness of the savage" (21). While Haas also sees the expressions of the two figures as the key to understanding the artwork, he explains the significance of the expressions more explicitly than Elliot or Mills:

[T]he artist has well and vigorously portrayed the ferocity of the Indian, and the cool deliberate courage of the intrepid white. In the contrast of the faces of these two men, brought into fearful connection, lies the great merit of this piece. It is the history of the two races, represented by the chisel of genius; the fierce revenge of the one, the calculating, calm courage of the other. (Haas, n.p.)

The point of this relief sculpture, according to Haas, is to define history as the visible manifestation of innate, unchangeable, and racially determined principles which exclude Indians from the American future.

Engendering the Citizen

The precise meaning of the principles that nineteenth-century Americans would have read into these expressions resonates in terms of gender as well as race. Elliot includes in his guidebook an anonymous review of the artwork of the Rotunda:

> The physiognomy and character of the savage are well portrayed in all [Causici's] Indian figures. Both he and Mr. Capellano have, however, fallen into a gross error in giving them so much muscle, and in placing the muscle, in some instances, in the wrong place. It is found, upon a close and accurate examination, that the body of a male Indian is as smooth, and devoid of every appearance of muscle, as that of the most delicate white female; and this may be easily accounted for from the indolent and inactive lives they usually lead. (121)

This reviewer's account of the Indian's effeminacy seems to jar with Elliot's description of the stereotypical "ferocity of the savage" (118). The logic behind these two very different perspectives gradually emerges when one considers a later section of the guidebook where Elliot discusses several portraits of George Washington. Instead of commenting upon the relative skill of the various artists, he focuses upon Washington's face, which he sees as a work of art comparable to "ancient statuary . . . where all the parts contribute to the purity and perfection of the whole" (297). Elliot elaborates on the qualities revealed in Washington's face: "Bred in the vigorous school of frontier warfare . . . he excelled the hunter and the woodsmen in their athletic habits, and in those trials of manhood which distinguished the days of his early life." Elliot concludes that "his physiognomy was decidedly Roman" (297). The connection here established between manliness and republican virtue echoes the political philosophy of the day.[5] Elliot's description of Washington, father of the country and model American, clearly aligns this vision of manly, republican virtue with the ideal of American citizenship.

Viewed through this ideological lens, Causici's relief sculpture implicitly justifies nineteenth-century American Indian policy. Like the vision of history as racially determined, which Haas saw as the central meaning behind the artwork, Elliot's reading of the sculpture in terms of gender would have supported American efforts during the 1830s to explain— and naturalize—the political exclusion, removal, and inevitable decline of Indians.

The way in which gender inflects constructions of race and national identity is further illuminated by the multiple representations of Pocahontas in the U.S. Capitol. Capellano's *Preservation of Captain Smith* portrays Pocahontas in a gesture of self-sacrifice as she shields Smith from the Indian's deathblow. As has already been noted (see chapter 3), this anecdote from Smith's *Generall Historie of Virginia* (1624) had previously been mythologized in a vast body of popular literature, drama, and art.[6] According to popular myth, the motivation ascribed to Pocahontas was generally twofold: an instant love based upon recognition of the European's cultural and personal superiority to men of her own race and an expression of her feminine and/or innately Christian virtue. In this reading of Pocahontas, gender supersedes race in determining the Indian's fate—but that fate still remains the exclusion of the Indian, as Indian, from the American future. Pocahontas's feminine virtue leads to the act of personal self-sacrifice pictured by Capellano, while her embrace of the European and his ways leads to cultural annihilation through assimilation, a point underscored by Chapman's *Baptism of Pocahontas at Jamestown, Virginia, 1613* (figure 5) also decorating the Rotunda.

According to the argument implicit in the Capitol artwork and made explicit in the guidebooks, the feminized male Indian lacks the republican virtue requisite for citizenship, while the idealized female Indian recognizes this lack as essential to her (feminine) nature and willingly offers herself to the superior (masculine) conqueror. This very recognition provides proof of her feminine virtue and serves as the basis of her idealization. It also provides an implicit justification of conquest.[7] The logic that George Custis's play *Pocahontas* (1830) dramatizes is enforced by the guidebooks in a different mode: the competitive individualism that actually drives conquest (or expansion) is deemphasized through an insistence upon the republican virtue of the ideal citizen, a virtue which Pocahontas can recognize but not embody.

While never attaining the heroic stature of Pocahontas, the virtuous Euro-American woman also plays a crucial role in constructions of U.S. national identity. Depictions of white women in the artwork of the Capitol fall into two categories: (1) to symbolize abstract ideals, such as Liberty, Justice, or America itself; (2) in a secondary but crucial supporting role as the helpless victim who requires and reveals the virtue and strength of the heroic Euro-American male. It is primarily this latter role I wish to examine for what it reveals about the gendered construction of a U.S. citizenry.[8]

The two Euro-American women most commonly singled out and praised for their beauty are the wives in Robert W. Weir's *Embarkation of the Pilgrims at Delf Haven, Holland, 22 July 1620* (figure 6) and Leutze's *Westward the Course of Empire Takes Its Way (Westward Ho!)* (figure 7) One anonymous commentator wrote in 1856:

Figure 5. John Chapman, *Baptism of Pocahontas at Jamestown, Virginia, 1613* (1836–40), oil on canvas. U.S. Capitol Rotunda. Courtesy of the Architect of the Capitol.

Figure 6. Robert W. Weir, *Embarkation of the Pilgrims at Delft Haven, Holland, 22 July 1620* (1836–43), oil on canvas. U.S. Capitol Rotunda. Courtesy of the Architect of the Capitol.

Figure 7. Emanuel Leutze. *Westward the Course of Empire Takes Its Way (Westward Ho!)* (1861–62), fresco. U.S. Capitol, House wing, west stairway. Courtesy of the Architect of the Capitol.

We have stood for hours before it [Weir's painting], and then returned again
and again, each time to see new beauties, and to gaze upon that face of
surpassing loveliness, the *wife of Miles Standish*. It is the very ideal of Saxon
beauty—the eyes clear, deep, fearless, as a woman's eyes may be, yet devo-
tional and confiding; they are turned upward, speaking the woman's trust in
her husband and the soul's faith in its God.[9]

In his 1865 guidebook Samuel D. Wyeth commented in a similar spirit
upon the beauty of female dependency as illustrated by the pioneer wife
in Leutze's fresco: "The mother looks pale, and patient, and as if she
tried to feel hopeful. . . . That mother's face is, to me, one of the most
beautiful faces I have ever seen in a picture. The father, a strong, stout
man, endeavors to cheer her; he is still behind, and points out with a face
of glowing hope, the land where his own good arm shall win for them
another home" (83). These descriptions make clear that the beauty of
female dependency lies in its relation to a particular model of male heroism. Female passivity and patience provide the occasion for male heroic
action. The woman's upward glance expresses faith in God *and* man in
the selfsame gesture, thus aligning the two and pronouncing benediction
upon whatever masculine action might be required to confirm this feminine confidence.

An 1855 review of Horatio Greenough's *Rescue* (figure 8) makes explicit the role of Euro-American women in the commemorative artwork
of the Capitol and the idea of the nation it represents. The reviewer, W.
J. Stone, begins by constructing an elaborate story:

A female and child, wife of a pioneer of the far west, is wending her way
through the forest; being weary, she rests on the side of a rock; whilst stealth-
ily and unobserved by her, a savage approaches within striking distance, his
tomahawk uplifted and ready to descend. A powerful and hardy hunter,
equally unobserved, approaches the Indian, and immediately pinions him by
the arms, and holds him as firmly as though bound with withes—evincing in
the entire group a beautiful conception. (393)

Beauty here consists in the relation of the parts to the whole, but it is
their relation to the woman that makes the parts cohere and gives them
meaning. "You may read volumes in the [woman's] countenance," the
reviewer asserts. In this statement lies the key to the woman's role. She is
imagined as entirely passive; the central action involving Indian and pioneer occurs beyond her gaze or comprehension. It is not the woman's
perspective or the viewer's identification with her perspective that be-
stows meaning. She remains in the background, overshadowed by the
action of the white man and Indian, yet her presence, as observed by the
viewer-interpreter, is what motivates and justifies the violent conflict

Figure 8. Horatio Greenough. *Rescue* (1837–53), marble. Photograph taken before 1920, showing the work in situ to the right of the staircase on the east facade of the U.S. Capitol. In storage since 1958. Courtesy of the Architect of the Capitol.

upon which the nation is built. "As Greenough has managed the group," the review concludes, "the story is plainly told, and the feelings of the beholder are not pained, but left calmly to admire the beautiful work of Art" (393).

Like nineteenth-century guidebooks, this review encourages citizens who visit the Capitol to dramatize and aestheticize the idea of the nation and to define citizenship as a position of symbolic authority claimed by Euro-American males through the interpretive stance they assume in relation to Indians and Euro-American women. The citizen is defined as the one who, in seeing the sights of the Capitol, interprets the meaning of the nation and, with each act of (guided) interpretation, reaffirms its power.

Re-membering a Nation Divided

During the decade leading up to and including the Civil War, as narratives of national identity foundered upon the politics of sectional division, a new wave of guidebooks attempted to enlist the symbolic power of the Capitol to preserve and renew the meaning of the nation. The politics of national union (and disunion) were addressed quite directly in these guidebooks and became the lens through which the Capitol—and the tour of the Capitol—was perceived. A two-part essay entitled "The Capitol at Washington," published in the *United States Magazine* in July and August 1856, urged American citizens to travel to their nation's capital. The essay, which could itself serve as a guide for those who made the trip, envisioned the role of the citizen-tourist as one of deep political significance.

The essay begins with an account of national history that locates the meaning of the Capitol in its power to unify the nation:

> The bands that held the Colonies together were feebler far than we at this late date realize; the fears of some, the ambitions of others, and a jealousy which the war had scarcely kept from exhibiting itself in some hideous form, all threatened the very existence of the Federal Government. Many of the leading men felt that a National Capitol, common to the people of each State, yet belonging to none, would be a strong link in binding the States together. The people could then see the palpable Government, which was as yet to most of them a mere political myth. (2)

Writing in the midst of mounting sectional tensions, when a new set of fears, ambitions, and jealousies threatened the continued existence of the federal government, the author clearly hoped this brief account of national history would instill in readers a sense of renewed faith in and commitment to the preservation of a united federal government. In this account the Capitol itself functioned as the palpable symbol of the nation.

The meaning of the Capitol tour likewise expanded in significance. Whereas the guidebooks of the 1830s tentatively hinted at the broader implications of the citizen's tour of the Capitol, here the nationalism is overt. The Capitol is defined as a holy shrine where the common, unifying ideal of nationhood is elevated to the status of the sacred and "the tour" becomes a holy pilgrimage for all true Americans:

> [The Capitol] is to the American almost what Jerusalem is to the believer in Christ, for it is hallowed by the great struggles and trials of our country during nearly sixty years of our momentous existence; and yet, alas! how few of the twenty-five millions to whom all this belongs have visited Washington. It is a truth, and one by no means creditable to the parties concerned, that numbers of Americans are found in Europe who have never seen Washington and know little of it. . . . We hold that there is nothing in Europe so well worth a visit—nay, which demands a pilgrimage to its altar—as the Declaration of Independence. (7)

In describing the Capitol tour as a pilgrimage, the writer urges citizens to go to Washington in order to confirm their identities as Americans, to become what they (in imagination) already are: citizens united by their shared vision of the nation.

Wyeth's guidebook to Washington, written during the Civil War and published in 1865, illustrates this impulse to make the Capitol a sacred space of civic ritual where the idea of the nation could be renewed by and for a patriotic American citizenry. The book's dedication—"To my Countrymen, / North, South, East, and West, / who Love the 'Old Flag'"—immediately focuses attention upon sectional division and proposes the book as a place where rifts are healed and a nation divided by war is reunited as "my Countrymen," rallying around the symbol of the "Old Flag."

In his introduction Wyeth makes clear that the book is as much about the war as the Capitol, for it is the war that gives motive and significance to Wyeth's narrative and the Capitol tour the guidebook describes: "The city of Washington is far dearer to the nation's heart now than it was before the breaking out of the Rebellion. The treasure expended and the blood spilled, in its defence, have made it seem to the patriots sacred as a shrine. To want to know all about it is a national longing, and to gratify this in some degree, is the design of the present book" (v). Like the author of "The Capitol at Washington," Wyeth imagines the Capitol as a shrine, but the power it thus accrues as a site of pilgrimage is intensified for Wyeth by the war. The meaning of the Capitol as a tourist site is infused with a sense of nostalgia; the Capitol is imagined as a place that offers the means to understand—and perhaps regain—what has been lost.

Wyeth elaborates upon the relationship of the war, the book, and the subject it describes: "The chapters have been written . . . over a period of between three and four years. The grand panorama of the war was enacting almost within sight and sound during all that time—and the fitful flashes of actual attack also really occurred. As a burning Bengal light throws a livid glare over all, so streaks of war paint fill in and enamel many pages" (vi). He conceives of the war as a theatrical or artistic effect, a "grand panorama" with "streaks of war paint" filling the pages of the text. The war is thus incorporated into the text as dramatic backdrop, setting the stage that the narrative, as main event, will then fill. This extended metaphor defines the text—and the Capitol as it is represented in the text—as imaginative spaces in which the meaning of the nation is to be enacted like a drama or composed like a picture.

Pushing the metaphor in a different direction, Wyeth goes on to describe the political activities of the Capitol in terms of artistic and theatrical effect. He inserts into the guidebook the character of a wounded Civil War soldier who asks author for directions to Congress. As the latter proceeds to guide the soldier, the reader sees the Capitol through the eyes of one whose perceptions have been shaped by the direct experience of war. As the soldier and his guide approach the Senate chamber, they encounter Emanuel Leutze in the process of painting *Westward the Course of Empire Takes Its Way*. Just as they open the door to the Senate chamber, the soldier exclaims, "What a splendid picture!" (67). The comment at first seems to apply to the fresco, the picture that has just been described, but as the narrative unfolds it becomes clear that the soldier is referring to the "picture" of Congress in session visible below the viewers' gallery. By means of this carefully constructed ambiguity, Wyeth blurs the line between politics and art, thus creating in his readers' minds, if only for a brief moment, a vision that perceives art as a political activity and politics as a work of art.

The actual history of Leutze's fresco illustrates just as powerfully as Wyeth's anecdote the relationship between art and politics. The sketch for Leutze's fresco of westward migration was approved by Captain M. C. Meigs, Superintendent of U.S. Capitol Extension, before the Civil War began. With the outbreak of war, however, orders were issued "putting a stop to all expenditures not absolutely necessary to that defence."[10] In a letter to the Secretary of War dated 20 June 1861, Meigs challenged this order: "The people of the country have so responded to the call of their Government that danger to the Capitol has now passed away, and it is a question worthy of consideration whether the Government by pursuing in some degree the project of completing its Capitol would not give to the people a welcome assurance of its confidence in its own strength and in the patriotism of its people" (quoted in Fairman, 202). This debate suggests that the activity of the artist engaged in representing the meaning of the nation is just as important as the activity of the army engaged in its military defense. Nathaniel Hawthorne, writing in 1862, called attention to Leutze's fresco:

> It was delightful to see him so calmly elaborating his design to go on the walls of the Capitol, while other men doubted and feared, or hoped treacherously, and whispered to one another that the nation would exist only a little longer. . . . But the artist keeps right on, firm of heart and hand, drawing his outlines with an unwavering pencil, beautifying and idealizing our rude, material life, and thus manifesting that we have an indefeasible claim to a more enduring national existence. (46)

The significance of the fresco for Hawthorne lies in the artist's activity in the midst of war.

The qualities Hawthorne associates with the artist—calm deliberation, firmness of heart, unwavering confidence—are similar to those that the guidebooks of the 1830s associated with the manly ideal of republican virtue, qualities which (by their absence) justified the Indians' exclusion from—and proved the Euro-Americans' right to—the American land and its destiny. In the 1860s these same qualities prove for Hawthorne Americans' claim to a national existence "more enduring" than the threat of dissolution posed by the war. The ideal citizen is defined here by his ability to envision (as the artist does) the *idea* of the nation even in the midst of discord and division. Such a vision affirms and makes manifest America's destiny to prevail and, as Leutze's fresco boldly proclaims, to expand.

Near the end of the guidebook, Wyeth returns to the subject of Leutze's fresco. His account emphasizes not the emigrants engrossed in the activity of crossing the pass—ostensibly the main focus of the painting—but those who pause to contemplate or commemorate the meaning of this activity. Wyeth describes a family sitting upon a peak gazing at their new homeland "with face[s] of glowing hope." He describes in detail the pioneers' *vision*: "[A]s glimpses of the opening view fall upon the faces of the pioneer men and women, they light, and glow, and seem almost to startle into life" (84). He chooses this moment to blur the line between representation and reality. In so doing, he invites the viewer/reader to participate in, realize, and "startle into life" the vision of national unity and destiny that the painting represents.

Wyeth goes on to describe another group of pioneers who commemorate the meaning of this climactic moment. "Away, far up, where rocks are piled upon rocks, as 'twere that veritable work of giants who made the futile attempt to scale the walls of Heaven, two men have climbed, and carry with them the glorious old Flag. They look tiny in the far-up distance, but you can see there, gleaming, over all, the 'Stars and Stripes'" (83). He returns to where he began in the dedication, proclaiming the power of "Old Flag" to unite his "Countrymen / North, South, East and West" (v). It is here that Wyeth locates both the meaning of Leutze's painting and the meaning of the Capitol as he has attempted to represent it in his guidebook. The meaning—and power, Wyeth hopes—of both the flag as represented in the fresco and the Capitol as represented in the guidebook lies in their symbolic function as markers which true citizens or informed citizen-tourists can recognize. Through this recognition the citizen-tourist affirms the authenticity of the experience (of nationhood and citizenship) and his own position of (interpretive) authority in relation to it.[11]

Wyeth concludes his guidebook to the Capitol with a description of a night session in the Senate. "It is all like looking on at, and hearing a marvellous play, the actors, men who have toiled the best part of their lives to gain this arena wherein to play their parts" (108). Wyeth once again encourages his readers to blur the line between reality and representation, but in this case the point of confusion is precisely the point he wishes to drive home. The meaning of the nation is achieved and affirmed by acts of representation. It is achieved by the political acts of legislators who, in a representative democracy, realize the ideal of rule "by the people," an ideal that exists only as an idea sustained by the people's faith that the few who govern do indeed represent the interests and views of the many who elect them. And it is affirmed by the imaginative acts of citizens who, by participating in a common vision (such as that encouraged by guidebooks to the Capitol), define themselves as "a people," thus preserving the idea and continued existence of the nation.

Inflecting the language of tourism by that of the pilgrimage, nineteenth-century guidebooks to the U.S. Capitol helped to (mass-)produce an idea of the nation and invest it with the power of the sacred. While pilgrimages are typically directed to places where great events have occurred, little had actually happened at the newly rebuilt Capitol featured in the first set of guidebooks. Guidebooks of the 1860s were written in the midst of events that threatened the "sacred" meaning of the Capitol and the nation it represented. The language of pilgrimage employed in these guidebooks thus invested the nation with history while simultaneously urging citizen-tourists to venerate a nation still in the making. The fulfillment of history that justified the language of the sacred lay in the present and in the future, which the gaze of the citizen-tourist helped create. To be a citizen, guidebooks of the nineteenth century insisted, was to see oneself *as* citizen—to become audience and actor in the ongoing drama of nationhood.

Between the approval in 1861 of Leutze's sketch for *Westward the Course of Empire Takes Its Way* and the completion of the mural in 1862, when the Civil War had become a reality, the artist changed the design in ways that significantly altered the relation of the parts to the whole. The most prominent change was the addition, near the center of the picture, of a black man leading a white woman and child seated upon a donkey. From the moment the mural was first unveiled, critics discussed at length the meaning of this group. Anne Brewster, writing for *Lippincott's Magazine* in 1868, reported asking Leutze:

> There is a group almost in the center of your picture—a young Irish woman seated on an ass holding a child—the ass is led by a negro. Did you not mean this group to teach a new gospel to this continent, a new truth which this part of the world is to accept—that the Emigrant and the Freedman are the two great elements which are to be reconciled and worked with? The young, beautiful Irish woman, too, is not she your new Madonna?

Brewster went on to say that Leutze approved of her interpretation: "[H]is eyes fairly laughed with joy at my comprehension of his thoughts. In the first flush of his pleasure he told me I was the first American that had understood his picture."[12]

Whether or not we accept Brewster's interpretation and her account of Leutze's affirmation, there can be no question that Leutze's revisions fundamentally altered the meaning of the mural as a representation of the nation and its future. Not only did the artist insert the black man into the final version of the mural, he also added a boy riding upon one of the oxen carrying "Indian arrows and a bow." The boy serves as the key to another figure in the painting, "a lad who has been wounded, probably in a fight with the Indians," according to Leutze's notes. While the black man is placed at the center of the painting, Indians are not actually present *in* the picture at all; rather, they are represented in the arrows the child carries as a souvenir of the journey, now past, that has brought Americans to this vision of the future. The only Indians Leutze includes are in the margins of the painting, entangled by the unfurling banner proclaiming, "Westward the Course of Empire Takes Its Way." Leutze describes the Indians "creeping and flying" before Union and Liberty, who stand shielded beneath the wings of the American eagle. Leutze concludes the account of his composition with a clear statement of his intention: "To represent as near and truthfully as the artist was able the grand peaceful conquest of the great West." The violence of conquest is erased, leaving barely a trace, except a few arrows for children to play with, souvenirs of a journey nostalgically remembered.

Leutze's mural illustrates—perhaps better than he realized—the meanings of race and nation in American culture during the nineteenth century. With the approach of the Civil War, African-Americans supplanted Indians in the national consciousness as a sign of the guilt and contradictions that unsettled the ideological foundations of American nationhood. But whether placed at the center or margin of the picture, race played a crucial role in constructions of American nationhood—not simply as a principle of alterity against which Americans defined their identity but as a central problem in American culture that threatened to reveal the nation as alienated from itself and its own ideals. This study has traced the insistent and destabilizing presence of "the Indian" in nineteenth-century popular culture—novels, melodramas, captivity narratives, autobiographies, tour guides—in order to show that even when Indians were marginalized, as in Leutze's patriotic art, they continued, through their very exclusion, to frame the meaning of the nation.

NOTES

CHAPTER ONE
THE "INDIAN PROBLEM" AND THE QUESTION
OF NATIONAL IDENTITY

1. "Or, l'essence d'une nation est que tous les individus aient beaucoup de choses en commun et aussi que tous aient oublié bien des choses. . . . Tout citoyen français doit avoir oublié la Saint-Barthélemy, les massacres du Midi au XIIIe siècle." Ernest Renan, (1882) "Qu'est-ce qu'une nation?" Unless otherwise noted, all translations are mine.

2. Over thirty years ago, in *The Return of the Vanishing American*, Leslie Fiedler noted the cultural power of the Indian to "haun[t] all Americans, in their dreams at least if not in their waking consciousness" as the marker of "our profoundest guilt" (Fiedler, 75). Richard Slotkin's monumental three-volume study of the American frontier examines the role of Euro-American violence against Indians in the formation of American national character and literature. But whereas Fiedler and Slotkin explored how the guilt and violence associated with Indian-white relations shaped "the myths which give a special character to art and life in America" (Fiedler, 7), I explore how the particular moral and political problems posed by American Indians during the first half of the nineteenth century participated, at a fundamental level, in the project of U.S. national identity formation and its ultimate ambivalences.

3. Cheryl Walker's recent book examines the intersection of American Indian relations and national formation from a complementary perspective. While I examine American attempts to grapple with the complex challenge posed by "the Indian problem," Walker focuses on the writings of nineteenth-century American Indians and their reflections upon nationhood (10).

4. Brian Dippie makes this argument in his excellent account of changing U.S.-Indian relations throughout the nineteenth century. My understanding of American Indian policy and nineteenth-century American culture has been informed—more deeply than can be reflected in specific citations—by my reading of works by Berkhofer, Dippie, Horsman, Pearce, Prucha, Rogin, Satz, Slotkin, and Washburn.

5. *Annals of Congress*, 15th Cong., 2d sess., 20 January 1819, 639; quoted in Dippie, 8.

6. See Dippie for an extensive and detailed analysis of American responses to the fate of the "Vanishing American."

7. Rogin opens his 1975 study of the Jacksonian era with this quotation.

8. *Correspondence of Andrew Jackson*, 2:279–81; quoted in Prucha 1962, 234.

9. See Foreman on Cherokee removal and resistance. See Satz (48–52) for a good discussion of the publicity surrounding the Cherokee cases and the political motivation behind it.

10. It is for this reason that I have chosen to focus primarily upon political events and cultural productions in the eastern region of the United States.

11. The definition of Indians as neither citizens, nor aliens is articulated in John Marshall's majority opinion in the 1831 Supreme Court case *Cherokee Nation v. Georgia*. See chapter 5 for a full discussion of this case.

12. The essay was originally published as "L'Instance de la lettre dans l'inconscient ou la raison depuis Freud," in *La Psychanalyse* 3 (1957): 47–81. I have chosen to use the translation by Jan Miel in the collection *Structuralism*, edited by Jacques Ehrmann.

13. On the popularity of Indians as the subject of American literature, drama, and art, see Barnett, Dippie, Keiser, and Sears.

14. My language here echoes that of Homi Bhabha. According to Bhabha, there is always a gap between the coherent narrative of national identity and the nation as a process of signification performed by each citizen, whose actual experience never quite fits the "signs of national culture" it supposedly enacts. "It is through this process of splitting," Bhabha argues, "that the conceptual ambivalence of modern society becomes the site of writing the nation" (1994, 145–46).

CHAPTER TWO
COOPER AND THE SOURCES OF AMERICAN NATIONAL IDENTITY

1. Edward Said distinguishes between beginning and origin as follows: "[T]he latter [is] divine, mythical and privileged, the former secular, humanly produced, ceaselessly re-examined" (xiii). I consciously echo Said's language to emphasize the fact that the project of nineteenth-century American nationalism was to make of the nation's historical beginnings a privileged myth of origin.

2. The review, entitled "Literature and Art Among the American Aborigines," originally appeared in the *Southern and Western Magazine* 1 (March 1845): 153–64.

3. John P. McWilliams, Brook Thomas, and, most recently, Charles H. Adams have examined at length the meaning of the law in Cooper's work. These critics are primarily concerned with understanding the function and representation of the law in Cooper's work as it reveals the condition of and attitudes toward the law in nineteenth-century America. While my aims differ somewhat from theirs, I share many of the same assumptions. For example, like Thomas I see literature and law sharing certain basic concerns and strategies: both respond to the historical situation and seek ways to resolve social contradictions through a process of narration; both reflect "the stories a culture tells about itself" (3–6). Informing this scholarship on Cooper and the law is a long critical tradition of viewing Cooper's work as it reflects or engages contemporary political and social issues. See, for example, Fisher, Franklin, McWilliams, Patterson, and Spiller.

I examine *The Pioneers* and *Johnson v. McIntosh* in order to determine how both participate in national identity formation and, in particular, how both deal with the challenges posed by an American history of revolution and conquest. I do not suggest a direct relationship or influence between these two texts. Rather, I attempt to illuminate from two different yet complementary angles a set of historically defined problems. Works that specifically discuss the relationship between *The Pioneers* and *Johnson v. McIntosh* include those by Cheyfitz and Scheckel.

Cheyfitz focuses upon the ways that both texts accomplish the work of dispossessing Indians by utilizing narratives in which Indians "always already" accept Euro-American notions of property. I examine the problem of dispossession in these texts as it impacts national identity formation during the 1820s.

4. *Johnson and Graham's Lessee v. McIntosh* [21 US (8 Wheaton) 543 (1823)].

5. Marshall defined this doctrine as the principle whereby "discovery gave title to the government by whose subjects, or by whose authority, it was made, against all other European governments, which title might be consummated by possession" (Washburn, 4:2538).

6. For further discussion of the debate over natural right as it arose in relation to questions of land rights, see Williams. For a history of natural right rhetoric in American literature, see Zuckert.

7. An anonymous reviewer writing for the *British Critic* [2 (July 1826): 437] noted, "In an infant state of society like that described in *The Pioneers*, the character of the old hunter stands out, as it is intended to do, in bolder relief than any of the other persons, including the beautiful and high-spirited Elizabeth Temple herself. . . . [H]e is the real hero of the scene in which he appears" (quoted in McWilliams, 73). The fact that Natty returns in four more Leather-Stocking Tales indicates Cooper's own recognition of the importance and popularity of this character.

8. For an alternative reading of the resolution that occurs when Judge Temple reads his will aloud in front of the cave, see Adams, 73–74. While Adams acknowledges that Temple acts because of private feeling rather than public law, he emphasizes that it is finally "a legal resolution" (73) that the book achieves. Judge Temple's will, a legal document, returns legitimacy to the law. The "renewed legitimacy" of the law "is synonymous with Edwards' rebirth from anonymity to authority." Since Edwards serves as symbolic heir and father to the nation, the law becomes "'parent' to the nation" (74). My reading differs from Adams's in placing more stress upon motivation. The judge writes the will and thus enacts justice because of personal rather than legal principles. Both Oliver and Judge Temple note that Temple's title to the land is perfectly legal. Temple's will denies him the rights (to the land) that the law sanctions. The judge may be redeemed by the will, but the law is not. The principles that guide the judge toward this act of justice are personal rather than legal. These are the principles that Cooper valorizes. This shift in authority from legal forms toward personal feeling as the basis of stability and legitimacy is important for understanding Cooper's strategy of national legitimation in *The Pioneers*.

9. From this account, Major Effingham's title seems much like that of the plaintiffs in *Johnson v. McIntosh*: a grant obtained directly from the Indians. But a later account by Judge Temple, and the fact that Oliver's father, Edward, appealed to the Crown to reimburse him for the loss of his lands during the Revolutionary War, suggests that Major Effingham's title was officially sanctioned by the Crown.

10. In a later discussion with Elizabeth, even Oliver agrees that it would be foolish—and impossible—to "convert these clearings and farms, again, into hunting-grounds, as the Leather-Stocking would wish to see them" (280). Although

both Oliver and Elizabeth express regret over the fate of the Indians, neither is willing to question the law of progress which informs the visions of America's bright future, which they will inherit.

11. One notable exception was Andrew Jackson. As early as 1817, while serving as military commander in the South, Jackson had denounced the treaty process because it implied that Indian "nations" had the right to decide whether or not to cede their lands to the U.S. government. According to Jackson, "Congress ha[d] full power, by law, to regulate all the concerns of the Indians," including the right to occupy and possess their lands whenever national interest, broadly defined, made this action necessary. See *Correspondence of Andrew Jackson*, 2:279–81; quoted in Prucha 1962, 234.

12. This notion of ownership, which includes all game that lives upon or passes through one's property, is a Euro-American concept wishfully projected onto the Indians, who, in Cooper's account, embrace Euro-American definitions of and battles over property rights. Eric Cheyfitz has argued that *The Pioneers* and *Johnson v. McIntosh* legitimize the usurpation of Indian land by the United States and ultimately "make the Other disappear" by incorporating Indians into a Euro-American narrative of property. I agree that the imposition of Euro-American notions of property does occur in both these texts, but I argue that the work of legitimation is more complex and reaches beyond this strategy.

13. See Clark and Ewart for further discussion of Cooper's writings on the Revolution.

14. Cooper is able to include Indians, the British, and Americans in one family lineage because this kinship remains purely metaphoric. Elsewhere in the Leather-Stocking novels, Cooper makes his attitude toward the actual mixing of races clear. In *The Last of the Mohicans* (1826), for example, Cooper raises the possibility of miscegenation only to suppress it vehemently. Cora, with her fraction of black blood, is rejected as an unsuitable mate for the British officer Duncan Heyward. Cooper rejects the idea of marriage between an Indian and a white woman even more forcefully. He seems able to imagine that only a "white" woman such as Cora, who is already racially impure, could be attractive to an Indian. Furthermore, he never explicitly refers to the possibility of a union between Cora and Uncas until both characters have died, and then it is represented as a misguided notion of the Indians.

The characterization of Natty also reflects Cooper's desire to imagine Americans' metaphoric kinship with Indians at the same time that he denies the possibility of actual kinship through the mixing of Indian and white blood. While Natty embodies the best qualities of both cultures, he is "a man without a cross" who repeatedly insists upon the importance of maintaining the "natural" distinctions between red and white gifts and, even more important, between red and white blood. Similarly, the political rhetoric of the day employed metaphors of kinship—describing Indians as "our red brothers" or "children of the Great Father"—while simultaneously excluding Indians from real political, social, and economic membership in the American "family."

15. Thomas C. Shevory's detailed analysis of Marshall's strategies of legal argument concludes that his "interpretivist" approach to language and law generally

locates a past point of reference from which legal intention is revealed un-problematically. See Shevory (15–73) for a historically detailed analysis of Marshall's interpretive practice in the context of Anglo-American ideas concerning law and language.

16. Critics have frequently noted that during the pigeon hunt Judge Temple appears to violate his stated moral principles. Kelly (23) sees him as a man whose impotence and moral failings disqualify him as an agent of American change. McWilliams (121) cites this scene as evidence of Cooper's belief that strong civil laws are necessary when men such as Judge Temple are capable of violating those very moral laws in which they profess to believe. Motley analyzes at length how shifts in narrative perspective throughout the scene force the reader to "witness the difficulty of transferring Natty's way of seeing nature to democratic society *en masse*" (92).

17. See Adams, Thomas, and McWilliams for excellent discussions of the trial scene in *The Pioneers*.

18. Henry Nash Smith has defined the conflict as a contest between the "old forest freedom" and the needs of the community, which must place the law above the individual. For Smith there is a basic and unresolved conflict in American views of the West (62). Others, such as Adams, Thomas, and McWilliams, identify Natty with natural law and Temple with civil law. In the context of American legal history, they explore the significance of the fact that the conflict is never really resolved. Both Thomas and Adams argue that the conflict between Natty's natural law and Temple's civil law reveals the transition in American law itself from the common-law tradition to a more democratic, instrumental vision of the law. Neither, however, considers at length the links connecting minority rights—in this case, the rights of the dispossessed Indians—the transformation of American law, and questions of national character and legitimacy. Thomas's main concern is to show how the transformation in American law—and Cooper's treatment of it—fostered the development of a capitalist economic system based upon principles of possessive individualism. Of the Indians' dispossession Thomas simply notes, "If Cooper shows that Temple's legal system might have dispossessed the rightful owners of the soil, that act of dispossession is easier to take once we believe that more "natural" souls like Natty and Indian John would prefer dispossessing themselves to compromising with the fallen ways of society" (43). Thomas does not pursue the significance of the questions of morality raised by Temple's uncertain claim to the land. Adams focuses upon problems of legitimation only in relation to the law. He argues that Judge Temple's will effectively bridges the gap between legal form and human motive which continually threatens to undermine the authority of the law. He mentions Indian rights only briefly (in a footnote) when asserting that Oliver's adopted Indian heritage ensures that "the historicity of both aboriginal and European laws coincide to sanction the inheritance that Cooper confers" (71), but he does not explore the implications or limits of Cooper's invocation of Indian rights. Adams accepts Cooper's simplified resolution (in terms of inheritance) to the much more complex problem of Indian dispossession. Both Thomas and Adams, in fact, follow Cooper's lead in allowing the problem of Indian dispossession to be absorbed and displaced by Euro-American conflicts.

19. Even more curious is the fact that no critics have commented upon Chingachgook's castration or its significance.

20. Thomas Philbrick has noted (593) that Oliver's double lineage makes him heir both to his father's legal claim and to the Indians' moral claim to the land. While true, this does not resolve the questions of national morality Cooper raises throughout the text; instead, such an interpretation follows Cooper's lead in allowing Oliver's legitimacy to stand in for the nation's.

21. My discussion of mourning throughout this section draws upon Sigmund Freud's study of mourning and melancholia. For a different analysis of the grave scene, see Thomas H. Schaub, who focuses on the thematic implications of the distinction between the written and spoken word as illustrated here.

22. In *The Prairie* (1827), which Cooper envisioned as the last novel in the Leather-Stocking series, Natty is finally laid in the grave. As Richard Slotkin has argued persuasively (111), at the time Cooper was writing *The Prairie* it was generally believed that the end of the frontier had been reached: the Great Plains seemed to represent a permanent barrier to further agrarian expansion and the Far West had not yet been opened for American settlement. Once the historical process of settlement, which Natty served even as he resisted it, has come to an end, Natty's existence and function become part of history. It is fitting that Natty is buried among the Indians on the "Great American Prairies," which, Cooper believed, would also be "the final gathering place of the red men" (1827, vii). For Cooper this is the place where the closing chapter in the history of American expansion occurred.

23. Natty's exclusion from actual participation in the march of "progress" helps to preserve the moral purity that contributes to his authority as hero. Philbrick has noted the ways in which Judge Temple's "position [of authority] is undercut by the principle of change that his whole life has served" (592). Unlike the judge, who actively presides over (and is somewhat tainted by) a period of rapid change, Natty serves as a catalyst, enabling change without being involved in the process itself.

24. See the epigraph at the head of chapter 1; for the French original, see note 1.

25. See also Homi K. Bhabha's reflections upon the significance of tense in Renan's formulation (1994, 160–61).

CHAPTER THREE
DOMESTICATING THE DRAMA OF CONQUEST

1. The enduring popularity and power of Pocahontas in American culture has been the subject of much reflection and scholarship. Philip Young's 1962 article represents one of the best attempts to make sense of what Rayna Green has called "the Pocahontas Perplex." Young locates the popularity of this "magical and moving explanation of our national origins" in its archetypal elements (392). He demonstrates its similarity to other legends popular in many lands and across several centuries, all of which follow the same general structure: adventurer becomes a captive and is rescued by the king's beautiful daughter, who gives up home and father for him (409). "The story will work for any culture," Young

NOTES TO CHAPTER THREE **159**

concludes, "informing us, whoever we are, that we are chosen or preferred" (413). Green's analysis focuses upon the legacy of Pocahontas as a "metaphor for Indian-White experience" and as a stereotype which American Indian women still live with (714). Both of these works discuss Pocahontas in very general terms, moving quickly to the archetypal structure of the story or the portrayal of *the* Indian woman in it; they do not concern themselves with exploring how any single version of the story actually functions as narrative or how it participates in the particular historical moment of its telling. For overviews of the Pocahontas story in American literature, see William Jenkins and Robert S. Tilton. Tilton's book is the most thorough study to date of Pocahontas's various appearances and persistent popularity in American culture, but its scope makes it difficult to develop a detailed reading of any given Pocahontas narrative it describes. (Tilton's discussion of all the Pocahontas plays occupies only four pages.)

2. On the authenticity of Smith's original account, see Lemay, Mossiker, and Williamson.

3. At a banquet honoring an American theatrical manager, one enthusiast of a national drama made a toast to "the Genius of Liberty and the Liberty of Genius," *Boston Weekly Magazine*, 18 December 1824, 158. See Grimsted (137–70) for a discussion of nineteenth-century attitudes toward a national drama.

4. Dunlap, who managed the Park Theatre in New York from 1798 to 1805 and wrote over sixty plays, is often identified as the first professional dramatist in America. As playwright, producer, critic, and historian, Dunlap exerted a powerful force shaping early American drama. See Meserve (1977, 102–9) for a brief account of Dunlap's career.

5. Because of its emphasis on moral and psychological legibility, the melodrama, which Dunlap helped to popularize in the United States during the early years of the nineteenth century, was especially well crafted to achieve the kind of emotional power he urges. Dunlap translated and produced several melodramas on the New York stage, including *The Voice of Nature* (1803) by L. C. Caigniez and *The Wife of Two Husbands* (1804) by Guilbert de Pixérécourt, in addition to a melodrama of his own entitled *Fontainville Abbey* (1795).

6. Dunlap's attitude toward the theater in many ways resembles the late-eighteenth-century notion that oratory is the most powerful means of reaching men's "common sense" of understanding and moving them to action. See Fliegelman for a penetrating analysis of theatricality as it pervaded the rhetoric and ideology of the Revolution.

7. "An Act to Prevent Stage Plays and other Theatrical Entertainment," quoted in "A Brief Account of the Boston Stage," *Boston Weekly Magazine*, 30 November 1816, 29.

8. On the class structure of theater audiences and the physical space of the theater, see Grimsted (52–59); on the changing class and gender composition of theater audiences, see Butsch and McConachie. For a discussion of riots, including the famous Astor Place riot of 1849, see Grimsted (65–73) and Moody 1958.

9. For an example of such antitheatrical arguments, see "On the Effects of Theatrical Exhibitions," *Weekly Magazine*, 21 April 1798, 357–62.

10. Such fears can be contrasted with the attitudes of the founders toward the

theatricality of public oratory. Fliegelman has argued that the founders envisioned the direct emotional appeal of oratory—the same kind of emotional appeal that many critics of the theater saw as dangerous—to lie at the very core of the workings of democracy. With commonsense faith in the moral sensibilities of all men, the ability of oratory, or performance in general, to move an audience was seen as a powerful and reliable means of encouraging men to recognize truth and act upon it. The fear that such power could be misused had always been present, but as the nineteenth century progressed and faith in man's innate morality waned, such fears grew.

11. See Grimsted (137–70), Benjamin T. Spencer (25–72), and, more recently, Gary A. Richardson for further discussion of nineteenth-century attitudes toward the national drama.

12. "The Drama," *The Albion* (New York), 13 January 1827, 248.

13. These reviews are quoted in Grimsted (59). See also McConachie (20–29) for a discussion of theater architecture and questions of class.

14. "The Drama," *The National Register* (Washington, D.C.) 10 April 1819, 225–27.

15. "The Drama," *The Critic* (New York), 22 November 1828, 62.

16. For overviews of nineteenth-century plays about Indians see Jones, Sears, and Wilmeth.

17. Odell refers not only to Indian characters in plays but also to the popular practice of bringing Indians to the theater either to view plays or to perform "authentic" war dances between shows (3:370–71).

18. Popularity is measured here by the number of plays on the subject. According to theater historian Montrose Moses, "numberless dramas . . . grew up around the character of Pocahontas" (569–70). Only five of the Pocahontas plays, written between 1808 and 1855, have survived. The single most popular Indian drama was *Metamora; or, the Last of the Wampanoags* (1829), by John Augustus Stone.

19. Smith's *Generall Historie* (1624) was the original source for the story of Pocahontas's act of courage. The fact that Smith did not mention this incident in such earlier writings as *A True Relation* (1608) and *Proceedings . . . of the Colony* (1612) has cast suspicion on its authenticity. Whether true or not, the story was retold several times by later historians. John Davis was the first author to develop the romantic potential of the plot by suggesting that love motivated Pocahontas to save Smith. See Tilton for a thorough account of the different versions of this cultural myth.

20. The first play dealing with Indians in America was *Le Père-Indian* (1753), written by Le Blanc de Villeneuve, an officer stationed at the French colony of New Orleans. It was never performed professionally. The Englishwoman Anne Kemble Hatton wrote an opera entitled *Tammany; or, The Indian Chief* which was first produced in New York in 1794. Major Robert Rogers's *Ponteach; or, The Savages of America* (1766) was the first play on an Indian theme to be written by someone born in the colonies, but it was never produced. Barker's play was first performed on April 6, 1808, in Philadelphia. In a letter to William Dunlap, Barker noted: "It has since been frequently acted in, I believe, all the theatres of the United States" (quoted in Dunlap, 379).

21. On the role of feeling in the national drama, see also Thespis, "Morality of the Stage—No. I," *The Correspondent* (New York), 10 March 1827, 100–102. This reviewer describes what might be termed a form of sentimental patriotism: "The sight of a hero, bleeding in the cause of his country, inspires us with courage; and, what is more, the misfortunes of the brave, the virtuous, and the innocent, teach us to feel and to weep; and of society, it is of no small consequence to humanize the mind of man, and render the heart tender and susceptible of these impressions."

22. See Annette Kolodny's landmark study (1975) of the history and implications of the "land as woman" metaphor in American literature. For more recent discussions of this metaphor in colonialist rhetoric, see Hulme and Zantop, both of whose works touch upon the Pocahontas story.

23. It is difficult to define with rigid consistency the generic conventions of stage melodrama. The word "mélodrame," meaning a drama accompanied by music, was first used by Jean-Jacques Rousseau in 1774 to describe a play which mixed soliloquy, pantomime, and musical accompaniment. The heightened emotional expressivity such plays achieved, along with the principle of hybridity itself, remain the most stable characteristics of stage melodrama. Because of its tendency to mix established genres such as comedy and tragedy, the melodrama was often referred to as illegitimate drama. The connotations of this label went beyond the form's violation of generic boundaries to include its association with the radical democratic politics of the postrevolutionary period in which it developed in France.

While individual melodramas vary greatly and exceptions can be found to any of the rules one might formulate, some of the most common conventions of the stage melodrama include: an aesthetic of heightened expressivity produced by music, tableaux vivants, and exaggerated gestures; a plot centered upon a clearly defined struggle between good and evil; and a hero or heroine whose virtue, after much persecution, emerges as triumphant in the end. The melodramatic heroine, whose virtue is typically defined in terms of sexual purity and filial piety, is usually passive and vulnerable; it is up to Fate or the melodramatic hero to relieve her suffering. At the end of the play virtue is recognized and vindicated, while evil is vanquished and expelled.

This brief description owes much to the work of Brooks, Grimsted, and Mason. While Brooks has been critized for his ahistorical, psychoanalytic approach to melodrama, I find his account of melodrama's emergence out of the specific political and social conditions of postrevolutionary France to be quite relevant to an understanding of American melodrama in the early nineteenth century. See Elaine Hadley and the collection of essays edited by Michael Hays and Anastasia Nikolopoulou for good examples of recent scholarship that considers melodrama not simply as a reified genre but as a historically specific, culturally embedded mode of production and critique.

24. Fliegelman includes a diagram and provides an interesting discussion of the proposed seal, including excerpts from the committee's report (160–64).

25. This pattern was not always rigid; occasionally the woman might take the initiative in order to influence the course of events, but only in a crisis, after which she would return to her customary passive, domestic state. Pocahontas

assumes the role of active heroine repeatedly in the play, saving first Smith and then the colony. Since the play ends with marriage, we never see Pocahontas assume a passive, domestic role.

26. An anonymous document attached to Smith's *Map of Virginia* suggests that "if he [Smith] would he might have married her [Pocahontas]" (Smith [1612], 1:274; quoted by Williamson, 373). In a letter to Queen Anne Smith suggested that Pocahontas might have been motivated by "affection" for him (Smith [1624], 2:259). See Williamson (374) for a discussion of the popular interpretation of this and other sources as evidence for romantic love between Pocahontas and Smith. Readers and viewers of the story consistently considered it a major flaw of the romantic plot that Pocahontas actually married Rolfe rather than Smith. Tilton (32–33) discusses John Davis's popular early-nineteenth-century versions of the Pocahontas story, which presented her motive as romantic love for Smith.

27. Lydia Sigourney's popular poem "Pocahontas" (1841) similarly generalizes Pocahontas's love for Rolfe into love for the Euro-American values he represents:

> Yet love, to her fair breast was but a name
> For kindling knowledge, and for taste refined
> A guiding lamp, whose bright mysterious flame
> Led on to loftier heights the aspiring mind.   (stanza 33)

Sigourney's characterization of Pocahontas also stresses the virtues that would identify her as a true woman according to nineteenth-century American middle-class standards. Lesley Ferris has noted how mid-nineteenth-century conceptions of the true woman intersect with the conventions of melodrama in the stock figure of the virtuous woman, "a figure who combines a mixture of age-old views and prejudices with a more modern, secular vision of the purity and goodness that restore moral order" (87).

28. The reader should here recall the distinction Said draws between beginning and origin—"the latter [is] divine, mythical and privileged, the former secular, humanly produced, ceaselessly re-examined" (xiii)—and Benedict Anderson's argument that the idea of the nation must be rooted in a mythic and "immemorial" rather than simply a historical past. For a detailed discussion of these ideas, see chapter 2.

29. Krupat (1992, 135–44) reads the Removal Act of 1830 in light of these complementary generic and rhetorical strategies.

30. This argument is deeply informed by Hayden White's extensive work on history as narrative.

31. Murray H. Nelligan briefly discusses the *Globe* incident. See Bank for a provocative reading of this performance.

32. Eric Lott has explored how blackface minstrelsy during the nineteenth century illuminated such questions of race, identity, and authenticity. See especially Lott's account of popular challenge dance contests in which white blackface performers would challenge other whites. The "Imitation Dance" of African-American performer Juba (William Henry Lane), which was popular in the mid-1840s, represented an exception to the standard white domination of racial representation. An 1845 playbill described the performance as follows: "The en-

tertainment to conclude with the Imitation Dance, by Mast. Juba, in which he will give correct Imitation Dances of all the principle [*sic*] [blackface] Ethiopian Dancers in the United States. After which he will give an imitation of himself— and then you will see the vast difference between those that have heretofore attempted dancing and this WONDERFUL YOUNG MAN" (uncatalogued playbills in Harvard Theater Collection; quoted in Lott, 115). Even as it acknowledges the superior authenticity of the black man's performance, the playbill underscores the fact that the notion of authenticity by which Juba is measured is constructed by whites, thus leaving the "authentic" black man no option but to enact an "imitation of himself." By imagining the Cherokee delegation entering into a challenge dance contest with whites, the white audiences of *Pocahontas* imposed upon the Cherokees their own definitions of "authentic" Indian character. As Bank has pointed out, John Ross was quick to counter with an alternative version of "Indian" identity (68). In chapter 5 I will explore more fully, in connection with the Sauk chief Black Hawk, how the very notion of authenticity itself can be made to perform the work of subjugation.

33. In fact, both Barker and Custis distort history significantly, for Rolfe did not arrive with the first Virginia Company colonists (which included Smith) in 1607.

34. Custis rearranges the historical record considerably to accomplish this, moving up the war that occurred after several years at the Jamestown settlement to just days after Smith's arrival in Virginia.

35. Pocock's seminal work traces the path, via Machiavelli and the English Whigs, by which classical republican theory influenced American political thought. Bernard Bailyn and Gordon Wood provide extensive and illuminating discussions of republican thought in early American history.

36. See Appleby and Hartz on the development of liberal thought in early America. Gould, McCoy, and Watts provide good discussions of the synthesis of liberal and republican values. See also the collection of essays edited by Klein et al.

37. Ruth Bloch has traced the evolution of the gendered meaning of virtue. Gould (23–29) discusses this change in the context of early American history and culture. See also Elizabeth J. Hinds for a book-length study of gender and virtue in the fiction of Charles Brockden Brown.

38. See Dippie on the pervasiveness of this particular version of "the vanishing American" in American culture. See Jones, Sears, and Wilmeth (1989) for discussions of the motif of "the dying Indian" on the popular stage.

39. John Augustus Stone's play *Metamora, or The Last of the Wampanoags* (1829), the most popular Indian play in the nineteenth century, features a hero who is similarly defiant and noble. Several critics have noted that Metamora is the embodiment of nineteenth-century ideals of American character, but they provide a different explanation of the significance of this fact and the contradictions it raises. McConachie (91–118) identifies in Metamora a series of binaries that remain unsynthesized: republican and liberal values; egalitarian and charismatic authority; history and utopia. He locates the power of *Metamora* in its hortatory style, which produced a "generalized patriotic ritual" (116) that subsumed its ideological contradictions. According to Jeffrey D. Mason, Metamora's function

as the embodiment of American values is related to the fact that a white man (Edwin Forrest) played the role of the Indian. This produced a double vision which let the audience embrace the "mythic Indian" while abusing real Indians. Mason concludes that "[this] version of the mythic Indian set a standard that no actual native—indeed no person of any background—could hope to match, and so vindicated both nostalgia and removal" (59). Mason fails to note that the melodramatic portrayal of the Indian as American hero also produces a version of the mythic *American* that "no person of any background . . . could hope to match."

Although both of these critics note the extent to which "the American," as presented on the popular stage, was defined as a masculine subject position, they do not explore how masculine and feminine stereotypes and values combined in these popular melodramas to justify American Indian policy while simultaneously producing nineteenth-century notions of the citizen and the nation. With their focus upon heroic male and female characters, the Pocahontas plays offer a richer opportunity than that provided by *Metamora* to explore such questions.

40. This creative synthesis differs slightly in its contours from the rebublican synthesis discussed by Klein, McCoy, and Watts, who tend to align individualism more closely with liberalism.

CHAPTER FOUR
MARY JEMISON AND THE DOMESTICATION
OF THE AMERICAN INDIANS

1. Page references to the Jemison narrative throughout the chapter refer to the twenty-second edition, which contains the original 1824 text together with all changes and additions made by later editors.

2. On 5 April 1758, Jemison was captured by a raiding party consisting of six Shawnee Indians and four Frenchmen and was forcibly taken from her family farm ten miles north of what is now Gettysburg in south-central Pennsylvania. She was given to the Senecas within a few days. For a detailed account of the chronological and geographical facts of the Jemison captivity, see Namias (1992, 3–33).

3. For detailed accounts of the narrative's publication history, see the appendix of the twenty-second edition or Namias (1992, 1993). Mott's discussion of American best-sellers places the Jemison narrative's popularity in context: in 1824 it outsold the novels of Cooper and Scott; between 1823 and 1827 only four works sold over one hundred thousand copies: three novels by Cooper (*The Pioneers, The Last of the Mohicans,* and *The Prairie*) and Seaver's Jemison narrative. Pearce's statement on the waning popularity of the captivity narrative is in some sense substantiated by Mott's statistics: between 1680 and 1720 three out of the four best-sellers were captivity narratives, whereas between 1823 and 1827 only one out of four best-sellers was a captivity narrative. Still, as the example of the Jemison narrative indicates, it is dangerous to generalize that the genre as a whole had lost cultural significance. Pearce does not account for the popularity of the Jemison narrative, which lasted for over a century as it went through twenty-three editions.

It is also worth noting that in two of the other three best-sellers between 1823 and 1827 (*The Last of the Mohicans* and *The Prairie*) captivity is central to plot and theme. Several other popular novels of the period, such as Lydia Maria Child's *Hobomok* (1824) and Catherine Maria Sedgwick's *Hope Leslie* (1827), also feature marriage between a white woman and an Indian.

4. Given the book's great popularity, it seems surprising that it was not widely reviewed. The only notice I have found in a major nineteenth-century literary magazine is a review of the fourth edition (1857). The reviewer stresses the usefulness of the book as history: "Finally, the book must be considered as not only very desirable for its truthful narrative, but as a record of events connected with the settlement and progress of civilization in Western New-York that ought to be found in every library" (*The Knickerbocker* 49 [March 1857]: 305–6). Other books on Indian and/or American history written at the time, such as Drake's *Indian Biography* (1832) and Parkman's *Conspiracy of Pontiac* (1851), were widely reviewed. But these authors were well known and the history they addressed was broader in scope than the necessarily limited history witnessed and reported by one old woman in western New York. The reviewer, in fact, praises the 1857 editor for providing more general information in the form of a glossary of Indian names and places which, he believes, "materially enhances the interest of the work" (306). Thus, it would appear that the Jemison narrative was not considered by the literary establishment to be serious literature or history. This does not change the fact that the public bought and read the book enthusiastically or alter its importance to the student of nineteenth-century American culture; it simply helps to clarify how nineteenth-century readers and critics viewed the book.

5. Gary Ebersole (98–143) provides an excellent analysis of these captivity novels as they progressed toward sentimentalism during the eighteenth century. See also Ellison for an illuminating reading of Bleecker's novel in the context of late-eighteenth-century notions of sensibility.

6. June Namias's 1993 study examines a wide range of captivity narratives published in the United States from the seventeenth to the late nineteenth centuries. Her main concern as a historian is to examine the narratives for what they reveal about "how Euro-Americans thought about gender and sexuality when confronted by a foreign enemy of another color and culture" (9) rather than to trace developments in the genre or its popularity. Jenny Franchot's *Roads to Rome* expands notions of the cultural significance of the captivity narrative during the nineteenth century by showing how the genre was enlisted to express anti-Catholicism. Franchot's analysis of popular nineteenth-century convent captivity narratives is illuminating for what it reveals about the structure and power of the captivity narrative in general. Among more recent scholars, Gary Ebersole has explored most directly and extensively the changing forms, context, popularity and cultural power of the captivity narrative in the United States from the seventeenth century to the present.

7. On the conventions of sentimental literature, see the studies by Herbert R. Brown and Jane Tompkins. For a wide-ranging consideration of the meaning and uses of sentiment in nineteenth-century American culture, see the collection of essays edited by Shirley Samuels.

8. In the "Preface to the Reader," Ter Amicum (most likely Mather writing under a pseudonym) presents Rowlandson as a figure representing the Puritan community, itself figured typologically as "Judea Capta." Slotkin, drawing upon this and other uses of the captivity narrative as a theme in American literature, identifies it as part of a larger myth of "American" identity. In this reading the captive again stands for the nation or culture as a whole.

9. There has been much scholarly debate in recent years regarding the use of the term "frontier." Mary Louise Pratt, for example, has defined the space of colonial encounter as a "contact zone" rather than a colonial "frontier," a term which she sees as grounded within a European expansionist perspective since "the frontier" is a frontier only in respect to Europe (6–7). Annette Kolodny (1992) and Arnold Krupat (1985, 1992) similarly conceive of the frontier as a space of contact and exchange where new hybrids are formed, while Amy Kaplan warns that such visions of the frontier as an implicitly neutral zone or space of contact risk overlooking the imperialist violence and power struggles that occurred there (15). I use the term "frontier" to designate the space of cultural contact defined geographically, conceptually and/or textually. Far from ignoring the power struggles and violence that so often characterize cultural contact, I intend to explore the complex dynamics of such struggles and the means by which they are culturally rationalized and inscribed.

10. See Fiedler for a discussion of what he sees as a defining paradigm in American literature.

11. John Gast's painting *American Progress* (1872) is an excellent example of such symbolic deployment of the white woman to represent (American) civilization. Patricia Hills provides an excellent discussion of this painting (97–148).

12. John Sekora has provided some particularly interesting reflections on this problem in relation to slave narrative, but virtually all scholars of the genre have had to deal with the question of textual authority. H. David Brumble, Ann E. Goldman, Arnold Krupat, Genaro Padilla, and Hertha Wong have also explored at length the textual and political dynamics of autobiographies produced through the collaboration of a nonliterate, speaking subject and an amanuensis or editor belonging to another culture.

13. See, for example, Doty, James H. Smith, and Van Dorn. The Letchworth State Park Museum in New York has a collection of materials on Jemison.

14. June Namias and Susan Walsh do an excellent job of situating Jemison in the context of Seneca culture and traditions. Although recognition of the influence of Seneca cultural and narrative traditions is important to illuminate aspects of the narrative's structure and Jemison's perspective, to view the narrative or Jemison herself only in terms of Seneca culture is to miss much of the complexity and power of the narrative and Jemison's cultural position. See Walsh and Oakes for interpretations of the Jemison narrative as Native American autobiography.

15. It also underscores the differences between the colonialist and post-colonialist models Bhabha draws upon and the American situation in which "the Indian" simultaneously represented a nostalgically idealized symbol of a distinctively American (postcolonial) identity and the (internally) colonized other.

16. For a suggestive discussion of cultural hybridity, see Robert Young's study. AnaLouise Keating's discussion of "threshold identities" is also quite relevant.

17. Castiglia notes that many captives continued to write "beyond the ending," describing their life after restoration in terms that did not always compare favorably with their captive state; such narratives performed a powerful cultural critique. Castiglia also argues that most scholars have overemphasized and thus reimposed the conventions of the captivity narrative. According to Castiglia, instability or subversion of conventions is common among captivity narratives and represents an important aspect of their power. I agree with Castiglia about the danger of standardizing *the* captivity narrative, but I also wish to emphasize that Jemison's narrative was extremely unusual. Castiglia notes only three examples of narratives "by" or about captives who did not return to Euro-American society. Of these, Eunice Williams (1707) did not write or tell her own story and Frances Slocum (1842) continued to live with her adopted tribe (Delaware) throughout her life; only Jemison's narrative is actually narrated from a position between Euro-American and Indian worlds.

18. Such interpretations generally draw upon Victor Turner's account of liminality and the *rite de passage*.

19. Far from feeling a sense of common ground and mutual understanding with Seaver and the white culture he represents, Mary Jemison is so uncomfortable and wary about sharing her story that she will not speak unless her friend and lawyer Thomas Clute is present in the room. This also suggests that with the aid of Clute Jemison was in a position to exercise a certain degree of narrative control.

20. Jemison's double vision, coupled with the double perspective of Jemison and Seaver, create a quality in the Jemison text similar to what M. M. Bakhtin describes in terms of the dialogical. Michelle Burnham applies the ideas of Bakhtin to the captivity narrative of Mary Rowlandson. Burnham identifies a deep "structural dissonance" in the Rowlandson narrative "between her orthodox Puritan belief that the Indians are savage and cruel heathens and her portrayal of individual Indians who are sympathetic and human." Rowlandson's own double "voice," reflecting the "altered cultural subjectivity" produced by prolonged contact with her Algonquin captors, generates the dialogism of the narrative (61). This dialogism is somewhat different from that of the Jemison narrative since it depends upon a gap between Rowlandson's experience among the Indians and an unwavering adherence to Puritan culture and values. Jemison's doubleness, on the other hand, arises from a self-identification with two cultures; in addition, the Rowlandson narrative does not include the voice of editor/collaborator to the same extent as the Jemison narrative.

21. Jemison here enters a long tradition of Indian women mythologized as benevolent mediators between Native and Euro-American cultures. The list includes Pocahontas, Sacagewea, and Doña Marina. See chapter 3 for a further discussion of this particular type of colonial fantasy.

22. Such appendixes were common in Indian ethnographic texts published at this time. Mary Louise Pratt points out that even frontier romances of the period tended to include a good deal of ethnographic information. She sees such attempts to memorialize Indian manners and customs as part of a "normalizing discourse whose work is to codify difference, to fix the Other in a timeless presence where all 'his' actions are repetitions of 'his' normal habits" (121).

23. See Heard and Namias (1993) on the question of rape among north-eastern tribes. See Lewis on nineteenth-century representations of captive rape. Joy Kasson's discussion of the popularity of Erastus Dow Palmer's sculpture *The White Captive* (1859) also illuminates nineteenth-century attitudes toward Indians as a sexual threat.

24. Henry Nash Smith (81–120) discusses the popularity of Western heroes, such as mountain men (1830s–1870s) and female Amazon characters (1860s–1870s), who violate conventional mores and inhabit the West as a realm of lawlessness and freedom from social restraint. Smith believes that the movement toward such unconventional heroes marks "a progressive deterioration in the Western story as a genre," a loss of "ethical and social meaning" (119). The presence of such unconventional elements in the person of Mary Jemison, whom Seaver nevertheless defines as a hero in quite conventional terms, shows that mainstream and subversive elements may be more closely intertwined than Smith's analysis suggests, and that the unconventional is not necessarily devoid of "ethical and social meaning." David Reynolds examines a broad range of literature, both popular and elite, to explore a variety of ways in which subversive writings can relate to more conventional forms.

25. Cass's and McKenney's articles appeared in the *North American Review* (January 1826) and the *National Intelligencer* 26 (April 1825), respectively. In his book-length study of Hunter, Richard Drinnon discusses the narrative as the site of national rivalry.

26. For a full discussion of the causes and significance of this theory during the nineteenth century, see Dippie (3–78). Frank E. Farley provides an interesting account of literary representations of "the dying Indian."

27. Namias (1992) describes some of the changes and additions made by later editors. The twenty-second edition includes them all.

28. It is difficult to believe that Jemison, who had been separated from her family (of Irish descent) since childhood, would still speak with a noticeable Irish accent. The fact that Seaver singles out this detail in his brief description of Jemison suggests that he considers it important for understanding her character. During the nineteenth century, even before the great waves of Irish immigrants resulting from the famine years of the late forties and early fifties, the Irish were associated with poverty and Catholicism and were viewed suspiciously as socially marginal, unwelcome additions to the American population. They were considered racially inferior in the sense that they were looked upon as ignorant, idle, childlike, lacking self-control, and fond of drink. In 1830, for example, one schoolbook even quoted an anecdote by Robert Bruce in which the Irish were referred to as "barbarians." The emphasis upon Jemison's Irish descent could thus be read as another indication of Seaver's difficulty in "placing" her. His solution here seems to be to situate Jemison in a somewhat marginal position in white society without denying her identity as a white woman. For a discussion of attitudes toward the Irish in the nineteenth century, see Elson (124–28), Knobel (82–99), and Wiebe (335–37). Roediger (133–63) explores nineteenth-century attitudes toward the Irish and African-Americans and their role in the racial formation of whiteness in the United States.

29. Namias (1992, 38) points out this important fact. While she sees this 1842

edition as the beginning of attempts to "whitewash" Jemison, I feel this change in the title page simply calls greater attention to what is already clearly present in the original text.

30. Idealized visions of home and motherhood were embraced and promoted in the United States during the nineteenth century as the foundation of cultural values and stability. For good accounts of nineteenth-century American domestic ideology, see the studies by Nancy Cott, Lora Romero, Jane Tompkins, and Barbara Welter. A large body of scholarship shows that such ideals only matched the experiences of members of a certain class and racial group. Gillian Brown has questioned the extent to which women's and men's spheres were ever truly separate or separable. Aside from the issues of its truth or exclusivity, the mere existence of a popular discourse that promoted certain domestic values as universal helps to explain how such values might structure the Jemison narrative.

I am not arguing that the emphasis on home and motherhood in the Jemison narrative is entirely a product of the editors' manipulation. There is good reason to believe that the story Jemison actually told placed strong emphasis on domestic and family matters. Jemison was, after all, speaking as a woman whose struggles to raise and care for her children required great effort. And it is not surprising that a woman whose home and family had been violently disrupted at age fifteen would place great value on both throughout her later life. The emphasis on home and family in the narrative, then, may very well be the result of a confluence of motives between narrator and editors.

31. Seaver's insistence upon incorporating the Seneca into nineteenth-century, middle-class American gender roles is dramatically revealed in the appendix entitled "Of Family Government." He blatantly misrepresents Jemison's account of gender roles in the matrilineal Seneca society—which gave significant social, political, and economic power to women—instead revealing his own cultural biases and ideological agenda: "One thing respecting the Indian women is worthy of attention, and perhaps of imitation, although it is now a days considered beneath the dignity of the ladies, especially those who are the most refined; and that is, they are under a becoming subjection to their husbands" (171).

32. A picture of this statue, sculpted by H. K. Bush-Brown, serves as the frontispiece to the twenty-second edition of the Jemison narrative.

33. See Scheick for a discussion of nineteenth-century Americans' racial identification of "half-bloods" as Indians.

34. Parkman, *Conspiracy of Pontiac*; quoted in Rogin 1975, 115).

35. Linda Kerber explores at length the social roles of women in the new Republic. The roles Kerber ascribes to "the republican mother" were incorporated and expanded in nineteenth-century domestic ideology. Eva Cherniavsky offers an incisive reassessment of republican motherhood.

36. Monroe's message is reprinted in Richardson, 2:281–82. Lucy Maddox has explored at length the logic of "civilization or extinction" as it informed nineteenth-century Indian policy and literary production. Whereas Maddox stresses this reasoning as the dominant response to the Indian question during the first half of the nineteenth century, I argue that it was simply one of several strategies by which Americans attempted to define and rationalize the status and rights of Indians in the United States.

37. Mary E. Young discusses the gendered meanings of allotment for nineteenth-century Americans. According to T. Hartley Crawford, Van Buren's Commissioner of Indian affairs, "at the foundation of the whole system lies individual property. It is perhaps nine times in ten, the stimulus that manhood first feels" (1838; quoted by Young, 99). While Crawford briefly attempted to enlist the ideology of domestic feminism in the service of the "civilizing" project, he did so by educating Indian women in domestic skills and sensibilities rather than by reimagining the "civilized" Indian (of both sexes) in feminized terms, as the Jemison narrative implicitly does. For a further discussion of the policy of allotment, see Dippie (141–76) and Prucha (1976).

38. Joseph E. Brown, *Congressional Record*, 46th Cong., 3d sess., 24 January 1881, 879 (quoted in Dippie, 163).

39. These statistics are drawn from a report to Congress by Edgar Howard, *Congressional Record*, 73rd Cong., 2d sess., 15 June 1934, 11726; quoted in Dippie, 314.

40. Roy Harvey Pearce has pointed out other contradictions undermining the policy of Indian removal. He argues that removal policy was actually premised upon an idea of "savagism" that precluded the possibility of ever "civilizing" the Indian. Defined as the antithesis of the "civilized," the "savage" belonged to a completely different order, with its own set of virtues and vices, and thus could never be incorporated into the "civilized" order. Removal or extinction were the only logical consequences of such a vision (1953, 48–58).

41. My understanding of the Jemison narrative and the "cultural work" it performs is indebted to Philip Fisher's account of popular literature. He discusses the power of popular literature to stabilize new and disturbing realities—what he terms "hard facts"—of social experience (19). According to Fisher, the predictable, often formulaic, narrative conventions of popular literary forms help to make complex issues seem simple and new experience seem familiar (20).

CHAPTER FIVE
BLACK HAWK'S *LIFE*

1. While he did not plan to start a war, Black Hawk did explore his military options in case hostilities broke out. When the Winnebago Prophet assured Black Hawk that neighboring tribes and the British government would support him, Black Hawk was prepared to respond to any attack by the Americans with force. However, after discovering that the Winnebago Prophet's assurances of assistance were unfounded, Black Hawk realized that a war would be futile and determined simply to occupy his village and fields as an act of protest until the U.S. government sent troops to force him out. Until such time that fighting actually began, Black Hawk did not believe that the Americans would dare to attack since they were bound by the Treaty of Ghent (which ended the War of 1812) to respect the rights of all Indians behaving peaceably. See Wallace (40–51) for a thorough analysis of Black Hawk's rationale and motivation for returning to his village.

2. Wallace provides the best account of the Black Hawk War and events leading up to it; see also Eby. For accounts of Black Hawk's tour as a prisoner of war,

see Drake (193–96), Eby (262–80), and Donald Jackson's introduction to Black Hawk's autobiography.

3. John B. Patterson was born in Virginia in 1806. He came to Illinois in 1832 to visit his relatives, the wealthy Davenport family of Rock Island. When the publisher of the local newspaper left to fight in the Black Hawk War, Patterson took over the *Galenian*. He also worked for a time as a clerk in George Davenport's Rock Island commercial establishment before starting his own newspaper, the *Spectator*, in 1848. For further information on Patterson, see Allaman and the anonymous *History of Mercer and Henderson Counties*.

4. According to Rourke, these treaties, which were "set down in amplitude as early as 1677," were essentially "chronicle plays—recording what was said in the parleys, including bits of action, the exchanges of gifts, of wampum, the smoking of pipes, the many ceremonials with dances, cries and choral songs. Even the printed form of the treaties was dramatic: the participants were listed like a cast of characters, and precise notations were made as to ceremonial action" (61–62). See also Drummond and Moody.

5. A good illustration of Jackson's reasoning can be found in *Correspondence of Andrew Jackson*, 2:279–81; quoted in Prucha 1962, 234.

6. Arnold Krupat provides a detailed rhetorical analysis of the Removal Act of 1830 (1992, 129–44). According to him, the maintenance of Indian free will in the provisions of the act was crucial in the sense that it enabled Americans to script the Indians' "fate" in the reassuring terms of classical tragedy: "This paradoxical situation [the Indians' "freedom" under the provisions of the act] reproduces the paradox also central to pre-Christian classical tragedy where the protagonist cannot escape his fate yet nonetheless affirms his status as tragic (rather than, say, merely pathetic) by taking responsibility for his fate: it is as if he chose it" (137–38).

7. Debate generally split along lines of party and region. Religious and philanthropic groups in the North and East expressed the strongest opposition. See Satz (20–21) for a further discussion of the partisan nature of the debate.

8. Krupat discusses at length the Cherokees' use of textual means to fight for self-determination. He reprints in full the Cherokee memorials presented to the Senate and House of Representatives on 15 March 1830 and provides a detailed rhetorical analysis of these texts (1992, 164–72).

9. See McLoughlin (388–451) for a detailed discussion of the conflict.

10. See Satz (48–52) for a discussion of the publicity surrounding the Cherokee cases and the political motivation behind it.

11. Drawing upon the work of Homi Bhabha (1984), Priscilla Wald reads the Cherokees' nationalist efforts as acts of mimicry. According to Wald, the threat posed by Cherokee nationalism can be seen by studying the implications of the Cherokee constitution:

> If it accepted the Cherokee Constitution, the United States government would have to acknowledge either the consistent violations of the Cherokees' natural rights or the possibility of a government that defined rather than was authorized by natural rights— a government that distinctly resembled the United States government. The Cherokee Constitution in effect mimicked de facto United States policy. (29)

While I agree that the Cherokee cases were threatening by virtue of their capacity to reveal deep anxieties and inconsistencies at the heart of American national character, I take issue with the terms of mimicry Wald applies. The "menace" of mimicry depended upon the existence of a firm binary opposition—us versus them—which is then subverted. Wald tends to elide nineteenth-century American responses to Indians and blacks as the Other, who then reappears in court cases, such as the Cherokee cases or the Dred Scott decision, as uncannily similar. I wish to argue that responses to Indians and blacks were profoundly different—especially during the period of nineteenth-century nation-building, when "the Indian" played an important symbolic role in American efforts to define a sense of national identity distinct from Europe and its Old World values. The binary opposition that Wald takes as a given I see as more fluid, changing as the symbolic function of Indians altered, providing the imaginative ground upon which American national identity and character were formed and reformed. In the Cherokee cases, for instance, we see the binary opposition emerging in struggles to justify the unequal treatment of Indians and collapsing when faced with the impossibility of defining the Indians as Other. Thompson's vision of the Cherokees replicating the structure of the U.S. government and Marshall's definition of the Cherokees as neither citizen (us) nor alien (them) both reveal the kind of problem posed by American Indians during the first half of the nineteenth century.

Cheryl Walker has also applied the notion of mirroring to explore the relationship between American Indian and Euro-American ideas of nationhood during the nineteenth century. While Walker focuses upon the writings of American Indians rather than Euro-Americans, her conception of mirroring is similar to mine in many ways. Walker stresses the fact that Indians did not completely occupy the position of Other for nineteenth-century Americans—for example, America was commonly personified as an Indian—and explores how Indian writers made use of this ambivalence to subvert dominant iconography and ideology through parodic acts of mimicry.

12. In his excellent analysis of the Cherokee cases (716–40), G. Edward White notes the emphasis on history in Marshall's opinion. White stresses the significance of Marshall's decision to make history rather than natural rights the fundamental source of law. Just a decade earlier, in 1822, Judge Joseph Story had primarily based his decision in *La Jeune Eugenie v. Alligator*, (a slavery case) upon the principle of natural law. The decisions of the Marshall court, and Marshall's articulation of the principles informing these decisions, marked a turning point in American legal history. According to White, during this period natural rights "disappeared as a source of law" (735). See White (692–703) for a further discussion of the slavery case and its legal implications.

13. Several historians have argued that loopholes in the law plus bad timing—the Court went into recess shortly after the decision was handed down—explain Jackson's failure to enforce the decision, making it not quite the blatant act of defiance it at first seems. For fuller accounts of this argument, see Burke, Miles, and Satz.

14. This excerpt from Richard Peters's pamphlet on the Cherokee cases was reprinted in an 1831 review that appeared in *The Spirit of the Pilgrims* 4(9):503.

15. My summary of the resolution of the nullification crisis relies heavily upon Ellis, McLoughlin, and Miles.

16. See the text of Jackson's speech in *Niles Weekly Register* 44, 15 June 1833, 256.

17. Ibid., 256, 282. For descriptions of Black Hawk's tour, see Drake (193–96), Eby (262–80), and Donald Jackson's introduction to Black Hawk's autobiography.

18. It is worth noting the irony surrounding the differing motivations behind these two tours. While the Cherokees hoped to show Americans the progress of the Cherokee nation, Black Hawk was sent to view the progress of the American nation. The Cherokees wished to call attention to the legal and political battles in which actual power was being exercised and policies shaped, whereas Black Hawk diverted Americans' attention to a sensationalized Indian "war" which posed no real threat to the Americans and made no appreciable difference in the Indians' fate. In the end, the Cherokees' efforts did little to alter their fate. Americans were impressed by the Cherokees' progress—McLoughlin noted that "almost all of the petitions received by Congress in opposition to removal cited the progress of the Cherokees as the principal argument for allowing the Indians to remain where they were" (435)—but this still did not convince Congress to defeat the Removal Act or to protect the Cherokees' rights to their land.

19. This passage illustrates the sense of nostalgia that pervaded nineteenth-century accounts of Indian decline and U.S. national development. *American Quarterly Review* 15 (June 1834):426.

20. David Murray examines "the transformations forced upon, and the uses made of, Indians in the American popular imagination and media as they moved from independent, alien and, therefore, profoundly threatening figures during the nineteenth century, to defeated, anachronistic survivors, material for the exercise of suitable white emotions, whether the frisson of horror or idealized nostalgia or pity" (1988, 34). Murray's comments seem to describe quite accurately the uses made of Black Hawk in the popular imagination, even though he became popular much earlier than the Indians whose stories Murray focuses on. This is not surprising, given the image of the Indians as Vanishing Americans, which was already quite popular by the 1820s. Although scattered conflicts continued until late into the nineteenth century, Brian Dippie has argued persuasively that after the War of 1812 the Indians were no longer seen as a real threat to the United States.

21. Increase Mather, *A Brief History of the War with the Indians in New-England* (Boston, 1676), quoted in Slotkin and Folsom (139). See Thatcher (1973 [1832] 1:173–74) for a more detailed description of King Philip's death and mutilation. Black Hawk's skull was put on display after his death, but the motive was not so much to assert triumph as to turn a profit. In 1839 graverobbers stole the body of Black Hawk and sold his skull to a museum in Burlington, Iowa, where it was briefly exhibited until it and the musuem were destroyed by fire (Cole, 272–73).

22. From *An Account of the Indian Chief Black Hawk* . . . (Philadelphia, 1833), reprinted in Donald Jackson's introduction (12).

23. See chapter 2 for a more extensive discussion of *Johnson v. McIntosh* in relation to American Indian policy.

24. *Niles Weekly Register* 44, 20 July 1833, 348. This statement is particularly ironic given that Black Hawk's War was fought precisely to oppose such a move.

25. Such use of the Indian perspective to frame American history was to become a regular part of the tradition of historical pageantry that blossomed in America toward the end of the nineteenth century. These pageants (which included hundreds of participants) were usually held to commemorate the history of a particular community or event, and almost all included depictions of Indians as representative of the nation's early history, against which the progress of the present era could be measured. The role of the Indian perspective as a frame for American history is illustrated by a 1916 poster advertising the celebration of Fort Wayne, Indiana, as "The Glorious Gateway of the West." The poster depicts an Indian in the foreground, dressed in a loincloth, with bow in hand, creeping over the crest of a hill as if stalking his prey. What he sees is a vision of American progress: a modern, industrial city complete with factories spewing forth smoke. The viewer's perspective is located just behind the Indian, gazing at the city from his vantage point, yet still encompassing the Indian himself, observing him as he views the display of American progress in the distance. In many ways Black Hawk's tour through the East—during the course of which American progress and power were displayed in contrast to and from the vantage point of the Indian—offered Americans a similar perspective from which to view themselves and their history. For an excellent discussion of the tradition of historical pageantry, see the studies by Susan G. Davis and David Glassberg. A photograph of the Fort Wayne poster serves as the frontispiece to Glassberg's book.

26. The quotation is from the translator's statement, which follows the title page of the 1833 (first) edition. All page numbers refer to Donald Jackson's edition of this text.

While some have claimed that Black Hawk's *Life* was a money-making scheme initiated—or even fabricated—by its editor, John Patterson, there is no concrete evidence to disprove the translator's claim that Black Hawk first suggested the publication of his autobiography. Several scholars have attempted to reconstruct how it might have served Black Hawk's own purposes. H. David Brumble considers Black Hawk's motives and the structure of the *Life* in the context of Native American preliterate "autobiographical" traditions. Brumble identifies Black Hawk's narrative as an example of the traditional tale of self-vindication, which typically would be recounted "when a ceremony failed, when a war party met disaster, or when hunters came home with empty parfleches." Brumble concludes: "In hoping to justify himself by producing an autobiographical narrative, Black Hawk was acting in a perfectly traditional manner, however innovative may have been the idea of having his self-vindication written down and published" (38–39). Timothy Sweet also interprets the *Life* in relation to strategies of "self-performance" central to Sauk culture. He shows how Black Hawk affirms his self-definition as a Sauk warrior throughout the text and argues that he uses the text to assert the "translatability of the warrior code in order to promote an understanding and dissemination of the terms of his identity" (495). Like Sweet, William Boelhower sees Black Hawk quite self-consciously employing the strategies of textualization for his own purposes. According to Boelhower, "It is hard to believe that Black Hawk was not aware of the conditions implied in his narrative limits. In fact, it is more likely that he considered himself less a narrator than a rhetor self-consciously speaking in public" (336). He demonstrates how Black Hawk subverts the dominant narrative of movement (American westward expansion) that overtly structures the text with an emotionally "moving" counternarrative of Indian dwelling centered upon descriptions of his lost home of Saukenuk. Cheryl Walker likewise ascribes self-conscious agency to Black Hawk, exploring how he wields the "moral force of transposition" in the *Life* (60). While it is impossible to know the extent to which the autobiography was motivated or controlled by Black Hawk, these scholars make plausible the interpreter's claim that Black Hawk wanted his story to be published.

27. For scholars such as H. David Brumble and Hertha Wong, working to establish a Native American autobiographical tradition, the contributions of white editors and amanuenses are viewed as barriers obstructing access to authentic traditions. According to Brumble, collaboration contributes to "the problematic nature of the published texts, embodying as they do the conflicting motivations and autobiographical assumptions of both the Indians and their Anglo collaborators. Responsible analysis, then, must largely wait upon descriptions of the assumptions and narrative conventions native to both the Indians and their editors" (18).

David Murray and Arnold Krupat take a different approach to the "problem," focusing on the nature and implications of the collaborative process itself. Murray sets out "to demonstrate the complex and various ways in which the process of translation, cultural as well as linguistic, is obscured or effaced in a wide variety of texts which claim to be representing or describing Indians, and what cultural and ideological assumptions underlie such effacement" (1991, 1). Krupat specifically chooses to focus upon those Indian autobiographies characterized by a "principle of original bicultural composite composition" since he sees the collaborative nature of these texts as a central source of their significance: "The principle, . . . which provides the key to the Indian autobiography's discursive type, provides as well the key to its discursive function, its purposive dimension as an act of power and will. For to see the Indian autobiography as the ground upon which two cultures meet is to see it as the textual equivalent of the frontier." According to Krupat, this same principle provides a rationale for poststructural approaches to the study of Indian autobiography: "Given the presence of two persons, two cultures, two modes of production, as well as two languages at work in the formation of the Indian autobiography, it seems reasonable to examine the signifier and the text's signifying practices in some detail, regardless of whether—and how—one may seek passage to the world beyond the text" (1985, 31–33). The "passage to the world beyond the text" is precisely what I intend to explore, not only in an effort to understand the cultural implications of Black Hawk's popularity but also in order to examine the interplay between "reality" and representation that structures Black Hawk's *Life*.

28. Upon his capture, Black Hawk delivered a defiant speech criticizing the whites and justifying his own actions. The following passage is representative:

> Black Hawk is an Indian. He has done nothing of which an Indian need be ashamed. He has fought the battles of his country against the white man, who came year after year to cheat his people and take away their lands. You know the cause of our making

war. It is known to all white men. They ought to be ashamed of it. The white men despise the Indians and drive them from their homes. (Wallace, 43)

It is significant, for my argument, that this speech was omitted from Major Joseph M. Street's official report of the surrender ceremony on 27 August 1832. While such criticism was printed, and even emphasized, within the pages of the *Life*, it could not so easily be accommodated within "official" accounts (or presentations) of Black Hawk and Black Hawk's War. This may reflect the different strategies of containment available within the private space of reading and the public sphere of "official" discourse. For the full text of this speech, see Wallace.

29. See Walker (60–83) for a different account of the effect of Black Hawk's *Life* on white readers. Whereas Walker believes that Black Hawk achieves the "moral force of transposition," I wish to stress the textual limits of the auto-biography's moral force.

30. *North American Review* 40, no. 86 (January 1835):68–87. The reviewer's account of justice (or its failure) underscores the connection among history, judgment, and interpretation.

31. The treaty of 13 May 1816, signed in St. Louis, was officially a treaty of peace between the United States and the Sauk of Rock River, who had fought on the side of the British in the War of 1812. In this treaty the Sauk unconditionally agreed to the terms of the disputed treaty of 1804.

32. G. Edward White's chapters on "The Origins of Marshall Court Jurisprudence" discuss the central principles and debates that shaped the Court's understanding and implementation of the law between 1815 and 1835. According to White

> The most fundamental, and at the same time the most unsettled, issue of early-nineteenth-century American jurisprudence involved the nature and source of law in the American republic. Since "frequent recurrence to first principles" was taken to be a vital exercise in the preservation and development of republican forms of government, and republican governments were acknowledged to be quintessentially governments of laws, it seemed necessary to identify what was meant by "law" in America and where legal principles originated. (112)

White lists, in descending order of authority, what were generally agreed to be the primary sources of law: the Constitution, the common law, the law of nature, the civil law, and specialized sources such as statutes. Not all of these sources were seen to be dependent on interpretation. The common law, for instance, "was treated as a source of timeless principles, consistent with natural justice, founded in reason, conforming to custom, and influenced by divine revelation" (129). The law of nature was similarly considered to consist of unchanging, universal, self-evident principles. Early-nineteenth-century Americans were reluctant to envision Supreme Court Justices as "making law." The nature and scope of legal interpretation was thus the source of considerable debate.

33. Thomas Gustafson provides an illuminating analysis of the relationship between the politics of representation and interpretation in American culture throughout the nineteenth century. Language—with its indeterminate meanings,

its openness to interpretation, and its vulnerability to corruption—was seen to have political consequences and became the source of considerable anxiety.

34. In *The Last of the Mohicans* (1826) Cooper considers the implications of differences between literate and oral cultures. Readers are introduced to Natty and Chingachgook as they engage in an intense debate over the veracity of Indian and Euro-American versions of history. The argument soon comes to rest upon the fact that Indian history is transmitted orally, while Euro-American history is written. On this point Natty seems forced to admit his disadvantage: "I am willing to own that my people have many ways, of which, as an honest man, I can't approve. It is one of their customs to write in books what they have done and seen, instead of telling them in their villages, where the lie can be given to the face of a cowardly boaster, and the brave soldier can call on his comrades to witness for the truth of his words" (Cooper [1826] 1980, 35). Although oral tradition is more truthful, it is also less flexible than writing. Cooper associates the Indians' reliance upon experience and tradition with their inevitable decline. "[Y]our young white," Natty explains, "who gathers his learning from books and can measure what he knows by the page, may conceit [*sic*] that his knowledge, like his legs, outruns that of his father; but where experience is the master, the scholar is made to know the value of years, and respects them accordingly" (253). The written language of the Euro-Americans ultimately allows them to shape history. Each generation moves forward beyond the world of their fathers, while the Indians remain the same, becoming history as "progress" overtakes them.

Marshall's definition of the concept of interpretation is interesting in light of these ideas regarding the power and limits of writing. Marshall legitimates interpretation by asserting that it is possible to return, in one's imagination, to an originary moment when meaning was created as a speech act performed within a community that authorizes its truth. Marshall's reasoning helps to illuminate nineteenth-century attitudes toward writing, especially the way in which textual strategies were employed to construct legitimizing versions of American history and "the nation" as imagined community.

35. Richardson, *Messages and Papers*, 2:459. Jackson's first (quoted here) and second annual messages to congress both discuss the Indian problem at some length.

36. *North American Review* 40, no. 86 (1835):68–69. *A Son of the Forest* (1829), the autobiography of the Ojibway Indian William Apes (or Apess), was the first published autobiography written by an Indian.

37. For a provocative discussion of the complex relationships among authenticity, (racial) identity, and performance, see the studies by Bank, Lott, and Roach. Bank's comments on commodified cultures seem especially relevant: "[I]n commodified cultures the counterfeit is also true performance. Here, the text is not that the representation stands for the real, but that the representation (counterfeit) is itself real. Cultural performance can only enact (represent, symbolize, counterfeit) subjects, an enaction that is the product of the resistance between subjects and performances" (163). As Black Hawk is commodified in the space of cultural performance provided by the text of the *Life*, he is transformed into a representation or a sign that readers interpret. While the text incorporates the resistance between Black Hawk the subject and Black Hawk the performance, it

enacts that resistance in a space (of the reading act) that derealizes the resistance that Black Hawk voices throughout the narrative.

38. For a good overview of American attitudes toward speech and writing, see Murray (1991).

39. Henry Louis Gates offers another perspective on the effect of representing within the pages of a text that is ultimately under white control the "voices" of those generally denied access to written language. Referring to slave narratives, Gates states: "Blacks had to establish themselves as 'speaking subjects' before they could even begin to destroy their status as objects, as commodities, within Western culture." Gates's comments point to important differences in the historical conditions that defined the status of African-Americans and Native Americans in the United States before the Civil War. From the time of their arrival in America, African-Americans had been defined by white Americans as objects to be owned and used. Native Americans, on the other hand, occupied a position of relative power when whites first encountered them in America. Down through the years, Indians were variously defined by whites as demons, enemies, allies, subject peoples, or vanishing Americans—but never as objects. Thus, the representation of African-Americans within the pages of a slave narrative might serve as a liberating opposition to the prevalent antebellum definition of African-Americans as objects. For the Indians, however, the competing categories of definition were not subject-object but (independent) subject–(dependent) subject. The subtlety of this opposition makes it easy for slippage to occur between these different definitions of the Indian as subject. Within the pages of the *Life*, for example, the textual representation of Black Hawk as independent autobiographical subject serves to mask and reinforce the political redefinition of the Indians' status in the United States as subject peoples.

40. The play was performed in the Bowery on 27 January 1834. George C. Odell (3:680) described the cast and production. Black Hawk was played by Mr. Collins and the Town Marshall by T. D. Rice, the blackface entertainer who had risen to instant fame after his "Jim Crow" debut in November 1832. The playwright's name was not recorded. Theodore Shank (372) claims that T. D. Rice wrote the play, while Schmitz (7) presents evidence that John B. Patterson wrote and performed in the play himself. Eugene H. Jones (86) suggests that the play was probably a *piece d'occasion* which was performed only once.

CHAPTER SIX
A GUIDE TO REMEMBRANCE

1. Literature on the grand tour and its cultural significance is extensive. James Buzard's excellent analysis discusses both European and American tourists in Europe during the nineteenth century. Robert Lemelin and John Sears discuss the cultural significance of American domestic tourism in the nineteenth century. While both attach a nationalistic meaning to domestic tourism, neither explores in detail the specific strategies and effects of tourism as civic ritual. Both works cite natural wonders—such as Niagara Falls, Yosemite, and Yellowstone—as the most popular nineteenth-century tourist attractions; neither mentions the U.S. Capitol.

2. This conception of the Capitol as ritual site for the performance of citizenship draws upon the work of Carol Duncan on the "civilizing rituals" of public art museums. According to Duncan, "A ritual site of any kind is a place programmed for the enactment of something. It is a place designed for some kind of performance. It has this structure whether or not visitors can read its cues. . . . But a ritual performance need not be a formal spectacle. It may be something an individual enacts alone by following a prescribed route, by repeating a prayer, by recalling a narrative, or by engaging in some other *structured* experience that relates to the history or meaning of the site . . ." (12). My analysis of the Capitol tour as ritual drama also relies on past scholarship on tourism as ritual (MacCannell) or performance (Adler).

3. See Vivien G. Fryd for an excellent book-length study of the artwork of the Capitol focusing upon "the politics of ethnicity." While Fryd focuses on the meanings of the artwork itself, I am more interested in the narrative strategies by which the guidebooks describe the artwork and position the reader in relation to it.

4. For a full account of this event, see Filson (57).

5. While the ideal of republican virtue was extremely important to formulations of citizenship during the Revolutionary period, by the middle of the nineteenth century a new, more liberal notion of citizenship based upon individualism, competition, and sentimental patriotism became dominant. The emphasis in nineteenth-century guidebooks upon the earlier model is thus noteworthy. For a further discussion of the relationship between republican virtue, manliness, and American national identity, see chapter 3.

6. Robert S. Tilton provides an excellent account of the development of the Smith-Pocahontas story in American culture.

7. As Louis A. Montrose has argued, narratives of discovery often describe the European conquerors' self-possession and sexual self-restraint as a means of legitimizing their exploitation of the land. Europeans are represented "not as territorial aggressors but rather as passive beneficiaries of the animated land's own desire to be possessed" (1991, 195). Capellano's *Preservation of Captain Smith by Pocahontas*, in which the bare-breasted Pocahontas is pictured as throwing herself upon the passive figure of Smith, would certainly support such a reading. The guidebooks' repeated comment upon the "self-possession" of Euro-Americans such as Boone, as contrasted with the "frantic" face and passions of the Indian, could also be understood in light of this analysis.

8. See Joy S. Kasson's study for an excellent discussion of representations of women in nineteenth-century American sculpture.

9. "The Capitol at Washington," *United States Magazine* 3, no. 2 (August 1856):100.

10. Letter of M.C. Meigs to Simon Cameron, Secretary of War, 20 June 1861; quoted in Fairman, 202.

11. Authenticity is a loaded term in studies of travel and tourism. "Tourists" are generally associated with inauthentic, mediated, or scripted experience as distinguished from the more direct and authentic experience of the "traveler"; see, for example, studies by Buzard, Culler, Fussell, MacCannell, and Urry. However, I wish to emphasize that the regulated and regularizing quality which has made

the tourist an object of scorn for Romantics such as Wordsworth and for twentieth-century critics nostalgically lamenting a lost authenticity is precisely what nineteenth-century guidebooks to the Capitol desired in their effort to (mass-) produce a certain idea of the citizen and the nation through the (real or imagined) tour of the national Capitol.

12. *Lippincott's Magazine* 2 (November 1868):536; quoted in Groseclove, 61, and Hills, 119. In his own notes to the composition, Leutze said of this group: "Below is a mother kissing her babe with tears of joy, mounted on a mule led by a negro boy who caresses the beast for the work done—She hopes to meet the father of her child who has preceded them." There is no suggestion that the woman is an Irish immigrant, as Brewster claims, or that the black man is a freed slave. The complete text of Leutze's notes can be found on microfilm in the *Archives of American Art*, roll 3091, frames 51–67; they have been reprinted by Justin G. Turner.

WORKS CITED

Adams, Charles H. 1990. *"The Guardian of the Law": Authority and Identity in James Fenimore Cooper*. University Park: Pennsylvania State University Press.

Adler, Judith. 1989. "Travel as Performed Art." *American Journal of Sociology* 94, no. 6 (May):1366–91.

Allaman, John Lee. 1988. "The Patterson Family of Oquawka." *Western Illinois Regional Studies* 11, no. 1 (Spring):55–70.

Anderson, Benedict. 1991. *Imagined Communities: Reflections on the Origin and Spread of Nationalism*. Rev. ed. London: Verso.

Appleby, Joyce. 1992. *Liberalism and Republicanism in the Historical Imagination*. Cambridge: Harvard University Press.

Bailyn, Bernard. 1967. *The Ideological Origins of the American Revolution*. Cambridge: Harvard University Press.

Bakhtin, Mikhail M. 1981. *The Dialogic Imagination*. Edited by Michael Holquist. Austin: University of Texas Press.

Bank, Rosemarie K. 1997. *Theatre Culture in America, 1825–1860*. Cambridge: Cambridge University Press.

Barker, James. 1808. *The Indian Princess; or, La Belle Sauvage. An Operatic Melodrame. In Three Acts*. Philadelphia: T. & G. Palmer. Reprinted in Moses.

Barnett, Louise. 1975. *The Ignoble Savage: American Literary Racism, 1790–1890*. Westport, Conn.: Greenwood Press.

Berkhofer, Robert F., Jr. 1978. *The White Man's Indian: Images of the American Indian from Columbus to the Present*. New York: Knopf.

Bhabha, Homi K. 1990. *Nation and Narration*. London: Routledge.

———. 1994. *The Location of Culture*. London: Routledge.

Black Hawk. [1833] 1964. *Life of Ma-ka-tai-me-she-kia-kiak, or Black Hawk*. Edited by J.B. Patterson. Cincinnati. Reprinted as *Black Hawk: An Autobiography*. Edited by Donald Jackson. Urbana: University of Illinois Press.

Bloch, Ruth. 1987. "The Gendered Meanings of Virtue in Revolutionary America." *Signs: Journal of Women in Culture and Society* 13: 37–58.

Boelhower, William. 1991. "Saving Saukenuk: How Black Hawk Won the War and Opened the Way to Ethnic Semiosis." *Journal of American Studies* 25, no. 3:331–61.

Brooks, Peter. 1976. *The Melodramatic Imagination: Balzac, Henry James, Melodrama and the Mode of Excess*. New Haven: Yale University Press.

Brougham, John. [1855] 1966. *Po-ca-hon-tas, or The Gentle Savage*. Rpt. in Moody.

Brown, Gillian. 1990. *Domestic Individualism: Imagining Self in Nineteenth-Century America*. Berkeley: University of California Press.

Brown, Herbert R. 1940. *The Sentimental Novel in America, 1789–1860*. Durham, N.C.: Duke University Press.

Brumble, H. David. 1988. *American Indian Autobiography*. Berkeley: University of California Press.

Burnham, Michelle. 1993. "The Journey Between: Liminality and Dialogism in

Mary White Rowlandson's Captivity Narrative." *Early American Literature* 28:60–75.

Burke, Joseph C. 1969. "The Cherokee Cases: A Study in Law, Politics, and Morality." *Stanford Law Review* 21:500–531.

Butsch, Richard. 1994. "Bowery B'hoys and Matinee Ladies: The Re-Gendering of Nineteenth-Century American Theater Audiences." *American Quarterly* 46, no. 3:374–405.

Buzard, James. 1993. *The Beaten Track: European Tourism, Literature, and the Ways to Culture, 1800–1918.* New York: Oxford University Press.

"The Capitol at Washington." 1856. *United States Magazine* 3, nos. 1–2 (July–August):1–18, 93–109.

Castiglia, Christopher. 1996. *Bound and Determined: Captivity, Culture-Crossing, and White Womanhood from Mary Rowlandson to Patty Hearst.* Chicago: University of Chicago Press.

Cherniavsky, Eva. 1995. *That Pale Mother Rising: Sentimental Discourse and the Imitation of Motherhood in Nineteenth-Century America.* Bloomington: Indiana University Press.

Cheyfitz, Eric. 1993. "Savage Law: The Plot Against American Indians in *Johnson and Graham's Lessee v. M'Intosh* and *The Pioneers.*" In *Cultures of United States Imperialism.* Edited by Amy Kaplan and Donald E. Pease. Durham, N.C.: Duke University Press.

Choate, Rufus. 1862. *The Works of Rufus Choate.* 2 vols. Ed. Samuel Gilman Brown. Boston: Little, Brown.

Clark, Robert. 1985. "Rewriting Revolution: Cooper's War of Independence." In *James Fenimore Cooper: New Critical Essays.* Edited by Robert Clark. London: Vision Press.

Cole, Cyrenus. 1938. *I Am a Man: The Indian Black Hawk.* Iowa City: The State Historical Society of Iowa.

Cooper, James Fenimore. 1980. *The Last of the Mohicans: A Narrative of 1757.* Ed. James F. Beard. 1826. Reprint, Albany: SUNY.

———. 1991. *Notions of the Americans Picked Up by a Travelling Bachelor,* 2 vols. Ed. James F. Beard. 1828. Reprint, Albany: SUNY Press.

———. 1980. *The Pioneers; or, The Sources of the Susquehanna.* Ed. James F. Beard. 1823. Reprint, Albany: SUNY.

———. 1964 *The Prairie.* 1827. Reprint, New York: Signet.

Cott, Nancy. 1977. *The Bonds of Womanhood: Woman's Sphere in New England, 1780–1835.* New Haven: Yale University Press.

Culler, Jonathan. 1988. "The Semiotics of Tourism." *Framing the Sign: Criticism and Its Institutions.* Norman: University of Oklahoma Press.

Custis, George Washington Parke. 1830. *Pocahontas; or, The Settlers of Virginia. A National Drama.* Philadelphia, n.p. Rpt. in Quinn.

Dane, Nathan. 1823–29. *A General Abridgement and Digest of American Law, with Occasional Notes and Comments.* 9 vols. Boston: Cummings, Hilliard.

Davis, John. 1805. *Captain Smith and Princess Pocahontas.* Philadelphia: T. C. Plowman.

Davis, Susan G. 1986. *Parades and Power: Street Theatre in Nineteenth-Century Philadelphia.* Philadelphia: Temple University Press.

Dippie. Brian W. 1982. *The Vanishing American: White Attitudes and U.S. Indian Policy.* Middletown, Conn.: Wesleyan University Press.

Doty, Lockwood L. 1876. *A History of Livingston County, New York: From Its Earliest Traditions, to Its Part in the War for Our Union.* Geneseo, N.Y.: Edward E. Doty.

Drake, Benjamin. 1838. *The Life and Adventures of Black Hawk.* Cincinnati, Ohio: George Conclin.

Drinnon, Richard. 1972. *White Savage: The Case of John Dunn Hunter.* New York: Schocken.

Drummond, A. M., and Richard Moody. 1953. "Indian Treaties: The First American Dramas." *Quarterly Journal of Speech* 39 (fall):15–24.

Duncan, Carol. 1995. *Civilizing Rituals: Inside the Public Art Museum.* London: Routledge.

Dunlap, William. 1832. *History of the American Theatre.* New York: J. & J. Harper.

Ebersole, Gary L. 1995. *Captured by Texts: Puritan to Postmodern Images of Indian Captivity.* Charlottesville: University Press of Virginia.

Eby, Cecil. 1973. *"That Disgraceful Affair," the Black Hawk War.* New York: Norton.

Ehrmann, Jacques, ed. 1970. *Structuralism.* Garden City, N.Y.: Anchor.

Elliot, Jonathan. 1830. *Historical Sketches of the Ten Miles Square Forming the District of Columbia.* Washington, D.C.: J. Elliot, Jr.

Ellis, Richard E. 1987. *The Union at Risk: Jacksonian Democracy, States' Rights, and the Nullification Crisis.* New York: Oxford University Press.

Ellison, Julie. 1993. "Race and Sensibility in the Early Republic: Ann Eliza Bleecker and Sarah Wentworth." *American Literature* 65, no. 3 (September): 445–74.

Elson, Ruth. 1964. *Guardians of Tradition: American Schoolbooks of the Nineteenth Century.* Lincoln: University of Nebraska Press.

Ewart, Mike. 1977. "Cooper and the American Revolution: The Non-Fiction." *Journal of American Studies* 11:61–79.

Fairman, Charles. 1927. *Art and Artists of the Capitol of the United States of America.* Washington: U.S. Government Printing Office.

Farley, Frank. [1913]. 1967. "The Dying Indian." *Anniversary Papers by Colleagues and Pupils of George Lyman Kittredge.* Reprint. New York: Russell & Russell.

Ferris, Lesley. 1990. *Acting Women: Images of Women in Theatre.* London: Macmillan.

Fiedler, Leslie. 1968. *The Return of the Vanishing American.* New York: Stein and Day.

Filson, John. 1784. *Kentucke.* Wilmington, Del.: James Adams.

Fisher, Philip. 1985. *Hard Facts: Setting and Form in the American Novel.* New York and Oxford: Oxford University Press.

Fliegelman, Jay. 1993. *Declaring Independence: Jefferson, Natural Language, & the Culture of Performance.* Stanford, Calif.: Stanford University Press.

Foreman, Grant. 1953. *Indian Removal: The Emigration of the Five Civilized Tribes of Indians.* Norman: University of Oklahoma Press.

Forgie, George B. 1979. *Patricide in the House Divided: A Psychological Interpretation of Lincoln and His Age*. New York: Norton.

Franchot, Jennie. 1994. *Roads to Rome: The Antebellum Encounter with Catholicism*. Berkeley: University of California Press.

Franklin, Wayne. 1982. *The New World of James Fenimore Cooper*. Chicago: University of Chicago Press.

Freud, Sigmund. [1917] 1957. "Mourning and Melancholia." In *The Standard Edition of the Complete Psychological Works of Sigmund Freud*. 24 vols. Edited and translated by James Strachey. London: Hogarth.

Fryd, Vivien G. 1993. *Art & Empire: The Politics of Ethnicity in the United States Capitol, 1815–1860*. New Haven: Yale University Press, 1993.

Fussell, Paul. 1972. *Abroad*. New York: Oxford University Press.

Gates, Henry Louis. 1988. *The Signifying Monkey: A Theory of African-American Literary Criticism*. New York: Oxford University Press.

Glassberg, David. 1990. *American Historical Pageantry: The Uses of Tradition in the Early Twentieth Century*. Chapel Hill: University of North Carolina Press.

Goldman, Ann E. 1996. *Take My Word: Autobiographical Innovations of Ethnic American Working Women*. Berkeley: University of California Press.

Gould, Philip. 1996. *Covenant and Republic: Historical Romance and the Politics of Puritanism*. New York: Cambridge University Press.

Green, Rayna. 1975. "The Pocahontas Perplex: The Image of the Indian Woman in American Culture." *Massachusetts Review* 16, no. 4:698–714.

Grimsted, David. 1968. *Melodrama Unveiled: American Theater and Culture, 1800–1850*. Chicago: University of Chicago Press.

Groseclove, Barbara. 1975. *Emanuel Leutze, 1816–68; Freedom Is the Only King*. Washington, D.C.: Smithsonian Institution Press.

Gustafson, Thomas. 1992. *Representative Words: Politics, Literature and the American Language, 1776–1865*. Cambridge: Cambridge University Press.

Haas, Philip. 1839. *Picturesque Work of Washington City, or Public Buildings and Statuary of the Government*. Washington, D.C.: P. Haas.

Hadley, Elaine. 1995. *Melodramatic Tactics: Theatricalized Dissent in the English Marketplace, 1800–1885*. Stanford, Calif.: Stanford University Press.

Hartz, Louis. 1955. *The Liberal Tradition in America: An Interpretation of American Political Thought Since the Revolution*. New York: Harcourt Brace Jovanovich.

Hawthorne, Nathaniel. 1862. "Chiefly about War-Matters." *Atlantic Monthly* (July–December):43–61.

Hays, Michael, and Anastasia Nikolopoulou, eds. 1996. *Melodrama: The Cultural Emergence of a Genre*. New York: St. Martin's Press.

Heard, J. Norman. 1973. *White into Red: A Study of White Persons Captured by Indians*. Metuchen, N.J.: Scarecrow Press.

Hills, Patricia. 1991. "Picturing Progress in the Era of Westward Expansion." In *The West as America: Reinterpreting Images of the Frontier*. Edited by William H. Truettner. Washington, D.C.: Smithsonian Institution Press.

Hinds, Elizabeth. 1997. *Private Property: Charles Brockden Brown's Gendered Economics of Virtue*. Newark: University of Delaware Press.

History of Mercer and Henderson Counties. 1882. Chicago.

Horsman, Reginald. *The Origins of Indian Removal, 1815–1824.* East Lansing: Michigan State University Press, 1970.

Horwitz, Morton J. 1977. *The Transformation of American Law, 1780–1860.* Cambridge: Harvard University Press.

Hulme, Peter. 1986. *Colonial Encounters: Europe and the Native Caribbean, 1492–1797.* London: Methuen.

Jackson, Andrew. 1926–35. *Correspondence of Andrew Jackson.* 7 vols. Ed. John Spencer Basset. Washington, D.C.

Jackson, Donald, ed. 1964. "Introduction." *Black Hawk: An Autobiography.* Urbana: University of Illinois Press.

Jenkins, William. 1977. "Three Centuries in the Development of the Pocahontas Story in American Literature, 1608–1908." Ph.D. diss., University of Tennessee.

Jones, Eugene H. 1988. *Native Americans as Shown on the Stage, 1753–1916.* Metuchen, N.J.: Scarecrow Press.

Kaplan, Amy. 1993. "'Left Alone with America': The Absence of Empire in the Study of American Culture." In *Cultures of United States Imperialism.* Edited by Amy Kaplan and Donald E. Pease. Durham, N.C.: Duke University Press.

Kasson, Joy S. 1990. *Marble Queens and Captives: Women in Nineteenth-Century American Sculpture.* New Haven: Yale University Press.

Keating, AnaLouise. 1996. *Women Reading Women Writing: Self-Invention in Paula Gunn Allen, Gloria Anzaldua, and Audre Lorde.* Philadelphia: Temple University Press.

Keiser, Albert. 1970. *The Indian in American Literature.* New York: Octagon–Farrar, Straus & Giroux.

Kelly, William P. 1983. *Plotting America's Past: Fenimore Cooper and the Leatherstocking Tales.* Carbondale: Southern Illinois University Press.

Kerber, Linda. 1980. *Women of the Republic: Intellect and Ideology in Revolutionary America.* Chapel Hill: University of North Carolina Press.

Klein, Milton, et al., eds. 1992. *The Republican Synthesis Revisited: Essays in Honor of George Athan Billias.* Worcester, Mass.: American Antiquarian Society.

Knobel, Dale T. 1986. *Paddy and the Republic: Ethnicity and Nationality in Antebellum America.* Middletown, Conn.: Wesleyan University Press.

Kolodny, Annette. 1975. *The Lay of the Land: Metaphor as Experience and History in American Life and Letters.* Chapel Hill: University of North Carolina Press.

———. 1992. "Letting Go Our Grand Obsessions: Notes Toward a New Literary History of the American Frontiers," *American Literature* 64 no. 1 (March): 1–18.

———. 1984. *The Land Before Her: Fantasy and Experience of the American Frontiers, 1630–1860.* Chapel Hill: University of North Carolina Press.

Krupat, Arnold. 1985. *For Those Who Come After: A Study of Native American Autobiography.* Berkeley: University of California Press.

———. 1989. *The Voice in the Margin: Native American Literature and the Canon.* Berkeley: University of California Press.

———. 1992. *Ethnocriticism.* Berkeley: University of California Press.

Lacan, Jacques. 1957. "L'instance de la lettre dans l'inconscient ou la raison depuis Freud," *La Psychanalyse* 3: 47–81. Rpt. (in a translation by Jan Miel) in Ehrmann.

Lemay, J. A. Leo. 1992. *Did Pocahontas Save Captain John Smith?* Athens: University of Georgia Press.

Lemelin, Robert. 1974. *Pathway to the National Character, 1830–1861.* Port Washington, N.Y.: Kennikat Press.

Lewis, James R. 1992. "Images of Captive Rape in the Nineteenth Century." *Journal of American Culture* 15, no. 2 (summer):69–77.

Lott, Eric. 1993. *Love and Theft: Blackface Minstrelsy and the American Working Class.* New York: Oxford University Press.

MacCannell, Dean. 1976. *The Tourist: A New Theory of the Leisure Class.* London: Macmillan.

Maddox, Lucy. 1991. *Removals: Nineteenth-Century American Literature and the Politics of Indian Affairs.* New York: Oxford University Press.

Mason, Jeffrey D. 1993. *Melodrama and the Myth of America.* Bloomington: Indiana University Press.

Mather, Increase. 1978. *A Brief History of the War with the Indians in New-England.* 1676. Rpt. in Slotkin and Folsom.

McConachie, Bruce A. 1992. *Melodramatic Formations: American Theatre and Society, 1820–1870.* Iowa City: University of Iowa Press.

McCoy, Drew R. 1980. *The Elusive Republic: Political Economy in Jeffersonian America.* Chapel Hill: University of North Carolina Press.

McLoughlin, William G. 1986. *Cherokee Renascence in the New Republic.* Princeton: Princeton University Press.

McWilliams, John P., Jr. 1972. *Political Justice in a Republic: James Fenimore Cooper's America.* Berkeley: University of California Press.

Meserve, Walter J. 1986. *Heralds of Promise: The Drama of the American People During the Age of Jackson, 1829–1849.* New York: Greenwood Press.

Miles, Edwin A. 1973. "After John Marshall's Decision: *Worcester v. Georgia* and the Nullification Crisis." *Journal of Southern History* 39, no. 4:519–44.

Mills, Robert. 1834. *Guide to the Capitol and to the National Executive Offices of the United States.* Washington, D.C..

Montrose, Louis A. 1991. "The Work of Gender in the Discourse of Discovery." *Representations* 33 (winter):1–41.

Moody, Richard, ed. 1966. *Dramas from the American Theatre, 1762–1909.* Cleveland, Ohio: World Publishing.

———. 1958. *The Astor Place Riot.* Bloomington: Indiana University Press.

Moses, Montrose, ed. 1918. *Representative Plays by American Dramatists, 1765–1819.* New York: E. P. Dutton.

Mossiker, Frances. 1976. *Pocahontas: The Life and the Legend.* New York: Knopf.

Motley, Warren. 1987. *The American Abraham: James Fenimore Cooper and the Frontier Patriarch.* Cambridge: Cambridge University Press.

Mott, Frank. 1947. *Golden Multitudes: The Story of Best Sellers in the United States.* New York: Macmillan.

Murray, David. 1988. "From Speech to Text: The Making of American Indian Autobiographies." In *American Literary Landscapes: The Fiction and the Fact.* Edited by Ian F. A. Bell and D. K. Adams. New York: St. Martin's Press.

———. 1991. *Forked Tongues: Speech, Writing & Representation in North American Indian Texts.* Bloomington: University of Indiana Press.

Namias, June, ed. 1992. *A Narrative of the Life of Mrs. Mary Jemison.* Norman: University of Oklahoma Press.

———. 1993. *White Captives: Gender and Ethnicity on the American Frontier.* Chapel Hill: University of North Carolina Press.

Nelligan, Murray H. 1950. "American Nationalism on the Stage: The Plays of George Washington Parke Custis, 1781–1857." *Virginia Magazine of History and Biography* 58, no. 3 (July): 291–323.

Norton, Anne. 1986. *Alternative Americas: A Reading of Antebellum Political Culture.* Chicago: University of Chicago Press.

———. 1988. *Reflections on Political Identity.* Baltimore, Md.: Johns Hopkins University Press.

Oakes, Karen. 1995. "We Planted, Tended and Harvested Our Corn: Gender, Ethnicity, and Transculturation in *A Narrative of the Life of Mrs. Mary Jemison.*" *Women and Language* 18, no. 1 (spring): 45–51.

Odell, George C. 1927–49. *Annals of the New York Stage.* 15 vols. New York: Columbia University Press.

Orgel, Stephen. *The Illusion of Power.* Berkeley: University of California Press, 1974.

Padilla, Genaro. 1993. *My History, Not Yours: The Formation of Mexican American Autobiography.* Madison: University of Wisconsin Press.

Page, Eugene R., ed. 1941. "*Metamora*" *and other plays by John Augustus Stone [and others].* America's Lost Plays, 14. Princeton, N.J.: Princeton University Press.

Pateman, Carole. 1989. *The Disorder of Women: Democracy, Feminism and Political Theory.* Stanford, Calif.: Stanford University Press.

Patterson, Mark R. 1988. *Authority, Autonomy, and Representation in American Literature.* Princeton: Princeton University Press.

Paulding, James K. 1827. "The American Drama." *American Quarterly Review* 2 (June): 331–57.

Pearce, Roy Harvey. 1947. "The Significances of the Captivity Narrative." *American Literature* 19:1–20.

———. 1953. *The Savages of America: A Study of the Indian and the Idea of Civilization.* Baltimore, Md.: Johns Hopkins University Press. Rev. ed. 1967. *Savagism and Civilization: A Study of the Indian and the American Mind.* Baltimore Md.: Johns Hopkins University Press.

Peters, Richard. 1831. *The Cherokee Nation Against the State of Georgia.* Philadelphia: John Grigg.

Philbrick, Thomas. 1964. "Cooper's *The Pioneers:* Origins and Structure." *PMLA* 79: 579–93.

Pocock, J. G. A. 1975. *The Machiavellian Moment: Florentine Political Thought and the Atlantic Republican Tradition.* Princeton, N.J.: Princeton University Press.

Pratt, Mary Louise. 1992. *Imperial Eyes: Travel Writing and Transculturation.* London: Routledge.

Prucha, Francis Paul. 1962. *American Indian Policy in the Formative Years: The Indian Trade and Intercourse Acts, 1790–1834.* Cambridge: Harvard University Press.

———. 1976. *American Indian Policy in Crisis: Christian Reformers and the Indian, 1865–1900.* Norman: University of Oklahoma Press.

Quinn, Arthur H., ed. 1925. *Representative American Plays, 1767–1923.* New York: Century.

Reynolds, David. 1988. *Beneath the American Renaissance: The Subversive Imagination in the Age of Emerson and Melville.* New York: Knopf.

Richardson, Gary A. 1996. "Nationalizing the American Stage: The Drama of Royall Tyler and William Dunlap as Post-Colonial Phenomenon." In *Making America/Making American Literature: Franklin to Cooper.* Edited by A. Robert Lee and W. M. Verhoeven. Amsterdam: Rodopi Press.

Richardson, James D. 1897. *A Compilation of the Messages and Papers of the Presidents,* vol. 2. 20 vols. Washington, D.C.: United States Congress.

Roach, Joseph. 1996. *Cities of the Dead: Circum-Atlantic Performance.* New York: Columbia University Press.

Roediger, David R. 1991. *The Wages of Whiteness: Race and the Making of the American Working Class.* London: Verso.

Rogin, Michael. 1975. *Fathers and Children: Andrew Jackson and the Subjugation of the American Indian.* New York: Knopf.

———. [1970]. 1987. "Liberal Society and the Indian Question." *Politics and Society* 1:269–312. Rpt. 1987 in his *"Ronald Reagan," the Movie: And Other Episodes in Political Demonology.* Berkeley: University of California Press.

Romero, Lora. 1997. *Home Fronts: Domesticity and Its Critics in the Antebellum United States.* Durham, N.C.: Duke University Press.

Rourke, Constance. 1965. *The Roots of American Culture and Other Essays.* Edited by Van Wyck Brooks. Port Washington, N.Y.: Kennikat Press.

Said, Edward W. 1985. *Beginnings: Intention and Method.* Reprint. New York: Columbia University Press.

Samuels, Shirley, ed. 1992. *The Culture of Sentiment: Race, Gender and Sentimentality in Nineteenth-Century America.* New York: Oxford University Press.

Satz, Ronald. 1975. *American Indian Policy in the Jacksonian Era.* Lincoln: University of Nebraska Press.

Schaub, Thomas. 1989. "'Cut in Plain Marble': The Language of the Tomb in *The Pioneers.*" In *The Green American Tradition: Essays and Poems for Sherman Paul.* Edited by H. Daniel Peck. Baton Rouge: Louisiana State University Press.

Scheckel, Susan E. 1992. "Shifting Boundaries: The Poetics and Politics of the American Frontier, 1820–1850." Ph.D. diss., University of California, Berkeley.

———. 1993. "'In the Land of His Fathers': Cooper, Land Rights and the Legitimation of American National Identity." In *James Fenimore Cooper: New Historical and Literary Contexts.* Edited by W. M. Verhoeven. Amsterdam: Rodopi Press.

Scheick, William J. 1979. *The Half-Blood: A Cultural Symbol in Nineteenth Century American Fiction.* Lexington: University Press of Kentucky.

Schmitz, Neil. 1992. "Captive Utterance: Black Hawk and Indian Irony." *Arizona Quarterly* 48, no. 4 (winter):1–18.

Sears, John. 1989. *Sacred Places: American Tourist Attractions in the Nineteenth Century.* New York: Oxford University Press.

Sears, Priscilla. 1982. *A Pillar of Fire to Follow: American Indian Dramas, 1808–1859.* Bowling Green, Oh.: Bowling Green University Press.

Seaver, James E. 1925. *A Narrative of the Life of Mrs. Mary Jemison*, 22d ed., rev. C. D. Vail. New York: American Scenic & Historic Preservation Society.

Sekora, John. 1987. "Black Message, White Envelope: Genre, Authenticity, and Authority in the Antebellum Slave Narrative." *Callaloo: A Journal of African American Arts and Letters* 10, no. 3 (summer): 482–515.

Shank, Theodore. 1956. "The Bowery Theatre, 1826–1836." Ph.D. diss., Stanford University.

Shevory, Thomas C. 1994. *John Marshall's Law: Interpretation, Ideology, and Interest*. Westport, Conn.: Greenwood Press.

Sigourney, Lydia. 1841. *Pocahontas and Other Poems*. New York: Harper and Brothers.

Simms, William Gilmore. [1849] 1962. *Views and Reviews in American Literature, History and Fiction, First Series*. Ed. C. Hugh Holman. Cambridge: Harvard University Press.

Slotkin, Richard. 1973. *Regeneration Through Violence: The Mythology of the American Frontier, 1600–1860*. Middletown, Conn.: Wesleyan University Press.

Slotkin, Richard, and James Folsom, eds. 1978. *So Dreadful a Judgment: Puritan Responses to King Philip's War, 1676–1677*. Middletown, Conn.: Wesleyan University Press.

Smith, John. 1986. *The Complete Works of John Smith*. 3 Vols. Edited by Philip L. Barbour. Chapel Hill: University of North Carolina Press.

Smith, Henry Nash. 1950. *Virgin Land: The American West as Symbol and Myth*. New York: Vintage Books.

Smith, James H. 1881. *History of Livingston County, New York*. Syracuse, N.Y.: D. Mason.

Spencer, Benjamin T. 1957. *The Quest for Nationality: An American Literary Campaign*. Syracuse, N.Y.: Syracuse University Press.

Spiller, Robert E. 1931. *Fenimore Cooper: Critic of His Times*. New York: Minton, Balch.

Stewart, Susan. 1984. *On Longing: Narratives of the Miniature, the Gigantic, the Souvenir, the Collection*. Baltimore, Md.: Johns Hopkins University Press.

Stone, John Augustus. 1829. *Metamora; or, The Last of the Wampanoags, an Indian Tragedy in Five Acts*. Rpt. in Page.

Stone, W. J. 1855. "Sketchings." *The Crayon* 2:392–93.

Stowe, Harriet Beecher. 1981. *Uncle Tom's Cabin or, Life Among the Lowly*. 1852. Reprint, New York: Penguin.

Sweet, Timothy. 1993. "Masculinity and Self-Performance in the *Life of Black Hawk*." *American Literature* 65, no. 3:475–99.

Thatcher, B. B. 1973. *Indian Biography*. 1832. Reprint, Glorietta, N.M.: Rio Grande Press.

Thomas, Brook. 1987. *Cross-examinations of Law and Literature: Cooper, Hawthorne, Stowe, and Melville*. Cambridge: Cambridge University Press.

Tilton, Robert S. 1994. *Pocahontas: The Evolution of an American Narrative*. New York: Cambridge University Press.

Tocqueville, Alexis de. [1835] 1988. *Democracy in America*. Translated by George Lawrence. Edited by J. P. Mayer. Reprint, New York: Harper & Row.

Tompkins, Jane. 1985. *Sensational Designs: The Cultural Work of American Fiction.* New York: Oxford University Press.

Treuttner, William, ed. 1991. *The West as America: Reinterpreting Images of the Frontier.* Washington, D.C.: Smithsonian Institution Press.

Turner, Justin G. 1966. "Emanuel Leutze's Mural *Westward the Course of Empire Takes Its Way.*" *Manuscripts* 18, no. 2 (September):14–16.

Turner, Victor. 1974. *Dramas, Fields and Metaphors: Symbolic Action in Human Society.* Ithaca, N.Y.: Cornell University Press.

———. 1974. "Liminal to Liminoid in Play, Flow and Ritual: An Essay in Comparative Symbology." *Rice University Studies* 60:53–92.

Urry, John. 1990. *The Tourist Gaze: Leisure and Travel in Contemporary Societies.* London: Sage.

Van Der Beets, Richard. 1973. "The Indian Captivity Narrative: An American Genre." Ph.D. diss., University of the Pacific.

Van Dorn, Fred. 1924. "Memories of Mary Jemison." *Rochester Historical Society Publication Fund Series* 3.

Vaughan, Alden T. and Edward W. Clarke. 1981. *Puritans Among the Indians: Accounts of Captivity and Redemption, 1676–1724.* Cambridge: Belknap Press of Harvard University Press.

Wald, Priscilla. 1995. *Constituting Americans: Cultural Anxiety and Narrative Form.* Durham, N.C.: Duke University Press.

Walker, Cheryl. 1997. *Indian Nation: Native American Literature and Nineteenth-Century Nationalisms.* Durham, N.C.: Duke University Press.

Wallace, Anthony F. C. 1970. *Prelude to Disaster: The Course of Indian-White Relations Which Led to the Black Hawk War of 1832.* Springfield: Illinois State Historical Library.

Walsh, Susan. 1992. "'With Them Was My Home': Native American Autobiography and *A Narrative of the Life of Mrs. Mary Jemison.*" *American Literature* 64, no. 1: 49–70.

Washburn, Wilcomb E. 1973. *The American Indian and the United States: A Documentary History,* 4 vols. New York: Random House.

Watts, Steven. 1987. *The Republic Reborn: War and the Making of Liberal America, 1790–1820.* Baltimore, Md.: Johns Hopkins University Press.

Welter, Barbara. 1966. "The Cult of True Womanhood, 1820–1860." *American Quarterly* 18, no. 2:151–74.

White, G. Edward. 1988. *The Marshall Court and Cultural Change, 1815–1835.* The Oliver Wendell Holmes Devise History of the Supreme Court of the United States; Volumes 3–4. New York: Macmillan.

White, Hayden. 1973. *Metahistory: The Historical Imagination in Nineteenth-Century Europe.* Baltimore, Md.: Johns Hopkins University Press.

———. 1978. *Tropics of Discourse.* Baltimore, Md.: Johns Hopkins University Press.

Wiebe, Robert H. 1984. *The Opening of American Society: From the Adoption of the Constitution to the Eve of Disunion.* New York: Knopf.

Williams, Robert A., Jr. 1987. "Jefferson, The Norman Yoke, and American Indian Lands." *Arizona Law Review.* 29, no. 2:178–91.

Williamson, Margaret H. 1992. "Pocahontas and Captain John Smith: Examining a Historical Myth." *History and Anthropology* 5, nos. 3–4:365–402.

Wilmeth, Don B. 1989. "Noble or Ruthless Savage? The American Indian On-stage in the Drama." *Journal of American Drama and Theatre* 1, no. 2 (spring): 39–78.

———. 1989. "Tentative Checklist of Indian Plays (1606–1987)." *Journal of American Drama and Theatre* 1, no. 3 (fall): 34–54.

Wong, Hertha. 1991. *Sending My Heart Back Across the Years: Tradition and Innovation in Native American Autobiography*. New York: Oxford University Press.

Wood, Gordon. 1969. *The Creation of the American Republic, 1785–1787*. Chapel Hill: University of North Carolina Press.

Wyeth, Samuel D. 1865. *The Federal City; or, Ins and Abouts of Washington*. Washington, D.C.: Gibson Brothers.

Young, Mary E. 1980. "Women, Civilization and the Indian Question." In *Clio Was a Woman: Studies in the History of American Women*. Edited by Mabel E. Deutrich and Virginia C. Purdy. Washington, D.C.: Howard University Press.

Young, Philip. 1962. "The Mother of Us All: Pocahontas Reconsidered." *Kenyon Review* 24 (summer):391–415.

Young, Robert. 1990. *White Mythologies: Writing History and the West*. London: Routledge.

Zantop, Susanne. 1995. "Domesticating the Other: European Colonial Fantasies, 1770–1830." In *Encountering the Other(s): Studies in Literature, History and Culture*. Edited by Gisela Brinkler-Gabler. Albany: SUNY Press.

Zuckert, Catherine H. 1990. *Natural Right and the American Imagination: Political Philosophy in Novel Form*. Savage, Md.: Rowman and Littlefield.

INDEX

Adams, Charles, 155n.8, 157n.18
African Americans, 150–51, 178n.39; slave narrative of, 77, 166n.12, 178n.39; slavery of, 10, 172n.12
allotment, 93–94, 170n.37. *See also* Dawes Severalty Act.
American Revolution, 7–8, 15–18, 24, 29, 106; in *The Indian Princess*, 49–50, 55; *in Notions of the Americans*, 24; in *The Pioneers*, 23, 25, 34–35; as subject of national literature, 44–45
Anderson, Benedict, 3, 8, 16, 35, 39, 129, 162n.28
Apes, William, 124
Atkinson, Gen. Henry, 112
authenticity: as construction, 114, 118, 163n.32; racial, 59, 114, 162–63n.32, 177n.37; and tourism, 134–35, 149, 179–80n.11; and voice, 113–14, 117–18, 123–24

Bakhtin, Mikhail M., 167n.20
Baldwin, Justice Henry, 121
Bank, Rosemarie, 163n.32, 177n.37
Barker, James: *The Indian Princess; or, La Belle Sauvage*, 45–58, 160n.20
Berlant, Lauren, 74
Bhabha, Homi, 3, 10–11, 75, 77, 154n.14, 166n.15
Black Hawk (Sauk): commodification of, 177–78n.37; as defeated warrior, 108, 110–13, 173n.18; exhibition of his skull, 173n.21; resistance of, to removal, 99, 170n.1; as speaking subject, 112–13, 115, 117, 123–24, 174–75n.26, 178n.39; surrender speech of, 175–76n.28; tour by, 99, 106–11, 114, 116, 173n.18, 174n.25; as vanishing American, 108, 112, 125, 173n.20. *See also* Black Hawk War; *Life of Ma-ka-tai-me-she-kia-kiak, or Black Hawk*
Black Hawk (play), 125–26, 178n.40
Black Hawk War, 99, 106, 108, 115
Boelhower, William, 174–75n.26
Boone, Daniel, 89, 135, 137
Brewster, Anne, 150

Brooks, Peter, 49, 57–58
Brougham, John: *Po-ca-hon-tas, or The Gentle Savage*, 59–60
Brown, Gillian, 169n.30
Brown, Sen. Joseph E., 93–94
Brumble, H. David, 174n.26, 175n.27
Burnham, Michelle, 167n.20
Butler, Elizur, 106–7

Calhoun, John C., 90–91, 95
Capellano, Antonio: *Preservation of Captain Smith by Pocahontas*, 130, 131 (fig.), 138–39, 179n.7
capitalism, 61, 63, 69, 157n.18
Capitol. *See* United States Capitol
captivity narrative: conventions of, 79–80, 96, 167n.17; development of genre, 72–73, 165n.6; popularity of, 70, 72–74, 164–65n.3; rape in, 82, 168n.23; symbolic role of women in, 74
Cass, Lewis, 83
Castiglia, Christopher, 72, 167n.17
Causici, Enrico: *Conflict of Daniel Boone and the Indians*, 135, 136 (fig.), 138; *Landing of the Pilgrims*, 130, 133 (fig.), 134
Chapman, John: *Baptism of Pocahontas at Jamestown, Virginia*, 139, 140 (fig.)
Cherokee Indians: "civilization" of, 27, 95, 103, 108; conflict in Georgia, 6, 60, 101–6, 111, 124; constitution of, 102, 105, 124, 171–72n.11; delegation to Washington, 58–59, 107–8; removal of, 6, 59–60, 91, 102–3, 119–20, 122–23, 173n.18. See also *Cherokee Nation v. Georgia*; *Worcester v. Georgia*
Cherokee Nation v. Georgia, 6, 95, 102–5, 120
Cheyfitz, Eric, 154–55n.3, 156n.12
Choate, Rufus, 8, 16–17
citizenship, 42, 95, 128–29, 134–35, 138–39, 145, 148–49, 179n.5, 179–80n.11
Civil War, 24, 145–48, 150–51
Clarke, Edward, 79, 82
Clay, Henry, 4

About the Author

Susan Scheckel is Assistant Professor of English at the University of Memphis.